ECOLOGICAL DESIGN AND PLANNING

THE WILEY SERIES IN SUSTAINABLE DESIGN

The Wiley Series in Sustainable Design has been created for professionals responsible for, and individuals interested in, the design and construction of the built environment. The series is dedicated to the advancement of knowledge in design and construction that serves to sustain the natural environment. Consistent with their content, books in the series are produced with care taken in the selection of recycled and nonpolluting materials.

Gray World, Green Heart: Technology, Nature and the Sustainable Landscape
Robert J. Thayer

Regenerative Design for Sustainable Development
John T. Lyle

Audubon House: Building the Environmentally Responsible,
Energy-Efficient Office
National Audubon Society
Croxton Collaborative, Architects

Design with Nature
Ian L. McHarg

Wind Energy Comes of Age
Paul Gipe

Tomorrow By Design
Philip H. Lewis, Jr.

Ecological Design and Planning
George F. Thompson and Frederick R. Steiner, editors

ECOLOGICAL DESIGN AND PLANNING

GEORGE F. THOMPSON

and

FREDERICK R. STEINER

Editors

JOHN WILEY & SONS, INC.

New York • Chichester • Weinheim • Brisbane • Singapore • Toronto

This book was brought to publication with the generous assistance
of the Design Arts Program of the National Endowment for the Arts.

This text is printed on acid-free paper.

Frontispiece: *Prairie Walk 7,* by Alan Gussow, 1980. Brush and ink on paper.
Collection of the Land Institute, Salina, Kansas.

Library of Congress Cataloging in Publication Data:

Ecological design and planning / George F. Thompson and Frederick R.
    Steiner, editors.
        p.   cm. — (Wiley Series in Sustainable Design)
    Papers from an international symposium entitled: Landscape architecture: ecology and design and
    planning, held in Tempe, Ariz., Apr. 1993.
    Includes index.
    ISBN 0-471-15614-0 (cloth : alk. paper)   1001271942
    1. Landscape design—Environmental aspects—Congresses.   2. Landscape ecology—Congresses.
    I. Thompson, George F.   II. Steiner, Frederick R.   III. Series.
SB472.45.E36   1997
712'.2—dc20   96-12132

Printed in the United States of America
10 9 8 7 6 5 4 3 2

In memory of Aldo Leopold

That land is a community is
the basic concept of ecology,
but that land is to be loved
and respected is
an extension of ethics.

A SAND COUNTY ALMANAC
(1949)

CONTENTS

ACKNOWLEDGMENTS

In April of 1993 the School of Planning and Landscape Architecture in the College of Architecture and Environmental Design at Arizona State University and the Center for American Places of Harrisonburg, Virginia, and Mesilla, New Mexico, cohosted an international symposium in Tempe entitled *Landscape Architecture: Ecology and Design and Planning.* This event was funded largely by a $30,450 grant from the Design Arts Program of the National Endowment for the Arts in Washington, D.C. Hundreds of scholars, designers, planners, students, and writers from all over the world attended what has since been called a watershed event.

The purpose of the symposium was twofold: To provide a public forum at which the contributors to this book presented their essays for discussion, debate, and further refinement; and to produce this book. We convey our heartfelt thanks to Mina Berryman and Alan Brangman, who were, respectively, the director and acting director of the Design Arts Program at the time we received the grant, as well as their colleagues and those who supported our application. Their generous support of the symposium and the book is hereby acknowledged. It is a national disgrace that the Design Arts Program was shut down last year by Congress.

Peer reviewers of the manuscript and book proposal included David Schuyler, professor of American studies at Franklin and Marshall College; Charles E. Little, author and conservationist from Placitas, New Mexico; Bonnie Loyd, editor emeritus of *Landscape* magazine in San Francisco, California; Bob Scarfo, professor of landscape architecture at Washington State University; Arnold R. Alanen, professor of landscape architecture at the University of Wisconsin–Madison; Randall Arendt, vice president of the

Natural Lands Trust in Media, Pennsylvania; Warren T. Byrd, Jr., professor of landscape architecture at the University of Virginia; and Darrel G. Morrison, professor of landscape architecture at the University of Georgia. Dr. Hamid Shirvani, then dean of the University of Massachusetts-Lowell, also made a valuable contribution to the scholarly discourse at the symposium by presenting his ideas on the American grid.

Also of great importance in ensuring that the symposium and the book were completed according to plan are the following colleagues, whose efforts went beyond the call of duty: John Meunier, dean of the College of Architecture and Environmental Design at Arizona State University; Laurel McSherry, assistant professor at the School of Planning and Landscape Architecture at Arizona State University; Stefani Angstadt-Leto, Chris Duplissa, Sasha Valdez, and Gopinath Arunachalam of the School of Planning and Landscape Architecture at Arizona State University; and Purna Makaram of the Center for American Places, for assistance in preparing the manuscript.

This book was originally to be published under the imprimatur of the Johns Hopkins University Press, a leading publisher in the field. Inasmuch as *Ecological Design and Planning* became particularly well suited for inclusion in The Wiley Series in Sustainable Design, Johns Hopkins graciously permitted us to publish the book with John Wiley. We wish to thank Willis G. Regier, director, and Douglas Armato, associate director and head of the book division, at Johns Hopkins for this unselfish consideration.

We also wish to recognize, at John Wiley & Sons, Dan Sayre, senior editor, Professional, Reference and Trade Group. His faith in this book, and his belief in the importance of landscape architecture and planning, meant so much in getting this project to the finish line. We especially thank Dan and David Sassian, the terrific associate managing editor at John Wiley, among the other talented individuals who have assisted in the book's editing, design, production, promotion, and sales.

Our intellectual debts are too numerous to acknowledge, but we are most grateful for all that we have learned from our teachers and mentors, the authors of great books, and the contributors to the symposium and book. We regret any errors of fact or interpretation in this book; they are, of course, unintentional. We also welcome comments and corrections in the event that revisions are possible in another printing or edition.

The Editors
Harrisonburg, Virginia
Tempe, Arizona
19 November 1996

INTRODUCTION

GEORGE F. THOMPSON
AND FREDERICK R. STEINER

Ask any citizen walking down the street the question, What is landscape? and likely you will receive a typical response, Doesn't it have something to do with shrubs around the foundation of a house or building? Doesn't it have something to do with planting flowers and trees in backyards and alongside interstates and city streets?

Here, as we are poised to enter another millennium, the subject of *landscape* has yet to permeate the common reader's psyche beyond this narrow conception. There is still little or no connection to the larger relationships that exist between "the natural and humanly constructed worlds," to borrow Yi-Fu Tuan's phrase, or, even in the United States, to the physical characteristics that make this nation unique. From coast to coast, and since 1959 out into the Pacific to the Hawaiian Islands and into the north country of Alaska, the United States is blessed with deserts, prairies, great forests of primeval quality, tundra, swamps, near jungles, barrier islands, glaciers, great lakes and rivers, volcanoes and nearly threescore mountains more than fourteen thousand feet high. And consider the value of the incredibly rich and diverse cultural landscapes in America—great global and regional cities, corn belts and cotton belts, iron ranges and copper ranges, suburbs and exurbs, battlefields and airports, parkways and greenways, industrial parks and dry docks, Back of the Yards and Bourbon Street, Monticello and Taliesin, Indian pueblos and the Sand Hills, Big Sur and Wounded Knee, Bravo 20 and Natchez Trace. Yet *landscape*—as revealed in *place*—is still unknown territory to the majority of Americans and citizens worldwide.

We can do better. We must do better, if civilization is to advance beyond what Bret Wallach in *Losing Asia* calls "the culture of development." It is high time that we citizens of the world begin to understand that our situation on Earth is not one in which nature must rule over culture, or culture over nature, as if one can separate the two in the first place. It is high time to reflect upon the geographies and landscape histories of the past throughout the world so that we can bring forward—again—the concept that only by designing and planning with nature and culture can we begin to heal and improve the landscapes and places of everyday existence—urban, rural, and wild—in environmental *and* aesthetic terms. "God's own junkyard" need not continue to dominate our public landscapes, nor our own backyards and city streets.

It is important to note, also, that *landscape architecture* can be—again—the vital discipline and agency that it was during its formative years in the nineteenth century when pioneers of the profession—from Andrew Jackson Downing, Frederick Law Olmsted, and Calvert Vaux to H. W. S. Cleveland, Beatrice Farrand, and Charles Eliot—were trying hard and with much success to make our world more humane, more beautiful, and more civilized, even as they used and adapted nature to human handiworks. They were, for the most part, trying to get beyond the notion that Frank Lloyd Wright would later espouse to great cultural effect: That landscape is primarily an extension of architecture.

We often forget that the roots of landscape architecture are in art and science. As the profession developed between the Civil War and the early twentieth century, a concerted effort was made on the part of many of its practitioners to embrace the best qualities of artistic design, planning, and the emerging life and natural sciences, such as botany, horticulture, soil science, and forestry. Designs reflected an increasingly interdisciplinary approach—though practitioners had not yet discovered that phrase—to the management, planning, and design of landscapes, communities, parks, and cities throughout the United States and much of the world. Designs often reflected an application of a broad base of knowledge of and experience in art, geography, economics, history, sociology, and science. Landscape architecture emerged quickly from its European predecessor, landscape gardening.

The motivations for such maturation were rooted, for the most part, in the public good. Unlike in today's professional climate, the client was not only the wealthy socialite or corporate heavyweight, but also city, state, and federal governments and the common citizen. How else would we have achieved such masterpieces as Prospect Park in Brooklyn, Central Park in Manhattan, the Emerald Necklace in Boston, the Minneapolis–Saint Paul Parks System, Parc Mont Royale in Montreal, Yellowstone in Wyoming, or Mariposa Grove and Yosemite in California, to cite some obvious examples?

In 1969 Ian McHarg published his *Design with Nature*, now a classic. In a real sense, this book brought landscape architecture back home. During the interwar period of the 1920s and 1930s, landscape architecture became dramatically oriented to the Beaux Arts tradition, forgetting most of its ties to science, regional planning, and the public good. McHarg reminded us— and taught a new generation of scholars, students, and practitioners—that landscape architecture involves art and science, nature and culture, city and region, the public good as well as the need to make a living. His tone was revolutionary, and oriented heavily toward the use and implementation of ecological design and planning—so much so that a good portion of the field resented the seeming dismissal of art as a viable part of the profession.

The backlash against "McHargian" ideas within some leading landscape architecture programs and trade magazines was, at times, severe, perhaps a knee-jerk fear of science invading nineteenth-century traditional art, as if "science may yet prove to be the anti-Christ," to quote the late Kenneth Lash. After all, quantitative methods were invading and severely altering the core spirit and direction of such landscape-based disciplines as geography, to the detriment of society and the academy. This backlash—still ongoing in some professional circles more than twenty-five years after the initial publication of *Design with Nature*—is ironic, for the time has come—finally, some would say—when world leaders are advocating sustainability and partnership and when other disciplines as diverse as architecture, forestry, geography, planning, and soil science have embraced, or returned to, the ideas and approaches espoused by McHarg. As a point of fact, *Design with Nature* laid the groundwork for the emergence of geographic information systems (GIS) and environmental impact assessments, which today dominate practice in both academic and public-policy spheres.

Although McHarg is still the revolutionary mind and spirit in the profession's collective memory, he was not the first to blend art and science, and design and planning, in landscape architecture. He had heroes, too, who pointed him down this path, most notably Lewis Mumford, Loren Eiseley,

Charles Eliot, Eugene Odum, and Patrick Geddes. And other contemporary landscape architects have reestablished connections with the past—with the practice of Jens Jensen, for example, especially as regards his understanding and use of native plants. It was Jensen, after all, who wrote in 1939 in *Siftings*, "Every plant has its fitness and must be placed in its proper surrounding so as to bring out its full beauty. Therein lies the art of landscaping." Jensen's long-standing call to design and plan with nature—and to create regional landscape designs and plans based on the use of plants native to a region—is the call some landscape architects hear most loudly today.

Or they hear Aldo Leopold, whose land ethic for the United States and the world was first expressed in the *Journal of Forestry* in 1933 and later refined in his heroic book *A Sand County Almanac* (1949). Leopold's message is still the wake-up call for many landscape architects, conservationists, environmentalists, geographers, and citizens who believe that, as a scientist and a land manager, he first brought forward the intuition that ecology, aesthetics, and a land ethic are inextricable.

Charles E. Little, the renowned conservationist and writer, has suggested privately that Leopold may have gotten his idea for a land ethic by reading Ludwig Wittgenstein, the British philosopher who argued in his journals that "ethics and aesthetics are one." Wittgenstein's concept, Little continues, may well have informed Leopold's essays, his "conservation aesthetic," as well as his "land ethic." Landscape architects such as Phil Lewis and McHarg who emerged during the 1960s developed the linkage between ethics and aesthetics in the practical world of landscape design and land-use policy. The terminology changed somewhat with Lewis and McHarg, but the Olmsted-Eliot-Jensen-Leopold-*et alia* tradition continued with the revived notion of ecological determinism in landscape architecture.

Now, as we anticipate the arrival of the twenty-first century, landscape architecture is at a crossroads. If the discipline embraces ecological design and planning, then it has a leadership role in contemporary society throughout the world. If landscape architecture, however, turns inward and ignores its larger responsibility to the public good, then it will become marginalized and less relevant.

To address our collective present we have brought together in this book—for the first time—not only some of the pioneers who have advanced an ecological approach in landscape architecture since the 1960s, but also leading practitioners and scholars of the next generation whose work involves either an ecological approach or a more aesthetically based alternative. Our goal was to create a synthesis of perspectives in order to lay the foundation for the new theories in landscape architecture that may emerge in the next century as a consequence of the profession's ongoing development and maturity as an art and science. The book makes no claim of being encyclopedic, but it does offer a range of ideas by leading scholars, designers, and planners in landscape architecture about a topic—ecological design and planning—that is not going away.

We have reached a critical time in our society when the health and maintenance of our cities and communities—and even the earth itself—is more imperative than a generation ago. Today, as most of our open spaces, wildlife habitats, air, water, soils, and trees show stress and decline despite hopes for a better future, the often cantankerous debate about ecology and its relevance for landscape architecture must be enlarged. We must appreciate *landscape* and *place* as ideas, and apply these ideas to the design, management, and planning of our homes, places of work, communities, cities, and biocultural regions. What this book attempts to accomplish, then, is to put an outdated debate—art versus science, nature versus culture, design versus planning, development versus beauty—to rest, so that we can move to a new dialogue about art *and* science, land *and* culture, design *and* planning, development *and* environmental health, practical needs *and* beauty. This is the call that landscape architecture must inevitably follow, in which ecological approaches will be seen as a vital part of landscape architecture's purpose and promise.

PART 1

RETROSPECT

1

LANDSCAPE ECOLOGICAL PLANNING

FORSTER NDUBISI

*In a time before history, people and their earth were as one,
inseparable. No words separated the dynamics of life and land.
Learning was there, and over time mistakes were corrected. Life relied
on the ability to sustain land. People fostered landscapes that fed
animals that in turn fed people. People were intelligent, but slowly
they forgot what it was to experience life. People, life, land, and flora
became dissected. But the spark still glowed from those early days of
prehistory. In the mid to late 1800s, the likes of Olmsted, Muir, and
Marsh remembered the way of life of their ancestors and began to
struggle to introduce it in their time.*   BOB SCARFO[1]

These observations by landscape architect Bob Scarfo capture the essence of
this essay: The evolutionary awakening of life and land. The landscape is the
template for understanding the intricate interactions between life and land.
It implies the totality of natural and cultural features on, over, and in the
land. The blending of natural and cultural features that make up a landscape
includes visible features such as fields, hills, forests, rivers, and lakes. In
turn, these visible features reflect the culture of its inhabitants. I use the term
landscape to denote the interface between human and natural processes.

Landscapes change over time as people mold natural processes, sometimes in tune with the rhythms of natural processes and other times altering

them. Landscape ecological planning is a way of directing or managing change in the landscape to bring human actions in tune with natural processes.[2]

The concept of landscape planning is not new to the United States. In 1641, the Massachusetts Bay Colony passed the Great Ponds Act, which required landowners to maintain public access to any body of water ten acres or more for the purposes of "fishing" or "fowling." Even at that time, the idea of managing fragile natural and cultural resources for human use and enjoyment existed. Lewis and Clark's expedition between 1804 and 1806 up the Missouri River and beyond to Astoria brought to the attention of the federal government those vast and beautiful lands west of Saint Louis and the Mississippi River. Accordingly, questions about how and in what way to settle the land might well have been the first landscape planning issues addressed by the federal government.[3] A historical perspective of landscape planning illustrates the events, ideas, and people that have been central to its evolution. My intent is to explore how and why it has developed into what it is today.

Landscape ecological planning means different things to different people, so a clarification of terms is necessary. At the interface between people and their use, and abuse, of resources is planning. I define planning as the integration of scientific and technical knowledge that provides options for making decisions about alternative futures. Planning does not focus solely on scientific knowledge or on decision making, but rather on the integration of both. When we extend the definition of planning into the context of the landscape, decisions about alternative futures focus on the wise and sustained use of the landscape in accommodating human needs. The wise use of the landscape signifies the *best* use, everything considered. Implicit in the idea of the best use of resources is permanence and stability; that is, the recognition of the need to accommodate human needs while protecting significant natural and cultural resources. The sustained use of the landscape ensures that the ability of future generations to meet their needs is not sacrificed in handling the present needs.

Insights regarding what we need to know to formulate alternative futures for the landscape can be gleaned from Alexander Pope's advice: "to consult the genius of place."[4] Plato also remarked: "To command nature, we must first obey her."[5] The underlying wisdom here is that we need to understand the character of the landscape not only in terms of its natural

The Shenandoah River and Blue Ridge Mountains, Clarke County, Virginia, as viewed from Rolling Hills Farm. Here, the interface of natural and cultural systems is superb. Photograph by George F. Thompson, 1987.

processes, but also in terms of the reciprocal relationships between people and the landscape. The important word is *relationships*. Of all the natural and social sciences, ecology provides, perhaps, the most beneficial insights into understanding the landscape, because it deals with the "reciprocal relationship of all living things to each other [including humans] and to their biological and physical environments."[6] I emphasize people because, until the past few decades, North American studies in ecology have focused on environments that are unaffected or affected little by people. Even these studies constitute interactions between people and living and nonliving things.

Thus, landscape planning is a process of managing change while maintaining regard for the wise and sustained use of the landscape, based on the knowledge of the reciprocal relationship between people and land. It is a process, a domain of professional practice and research in the discipline of landscape architecture and, arguably, within the profession of planning. Moreover, it is a recognized activity of federal, state, and local governments. Landscape planning is a form of intervention that traditionally has been applied at a scale that is larger than a specific site. In addition, it can be applied in a variety of landscapes, including the urban, suburban, rural, and wild.

Since no profession by itself can understand fully all the intricacies involved in making decisions about the wise and sustained use of the land, the practice of landscape planning is a multidisciplinary effort, effectively undertaken by a team consisting of anthropologists, ecologists, foresters, geographers, historians, landscape architects, planners, sociologists, and soil scientists, among others. This does not mean that the landscape planner does not play a specific role, for he or she integrates and interprets information provided by the various disciplines and puts it in a form that offers options for decisions regarding the wise and sustained use of a landscape.

EVOLUTION OF A PARADIGM

Every profession has a life cycle, and so does landscape planning. The major phases of the development of landscape planning somewhat parallel those identified in Thomas Kuhn's work on the structure of scientific revolutions. He used the idea of a paradigm to assess the developmental progression of the scientific community. A paradigm is a scheme for understanding and explaining aspects of reality. It provides a basis or organizational principle that enables a professional community to solve problems that were previously deemed insolvable or overwhelming. The acquisition of a paradigm is a sign of maturity in the development of any professional community.

Kuhn asserted that major changes in scientific thought occur periodically when existing paradigms explain anomalies inadequately. The change takes the initial form of a new paradigm that provides another way of interpreting the older knowledge. Planners and landscape architects have used Kuhn's idea of paradigm development to examine the evolution of their professions.[7] In a similar manner, I extend its usage in exploring how landscape planning evolved. Like Kuhn, I refer to the developmental phases of landscape planning as Awakening, Formative, Consolidation, Acceptance, and Maturation.[8] I caution that these phases do not correspond exactly with the phases that Kuhn suggested.[9] But his ideas are instructive in explaining the progression from one phase to another.

Awakening

Landscape planning in the United States evolved as a part of the profession of landscape architecture in the mid-nineteenth century. The early phase in the evolution of landscape planning was when its basic shared values and beliefs were articulated. This phase is usually marked by a "continued competition between a number of distinct views of nature . . . all roughly compatible."[10]

Frederick Law Olmsted, who is credited with founding the profession of landscape architecture, developed a plan for California's Yosemite Valley in 1864. This plan is an outstanding example of landscape planning at that time. He proposed not only the landscape development of the valley, but also a national strategy for recognizing and managing similar areas of natural beauty. Another classic example of landscape planning was the plan he developed for the Fens and the Riverway in Boston. This plan, continued by Olmsted's protégé Charles Eliot, resulted in the first metropolitan park system planned around hydrological and other ecological features. The significance of the plan is that it combined a concern for recreation, preservation of natural scenery, and the management of water quality. An example of a planned park that showed similar concerns for protecting natural systems was H. W. S. Cleveland's plan for the park systems of Minneapolis and Saint Paul in 1888. The plan reflected Cleveland's earlier call for examining the "intrinsic character" of landscapes to accommodate human growth.

Olmsted's visionary ideas were numerous. One that impresses me is his view that the landscape is a living entity, a reflection of an ongoing, two-way interaction between people and their physical region. Such a view contrasted with the European garden park model, which depicted nature as an epitome of perfection that "could be observed from a vantage point somewhere outside of her influence."[11] Although Olmsted's primary interest was shaping the city for the benefit of society, he demonstrated that caring for human health and enjoyment was synonymous with caring for the landscape.

The call for planning with, rather than against, nature was echoed by visionary thinkers outside the emerging profession of landscape architecture. In his 1864 classic, *Man and Nature, or Physical Geography as Modified by Human Action*, geographer George Perkins Marsh put forth a convincing argument for using nature to "mitigate extremes" in human actions.[12] Shortly thereafter, John Wesley Powell, the renowned explorer and director of the U.S. Geographical and Geological Survey of the Rocky Mountain region, drew extensively on Marsh's ideas and formulated public policy for managing the arid lands of the western United States. He argued that the redemption of these lands should be based on knowledge of "the character of the lands themselves."[13] Ebenezer Howard, an English proponent of the Garden City concept, also argued vehemently for giving high priority to protecting agricultural land for its productive value and its ability to serve as a buffer between cities.[14]

The 1890s and 1900s marked an increasing involvement of landscape architects in large-scale planning activities. The passage of the Forest Reserve Act of 1891 accelerated the development of parks nationwide and provided the opportunity for landscape architects to demonstrate how an understanding of intrinsic features could be utilized in planning and designing large tracts of public land. Landscape architects participated in the design of Yosemite National Park in 1891, Bronx River Park in 1907, and Grand Canyon National Park in 1908, among others. By 1910, landscape architecture was well established as a profession whose practitioners dealt with site-specific projects and large tracts of land.

In terms of large-scale planning, what I would call a "belief system" for guiding the use of the landscape was beginning to emerge. The belief system was a loose aggregation of competing ideas proposed by many visionary thinkers, but the unifying idea was that of using an understanding of the intrinsic character of the land to guide landscape use. I call it a belief system because it was based primarily on faith; its tenets were not yet founded on rigorous proof. Nevertheless, this belief system was consolidated during the park movement and in other large-scale projects that landscape architects were involved in during the following two decades.

The Formative Era

The field of landscape planning was in its formative stage in 1910. Practice in the field was marked by a series of innovative and rather successful attempts to plan open space systems, urban parks, and national parks, based on the belief system outlined above. Kuhn reminds us that, with a belief system, "all the facts that could possibly pertain to the development of any given [professional community] are likely to seem roughly relevant."[15] Thus, the formative era was a period of experimentation in landscape planning: Consolidating and refining ideas in the belief system in numerous large-scale projects, sorting out which ones were more useful than others, and developing techniques for putting good ideas into practice. This era also coincided with the gradual emergence of landscape planning as a discipline within the profession of landscape architecture.

Warren Manning, a landscape architect who started his career working for Olmsted, developed an overlay technique for analyzing natural and cultural resource information. This innovative technique was applied in Manning's 1913 plan for the town of Billerica, Massachusetts, and validated the way plans were then developed by landscape architects. Through the overlay technique, landscape architects could better explain how relevant information is organized and combined to arrive at specific conclusions. Numerous questions, however, remained unanswered. For example, what is the effective unit for analyzing natural and cultural information, and why? What natural and cultural information should be identified and analyzed, and on what basis?

These questions were answered partially when, in 1915, a botanist and planner from Scotland, Patrick Geddes, provided insights on what constituted the unit for organizing and analyzing information for large-scale planning activities. He proposed a system for conducting regional surveys based on the idea that the complex relations between human action and the environment might best be understood in terms of "place-work-folk" attributes: "The types of people, their kinds of styles of work, the whole environment become represented in the community, and these react upon the individual, their activities, and their place itself."[16] What is impressive about the system that Geddes proposed is the emphasis he placed on examining not place, work, or folk, but the relationships among them. Indeed, the notion of relationships is a central feature of landscape planning as we know it today. Surveys were to be conducted based on a *systematic* understanding of the relationships between the regional landscape, people's economic activities, and their cultures. Interestingly, the "place-work-folk" attributes for understanding a region that Geddes proposed would become an underlying principle in the theory of human ecological planning proposed by Ian McHarg some fifty years later.

The concept of regionalism was promoted as a form of cultural philosophy in the 1920s and 1930s by the Regional Planning Association of America.[17] Members of this small group included Catherine Bauer, Benton MacKaye, Lewis Mumford, Clarence Stein, and Henry Wright. Others influenced by this group include Howard W. Odum and New Deal economist Rexford Tugwell, who guided the development of the greenbelt communities during the Depression. Despite the interest in regionalism, what actually constitutes a region is a thorny issue that landscape architects, geographers, and others continue to debate. For example, does a region imply a drainage basin, a watershed, a physiographic province, a cultural entity, a political unit, or some combination of all?

Advances in ecology, or the knowledge of the interrelationships between organisms and their living and nonliving environment, were already taking place in the biological and social sciences in the early decades of the twentieth century. For example, Frederick Clements, Henry Cowles, and Herbert Gleason studied plant communities in the 1920s and provided invaluable insights into how changes occurred in the landscape.[18] Their work showed that the landscape is a dynamic entity with a life history of its own. Plant communities go through a growth and developmental process that parallels that of an individual organism, insofar as they strive to reach a "climax stage." Cowles had a close association with the landscape architect Jens Jensen, whose pioneering work led to the "recognition of the aesthetic and functional values of native plant materials, and of the need to protect unique and significant natural landscapes."[19]

Although the evolution of landscape planning at this time was still fragmented, the ingredients of what would later become a paradigm for landscape planning were apparent. By the late 1920s, the notion of utilizing an understanding of the intrinsic character of the landscape to guide planning had been put to test in many large-scale planning endeavors, including the planning of parkways and state parks. For example, the ideas of Olmsted and Howard on utilizing natural principles were expounded upon and applied in the design of planned residential communities such as Radburn, New Jersey, and Chicopee, Georgia. Regions were already being used as a basis in conducting surveys. But integrating ecological ideas into planning was still rudimentary.

Another feature of the latter phase of the Formative Era in landscape planning was a shift from the *need* to understand the intrinsic character of the landscape to *how* such understanding might be applied with *rigor and consistency* in guiding human use and management of the landscape. When consistency is lacking, different outcomes may be reached using the same information. Kuhn pointed out that an early preparadigm phase can be distinguished readily by "insufficiency of methodological directives to dictate unique substantive conclusions" to the many questions that confront a professional community.[20] At this stage, explicit methodological rules governing landscape planning efforts were yet to be formulated.

Consolidation

Some of the key ingredients of a recognizable paradigm for landscape planning were consolidated between the late 1920s and the 1950s. The developments that would eventually lead to a recognizable paradigm evolved around three main issues: (1) The explicit linkage between ecology and planning, (2) the articulation of ethical principles governing human relations to the land, and (3) the refinement of techniques for applying ecological ideas in landscape planning efforts. These developments were in part shaped by United States social history in the years between the 1930s and 1950s.

The beginning of this era was marked by chronic economic, social, and environmental problems associated with the Great Depression. President Franklin D. Roosevelt pledged a New Deal for the American people aimed at addressing the problems associated with the Depression. Two noteworthy endeavors were the soil conservation movement and the Tennessee Valley Authority (TVA) project.

The larger conservation movement gathered steam when the federal government in the late nineteenth century initiated efforts to achieve a sustainable balance between accommodating the needs of peoples and protecting significant natural and cultural resources. In fact, one can claim that landscape planning is synonymous with conservation, at least in a philosophical way. During the New Deal, however, the focus of conservation efforts shifted with the emergence of public concern for soil conservation. The Soil Erosion Service was organized in 1933 largely through the efforts of H. H. Bennett. In 1935, the Soil Conservation Service (SCS) was established as a permanent agency under the Soil Conservation Act. One unique aspect of the work of the SCS contributed immensely to the refinement of techniques used in integrating ecological principles into landscape planning. This was the development of "land capability" maps designed to show an area's agricultural capacity, based on the intrinsic ability of the soil to support one type of agricultural use over another.

The TVA was established in 1933 mainly for flood control, rural electrification, and the development of commerce and river navigation in the South. It signified a recognition by the federal government of the need for the sustained and multiple use of social, natural, cultural, and economic resources. In addition, the TVA project demonstrated the effectiveness of using a river basin as a unit for landscape planning. Moreover, public agencies at the time provided the primary employment opportunity for landscape architects. Such opportunities not only bolstered the profession's recognition, but also illuminated the landscape architect's capabilities in large-scale planning endeavors including parks, recreation, and open-space planning and design. The New Deal era made clear the interdependencies of ecological, social, and economic factors, and the role landscape architects and planners could play in large-scale land planning.

In 1928, Benton MacKaye, a champion of the primeval landscape, published *The New Exploration,* which articulated objectives for regional planning and the specific tasks of a regional planner. He asserted that planners have a responsibility to understand a place by revealing both its physical and human aspects: "Here we have the function of every sort of planner: it is primarily to uncover, reveal, visualize—not only his own ideas but nature's; not merely to formulate the desires of man, but to reveal the limits thereto imposed by a greater power. Thus,...planning is two things: (1) an accurate formulation of our own desires, the specific knowledge of what we want; and (2) an accurate revelation of the limits, and the opportunities, imposed and bequeathed to us by nature."[21]

MacKaye advocated an approach to planning grounded in human ecology. He urged understanding the landscape in its totality: Its physical and natural attributes and processes, as well as the attributes of cultural values, processes, and meanings attached to the landscape. He later explicitly linked regional planning to ecology and, more specifically, to human ecology: "The region is the unit of environment. Planning is the charting of activity therein affecting the good of the human organism, its object is the application or putting into practice the optimum relation between humans and the region. Regional planning in short is applied human ecology."[22]

To accomplish the tasks of planning that MacKaye proposed, we would have to assume that an ethic or a set of moral principles existed that governed human relations to the land. This was not the situation. Ethical thoughts and behavior were based on individual relations to other individuals. Even when visionary thinkers such as Olmsted, Marsh, Powell, and Cleveland called for understanding nature as a basis for planning, the relations of people to the land were still predominantly governed by economic self-interest, not a land ethic. Because people-land relations were strictly economic, they entailed exchange and privileges, not moral obligations or responsibilities. New forms of ethical thought and behavior were urgently needed that would allow for an extension of human ethics to the natural environment.

The foundation for a "new" ethic was articulated in a series of essays written between the 1930s and late 1940s by Aldo Leopold, a wildlife biologist and forester who had been involved with the SCS in watershed planning as well. One underlying theme in his writings is the need to distinguish right and wrong actions on the land. To ensure the "healthy functioning" of land, he argued persuasively for an ethic that extends the boundaries of the biotic community, of which people are an integral part, "to include soils, water, plants, and animals, or collectively: the land." He regarded land as "all things on, over, or in the earth."[23] This inclusive view of an interdependent relationship between people and land calls people, whose survival is dependent on that of the other members of the community, to be responsible and caring members of the biotic community. Important, but often forgotten, is Leopold's plea for aesthetics in a land ethic.

Following the tradition of Marsh, Geddes, Jensen, and MacKaye, emerging leaders in the area of landscape planning and ecology continued to explore ways to use ecological principles to resolve the impact of human action on the landscape. The contributions were numerous, so I have chosen only a few. In many books, Mumford explored how human processes were intricately interwoven with natural processes in the city. He rarely used the term *ecology,* but his works dealt extensively with landscape planning in the city. Edward Graham proposed a method for integrating ecological principles in planning for different rural uses. In addition, he established a clear relationship between landscape planning and the public interest.[24] A relatively unknown biologist, William Vogt, proposed a "biotic equation" for achieving ecological health, which was a function of biological potential and environmental resistance.[25] Ecological health is, indeed, carrying capacity. The latter would became a powerful concept used by landscape architects and planners in resolving people-nature conflicts. In 1950, Jacqueline Tyrwhitt provided the first explicit discussion of how the overlay technique actually works. The overlay technique would later be an inherent feature of many landscape planning methods that were proposed during the 1960s.[26]

If a paradigm represents a body of consistent ideas, theories, data requirements, and techniques for putting ideas into practice, then a recognizable paradigm for landscape planning was developing by the 1950s. A rationale for extending human ethics into the natural environment had been articulated. The desirability of employing ecological ideas in planning was a value that was shared increasingly by landscape architects and planners, although the language of ecology was not explicitly used. Ecological ideas were applied in numerous large-scale public planning efforts. For example, the drainage basin was used to establish the boundaries for planning large areas. The notions of multiple use, sustained yield, and carrying capacity were employed as planning and management principles. Also, the techniques for integrating ecological ideas into planning continue to be refined, especially through the efforts of the SCS.

Although most elements for an established paradigm were sufficiently developed, a solid coherence among them was lacking. When coherence is lacking, the outcome usually is a proliferation of competing methods, which was evident during the Consolidation Era. Competition among the methods continues until one or more of the methods are able to yield consistent results. Kuhn suggested that "to be accepted as a paradigm, a theory [or method] must seem better than its competitors."[27]

After World War II, the United States became an economic powerhouse of consumer goods that depended largely on natural resources. The rapid increase in population and related production placed an unprecedented demand on the land. Air pollution and the contamination of water sources were two consequences of the rapid growth. A third consequence was a growing public recognition of abuse and degradation of the landscape. The fact that abuse of the landscape was seemingly uncontrolled raised serious concerns about the ability to plan for the wise and sustained use of the landscape. What happened to the call for a land ethic, to the call for planning with nature? The search for answers coincided with an international conference sponsored by the Wenner-Gren Foundation for Anthropological Research in New Jersey on "Man's Role in Changing the Face of the Earth."[28] An important outcome of the conference was a renewed commitment to increase public awareness about the consequences of degradation of the landscape and to develop management strategies to reduce degradation.

Acceptance

The beginning of this era coincided with many social and political upheavals that took place in the United States during the 1960s. Many Americans publicly began to question the basic values that had made the United States a dominant industrial and technological society. Protests against a growing technological culture bolstered a contemporary environmental crusade in a way that brought ecology and environmental ethics to the forefront of public attention. The Acceptance Era may well represent the period of "paradigm consensus" in the life cycle of landscape planning, when all the ingredients of an acceptable paradigm—the ethical foundation, working theories and concepts, techniques, and ideas for putting theory into practice—were woven together in a fairly coherent fashion.

While public consciousness of alienation and environmental degradation was growing, many influential people, especially in academic circles, sought to find ways to reconcile human abuses to the environment. Three people stand out from the rest: Angus Hills, Philip Lewis, and Ian McHarg. Hills, a soil scientist and geographer, and his colleagues from Toronto, Canada, developed a method for using the biological and physical capability of the land to guide land-use decisions for agriculture, forestry, wildlife, and recreation.[29]

From the Midwest, Lewis, a landscape architect and professor, first at the University of Illinois and then at the University of Wisconsin–Madison, made significant advances in developing methods for protecting unique and rapidly disappearing recreational resources. Unlike Hills, whose work was based primarily on examining biological and physical (biophysical) systems such as landforms and soils, Lewis was concerned more with perceptual features such as vegetation and outstanding scenery. In his *Quality Corridor Study for Wisconsin,* Lewis found that the unique perceptual resources in the Midwest were the surface water, wetlands, and significant topography. The resources were to be connected to form a linear pattern that he referred to as an "environmental corridor." In effect, he was able to develop an approach that linked the perceptual or visual qualities of the landscape, which had been little studied, to natural/environmental features.[30]

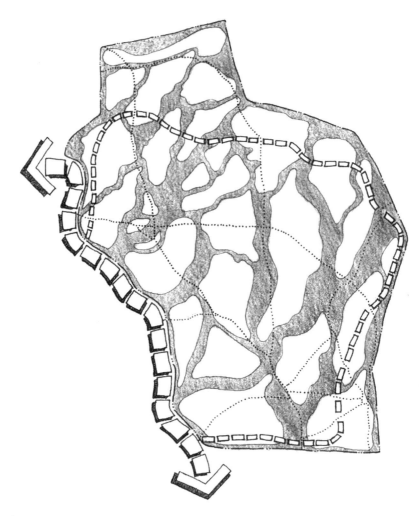

The quality corridor study for Wisconsin (Philip Lewis 1964) linked visual qualities of the landscape to natural environmental features. The shaded areas denote portions of the landscape that contained a unique perceptual resource. Drawn by Kirsten Barré.

Beginning in the early 1960s, McHarg, a landscape architect, city and regional planner, and educator, argued strongly and persuasively for employing ecology as a basis for reconciling human use and abuse of the landscape. He promoted ecology vigorously as the foundation science for landscape architecture and planning. Heavily influenced by the works of Geddes and, especially, Mumford's reverence for life, he may well have made the most significant advances in the field of landscape planning in the twentieth century. Through a series of lectures and writings, he outlined an ethos and a method that explicitly linked ecology to planning and design. The method is widely known as a *suitability analysis*. The ethical principles, working theory, and successful applications of the approach were skillfully presented in his seminal book, *Design with Nature,* published in 1969. McHarg's method, as it came to be known, revealed nature as a process and value that has rights for continued existence: "The basic proposition employed is that any place is the sum of its historic, physical and biological processes, that these are dynamic, and they constitute social values, that each area has an intrinsic suitability for certain land uses and finally that certain areas lend themselves to multiple coexisting land uses."[31]

McHarg's techniques involved superimposing hand-drawn translucent overlay maps of physiography, drainage, soils, and critical natural and cultural resource factors to reveal areas suitable for different types of human uses. McHarg viewed the method as a direct divergence from methods used in planning, in which the bulk of information employed was based on criteria that were often ambiguous and covert. In short, his was a thoroughly defensible approach. Perhaps this is the reason it continues to appeal to practitioners and scholars.

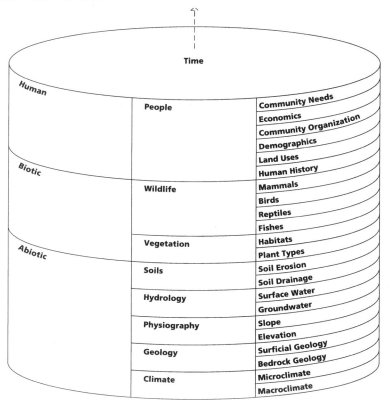

The Layer-Cake Model (Wallace, McHarg, Roberts & Todd 1971–74) illuminates the relationships among elements across a landscape. The elements are mapped and superimposed to reveal areas in the landscape suitable for different human activities. Reinterpreted by Steiner 1991a and drawn by Mookesh Patel, Sanft Design, Inc.

Meanwhile, other significant contributions took place that would solidify and confirm the importance of landscape planning. Artur Glikson, an Israeli planner and architect, further clarified the role of regions in landscape planning. In 1967, Carl Steinitz and his colleagues from Harvard University extended the application of computer technology to landscape planning. The application was applied in such projects as the Minneapolis–Saint Paul Metropolitan Region Study and the study of an interstate highway in Rhode Island. In the late 1960s, Burt Litton of the University of California at Berkeley began to develop approaches for protecting unique scenic and cultural qualities in the landscape. Others followed and introduced new ideas, including Jay Appleton, Rachael and Stephen Kaplan, Sally Schauman, and Ervin Zube.

The period between 1961 and 1972 was significant in the evolution of landscape planning theory and methods. The intensity of developments marks this as the Awakening Era in landscape planning. The environmental movement and the passage of the National Environmental Policy Act (NEPA) in 1969 opened the way for landscape architects to assess natural, cultural, and visual resources of large areas. Numerous successful applications made McHarg's suitability method the modus operandi for the bulk of landscape and environmental land-use planning work undertaken by practitioners at the time.

Indeed, the development of the suitability approach satisfied most of the conditions stipulated by Kuhn for achieving "paradigm-consensus." McHarg's approach proved its ability to examine, to set the parameters, and to solve with better precision the problems associated with human use and abuse of the landscape. A lingering question remained, however: Does the suitability approach help us to understand why human abuses still exist and to explain what ought to be done, or is it more an approach to better management of the changes inherent in any landscape?

Signs of Maturation

The passage of NEPA and the acceptance of the suitability approach as a paradigm for solving problems dealing with human actions on the landscape were only a foretaste of things to come. Many environmental regulations were passed during the late 1960s and early 1970s by the federal government, such as the Clean Water Act, the Clean Air Act, the Coastal Zone

Management Act, and the Wild and Scenic Rivers Act. States and localities followed suit by adopting programs aimed at protecting the natural landscape. By the end of the 1970s, environmental protection was entrenched in American life.

Moreover, major advances were made in understanding the myriad interactions between people and landscape. For example, scientific information about the effects of air and water pollution became increasingly available. Landscape architects and planners began to work more often with scientists to obtain pertinent information about the nature of human impacts on the landscape. Also, rapid advances in computer technology enabled landscape planners to store, analyze, and display large amounts of natural and cultural resource data, thereby laying the foundation for providing intelligent and diverse options for decision making. Computer technology and geographical information systems (GIS), though in their infancy, began to characterize a majority of work in landscape planning.

Increased involvement of local governments in environmental protection perpetuated the emotional debate about private versus public property rights. It became a necessity, therefore, to provide policymakers with defensible and precise information about the use and protection of the landscape in a timely manner. Taken together, these events vastly increased the nature, scope, and complexity of issues that landscape planning had to address.

Earlier, I argued that the suitability approach emerged as an accepted paradigm for problem solving in landscape planning. Kuhn, however, pointed out that a paradigm, once accepted, still "is an object for further articulation and specification under new or stringent conditions."[32] Unlike earlier eras, the evolution of landscape planning during the Maturation Phase of the 1970s and 1980s has four themes: (1) Landscape processes, (2) culture in landscape planning, (3) landscape planning and the city, and (4) landscape ecology.

Landscape Processes

A comprehensive understanding of the inner workings of the landscape requires us to look at it in terms of structure, processes, and location. By structure, I mean the composition of biological and nonliving elements in natural and human environments—the functional relationship between elements such as climate, landforms, soils, flora, and fauna. Process implies the movement of energy, materials, and organisms in the landscape; location refers to the distribution of elements and processes in the landscape in relation to climate and landforms.

McHarg's approach as described in *Design with Nature* recognizes the significance of landscape processes but, in hindsight, provides insufficient guidance on how they can be incorporated as options for managing change on and in the landscape. More precisely, it treats landscape elements such as soils and vegetation as if they were separate and independent features. To identify areas in the landscape that are intrinsically suitable or sensitive to different human activities, we identify relevant landscape elements and place them on translucent maps or into computers. We know the mapped elements are intimately related to each other from our knowledge of ecology. Only when we combine them by using the overlay technique do we actually display and "model" their functional relationship to each other, and how they are distributed over the landscape. The display, however, does not show how energy, materials, or organisms flow among the landscape elements under study. To do that, we need to make assumptions about the nature of the flows when we select the relevant elements that are overlaid. A related problem is that, since we focus on identifying areas that are sensitive as well as suitable for human activities, we may neglect those areas in the landscape that do not have any consequences for human use. An example is the capacity for long-term survival of a protected or endangered wildlife or plant species. I argue that the inadequacies in the McHarg method at that time were related to insufficient knowledge of the ecological theory and of human ecology.

The response of ecologists and landscape planners to integrating knowledge of the function of landscapes in their works has come in many forms. The Woodlands, Texas, for example, was a new community designed by McHarg and his colleagues. Among its successes is the manner in which the designers skillfully utilized land-use suitability analysis and ecological information to develop a master plan and performance criteria for implementing the plan. In fact, McHarg emphasized that "the natural balance of the hydrological regime was the key to successful environmental planning and an organizing concept for development."[33]

Eugene Odum, a prominent ecologist from the University of Georgia, shed insight into the manner in which ecosystems change in response to human actions. He developed a working model or theory that makes clearer the functional relationships between types of landscape required by people

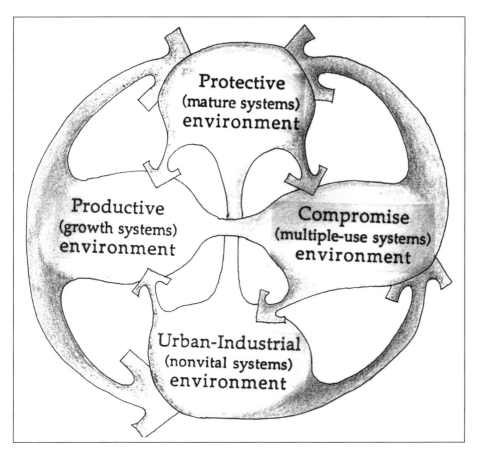

Eugene Odum's ecosystem compartment model (1969) relates the major types of landscape to the ecological functions required to support them. Drawn by Kirsten Barré.

and the ecological functions required to support them. The model divides the landscape according to its basic ecological roles: Production (e.g., agriculture, forestry); protection (e.g., wetlands, mature forests); compromise or multiple-use (e.g., suburbs under a forest canopy); and biologically nonvital uses (e.g., cities, industry). Odum's model provides a theoretical basis for understanding the functioning of landscapes. Julius Fabos and his coworkers at the University of Massachusetts in Amherst have, for two decades, used Odum's model as the basis for developing a comprehensive approach to regional land-use planning. Moreover, researchers from other disciplines, especially conservation biologists and environmental managers, have made significant advances in utilizing concepts about ecosystem structure and processes in their work.[34]

Culture in Landscape Planning

As an interface between natural and human processes, the landscape reflects the dialogue that has occurred between both processes over time. Ecological landscape planning, therefore, requires an in-depth understanding of the nature and evolution of the dialogue. In attempting to reconcile human use and abuse of the landscape, environmentally oriented planners and designers have tended to overemphasize natural processes in their understanding of the dialectic with human processes. The result is a constant struggle to understand the human side of the dialogue. When human processes are considered, they are usually relegated to such information as the social, economic, and demographic profiles of a community or region. Yet people have a culture or a "characteristic way of life." Their value systems guide their selection of alternative ways of doing things, including the way they use the landscape and adapt to it.

The Church of St. Francis of Assissi at Ranchos de Taos, New Mexico, was built in 1772 and speaks volumes about the interface of three cultures—Indian, Spanish, and Anglo-American—in the Land of Enchantment. Photograph by George F. Thompson, 1993.

What is often missing is a "deep" understanding of the accumulated experiences of people on a particular landscape, the meanings they attach to it, and how all of these change over time. Social scientists, landscape architects, and planners often have a difficult time in reaching this understanding. It "comes from not only a scientific overview of a region, but also from the voices of the residents themselves . . . the insiders' view . . . [which most planners hold] does not yet have a framework into which they incorporate such information, and insiders' views often conflict."[35]

Efforts to identify and incorporate the insiders' view have come from many directions. Landscape architects, including Litton, Schauman, and Zube, have considerably advanced our knowledge of landscape perception, which is considered a function of the interactions of people and the landscape, but we still lack agreement on a unifying theory of landscape perception.[36] The University of Pennsylvania has been at the forefront in integrating human processes into landscape planning, and the work of Narendra Juneja on Medford Township, New Jersey, in the early 1970s under the guidance of McHarg, in particular, continues to exemplify innovative efforts in integrating social values into landscape planning.

Also notable among the efforts to understand better how people affect and are affected by the natural environment is the Hazleton Human Ecological Study, undertaken by a University of Pennsylvania team of landscape architects, planners, and anthropologists. The study focused on how people in a mountainous region in rural Pennsylvania adapted to their natural environment. Still other significant efforts include the works of Jonathan Berger, Yehudi Cohen, Joanne Jackson, Dan Rose, and Frederick Steiner. Initially, these efforts suffered from the lack of a solid theoretical base. It was not until the early 1980s that McHarg articulated a theory of human ecological planning, which he summarized as follows:

All systems aspire to survival and success. This state can be described as syntropic-fitness-health. Its antithesis is entopic-misfitness-morbidity. To achieve the first state requires systems to find the fittest environment, adapt it and themselves. Fitness of an environment for a system is defined as that requiring the minimum work of adaptation. Fitness and fitting are indications of health and the process of fitting is health giving. The quest for fitness is entitled adaptation. Of all the instrumentalities available to man for successful adaption, cultural adaptation in general and planning in particular appear to be the most direct and efficacious for maintaining and enhancing human health and well-being.[37]

Planning that strives for fitness between people and the landscape, therefore, is one of the most promising ways to reestablish the form and content of the dialogue between human and natural processes. A majority of subsequent work in landscape planning explicitly considers human processes. The work of Berger and John Sinton on the New Jersey Pine Barrens is an example of how to develop a plan that responds "not only to place, but to people as well." My plans for Ojibway Indian communities in Canada during the 1980s also exemplify an attempt to understand the nature of the dialectic between human and natural processes in situations when the planner or designer comes from a social group whose culture is different from that of the client group.[38]

Landscape Planning and the City

During the 1960s McHarg called on landscape architects to extend ecological principles to landscape planning problems in the city. Unfortunately, most efforts in landscape planning have, until recently, ignored the city or have treated the city in terms of the demand it places on rural areas for recreation, food, energy, and waste disposal. Yet the city is a part of nature. Whatever processes occur in the city also take place in suburban and rural areas. In fact, the challenge the city poses to landscape planning is "both the greatest and the least recognized, because the human-built structure seems so dominant, because the contrast between nature's order and human order is particularly acute, and because cultural processes are so densely interwoven and overlain."[39]

Landscape architects, including Anne Spirn, Michael Hough, and John Lyle, have argued convincingly that landscape planning can play a major role in reconciling human use and abuse of urban landscapes. They contend that, whereas the intensity and the varieties of human activities may be of a different character, the natural processes are still the same: The flow of nutrients, energy, and organisms. In cities, however, most of these processes have been replaced by artificial ones that do not regenerate themselves. For example, many of the storm drainage systems in cities were located to interrupt or even destroy the rhythm that nature uses to move water. Over time, we will increasingly import most of the food, energy, and water we use in the city.

These landscape architects and others concerned about landscape planning in the city agree that it is essential to view urban landscapes as ecosys-

An evening concert along the redesigned banks of the Scioto River looking east at Columbus, Ohio. Photograph by Bob Thall, 1994, from the National Road Project.

tems; that is, as a collection of living organisms interacting with each other and their natural and built environment. This viewpoint makes sense only when people are regarded as an integral and essential component of living organisms. They advocate designing and planning landscapes that are rich, diverse, productive, and regenerative. A point of departure is to understand the inner workings of ecosystems and their visual expressions. Attention is paid to ecological processes essential to the functioning and sustenance of ecosystems: The flow of energy, material nutrients, and species. Interest in urban landscapes continue to thrive.

Landscape Ecology

Landscape architects and planners have often struggled with translating ecological principles into a scale that is practical for people. Most ecological studies are conducted on larger landscapes. Translating the resultant ecological principles to address issues in landscapes of a relatively small size is a problem with which ecologists and planners have struggled. Moreover, in numerous landscape planning efforts, ecologists have traditionally played the role of experts who organize ecological information in a format that is readily accessible to landscape planners and designers. The latter are then expected to create ecological and visual order as well as meaning in the landscape. Because most ecologists do not think visually, as do most designers, ecological information is rarely organized in a way that is immediately useful to landscape planners. This inhibits "the ecologically sound configuration of built and managed landscapes."[40]

Landscape ecology addresses some of these issues. Since Forman and Godron published their seminal book, *Landscape Ecology,* in 1986, an increasing fusion has occurred among ecologists, geographers, landscape architects, planners, and some historians in the United States. Landscape ecology seeks to understand the structure, function, and change in the landscape. There are many reasons for this fusion.

Landscape ecology provides a conceptual framework within which planners and designers can explore how the structure of land evolves along with relevant ecological processes. If the landscape is the interface between human and natural processes, by implication landscape ecology focuses on the medium in which the dialogue between both processes occurs. Landscape ecology also regards the landscape as an interacting mosaic of ecosystems, connected by flows of energy and materials. Over time, the ecosystems develop an identifiable visual and cultural identity. Since ecosystems of any size can be studied and the flows of energy and materials between ecosystems of different sizes can be identified, it follows that landscape ecology provides a key conceptual basis for studying landscapes at a scale that is practical for people. By extension, it focuses attention on understanding a landscape in relation to its social and natural contexts.

Landscape ecology strengthens the theoretical base of ecology by enabling both planners and ecologists to understand the landscape in terms of the relationship between three inseparable perspectives: The visual aspect, the chronological aspect, and the ecosystem aspect.[41] The point is that if planners and ecologists comprehend the landscape from a shared perspective, then ecological information can be interpreted better to provide both ecologically sound landscapes and landscapes that embody meaning, identity, and a sense of place. The application of landscape ecology in managing landscapes in North America, however, is still relatively new. Some pioneering works are emerging through the efforts of landscape architects, planners, and ecologists, including Jack Ahern, Edward Cook, Donna Hall Erickson, Frank Golley, Tom Hunt, James Thorne, and Joan Hirschman Woodward.

It is evident that diversity exists, both in the approaches that are currently in use in landscape planning as well as in the scope of its substantive areas of research and practice. Since the 1960s, the intensity of the evolutionary progression of landscape planning has almost surpassed that during the Awakening, Formative, and Consolidation eras. Unlike the earlier eras,

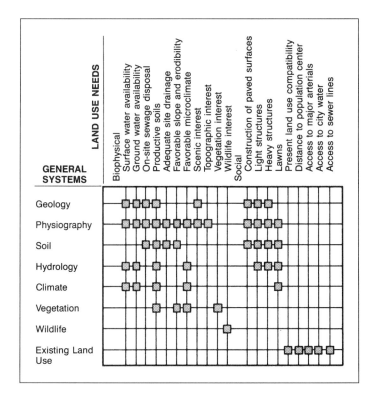

During the late 1970s and 1980s, Frederick Steiner was engaged in several ecological planning studies in eastern Washington and northern Idaho. One of those studies was for Asotin County, Washington, undertaken by a team of graduate students in planning and environmental science and senior landscape architecture students under the direction of Steiner and Kenneth Brooks.

Here land-use needs are compared with various biophysical processes. The shaded boxes indicate some relationship exists between the land-use need and the specific biophysical element.

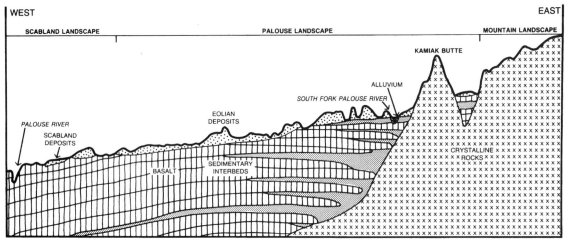

WEST   EAST

SCABLAND LANDSCAPE   PALOUSE LANDSCAPE   MOUNTAIN LANDSCAPE

KAMIAK BUTTE

ALLUVIUM

SOUTH FORK PALOUSE RIVER

EOLIAN
DEPOSITS

PALOUSE RIVER

SCABLAND
DEPOSITS   CRYSTALLINE
                                                                                   ROCKS

BASALT   SEDIMENTARY
            INTERBEDS

*Cross sections are a tool commonly used in ecological planning. Frederick Steiner adapted this
schematic east-west section through southern Whitman County, Washington, to illustrate the regional
geology. The cross section was used by Steiner in soil conservation planning during the mid-1980s.*

*Another common
ecological planning
tool is the thematic
map. This geology
map of the Palouse
River drainage basin
was used by Frederick
Steiner in a soil con-
servation study of the
region during the
mid-1980s.*

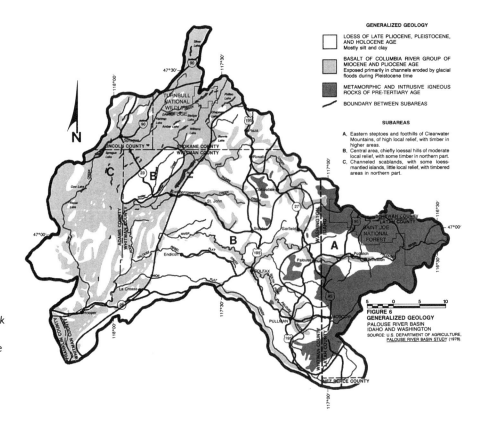

GENERALIZED GEOLOGY

LOESS OF LATE PLIOCENE, PLEISTOCENE,
AND HOLOCENE AGE
Mostly silt and clay

BASALT OF COLUMBIA RIVER GROUP OF
MIOCENE AND PLIOCENE AGE
Exposed primarily in channels eroded by glacial
floods during Pleistocene time

METAMORPHIC AND INTRUSIVE IGNEOUS
ROCKS OF PRE-TERTIARY AGE

BOUNDARY BETWEEN SUBAREAS

SUBAREAS

A. Eastern steptoes and foothills of Clearwater
Mountains, of high local relief, with timber in
higher areas.
B. Central area, chiefly loessal hills of moderate
local relief, with some timber in northern part.
C. Channeled scablands, with some loess-
mantled islands, little local relief, with timbered
areas in northern part.

FIGURE 6
GENERALIZED GEOLOGY
PALOUSE RIVER BASIN
IDAHO AND WASHINGTON
SOURCE: U.S. DEPARTMENT OF AGRICULTURE,
PALOUSE RIVER BASIN STUDY (1978).

in which the evolutionary progression focused on elaborating and clarifying the theme of planning with nature, the progression over the last two decades occurred in more divergent but related directions. The boundaries of landscape architecture and the field of landscape planning have broadened considerably. Moreover, new and complex problems regarding human actions on the landscape emerged as landscape architects and planners began to ask more diverse questions: Are we experiencing a fundamental shift in the values that have guided the practice of landscape planning? Is landscape planning experiencing a paradigm anomaly, as Kuhn would put it, or only a phase of maturation? Anomaly occurs when landscape planners cannot readily provide solutions to new and unsuspected problems that emerge regarding human actions on the landscape.

REFLECTION AND PROSPECT

From the late nineteenth century to the middle of the twentieth, the evolution of landscape planning was a slow and fragmented process in which new ideas were proposed and refined and others were added. A synthesis of the major themes in the evolution is offered as follows: The concern that human actions progressively degraded the landscape and that we should plan with nature; the consolidation of the idea of planning with nature in numerous large-scale planning efforts and the emigration of ecological ideas from biology into planning; the explicit linkage between ecology and planning and the continued refinement of methodological rules for integrating ecological ideas into planning; the consensus, especially among landscape architects and planners, that planning can and should be ecologically based, and the articulation of a consistent body of techniques and data requirements for integrating ecological principles into planning; and, recently, a diversity in the scope of substantive area applications of landscape planning. Kuhn's framework is instructive in explaining the evolution of landscape planning, but it provides no basis for speculating on future scenarios for its continuing evolution.

A shift in values is occurring within landscape architecture, and change is noticeable even in the profession's basic mission. The traditional definitions of design and planning have stressed fitting the landscape for human use and enjoyment. The themes of sustainability, ecological fit, ecological integrity and diversity, aesthetics, and maintenance of functioning landscapes are evident in recent definitions. Ecological fit is already in use as a major criterion for evaluating landscape planning projects. Ann Rosenberg puts it succinctly: "The key issue is a shift from ecology as an important consideration in the landscape architect's practice to ecology as a guiding principle at the deepest conceptual level of understanding."[42] Put simply, landscape architects and planners need to be proficient in understanding the science of ecology: "If doctors can know anatomy, then landscape architects and planners should know ecology."[43]

In response to this shift, which is still occurring, the suitability approach in landscape planning has undergone several revisions and has advanced beyond the theoretical-methodological construct presented in McHarg's *Design with Nature,* even as it continues to provide a bridge in relating human and natural processes to their spatial distribution on the landscape. Alternative approaches that complement and strengthen the suitability approach have been proposed, and I organize them into three broad categories that reflect subdisciplinary areas within ecology: Human ecological planning, applied ecosystem planning, and landscape ecology. Human ecological planning is useful where cultural matters are prominent. When an emphasis is placed on the relationships between the spatial distribution of human activities and ecological functions needed to support them, the applied ecosystem planning serves the role. Landscape ecology is valuable when land is the primary concern.

These new approaches reflect an ongoing maturation in landscape architecture and planning. The majority of developments during the past two decades have occurred in the research domain and are not yet an integral part of the professional practice of landscape design and planning. Such maturation enables landscape architects and planners to respond effectively to the increasing complexity of design and planning issues, and to permit better understanding and integration of ecological information into planning and design decisions at all levels.

With the expanded scope of decision making comes an increased need for a theoretical foundation to provide coherence to the current diversity that characterizes landscape planning. A scholarly debate exists over whether or not the field has a theory that addresses the following questions: What precisely is the process by which a landscape undergoes change in response to human actions and values? What are the impacts of human actions on other members of the biotic community, and how are the impacts expressed in the landscape? Which landscapes undergo what types of change, and in response to which human actions and values? Which natural processes in the landscape are most influenced by what human actions and values, under what conditions, and why? In the absence of a comprehensive theory, we encounter difficulties in establishing the identity of the profession, in defining its boundaries, and in articulating the theoretical basis for research. As Zube has said, "When theories are advanced, they are often in the form of models of spatial or functional relationships, or statements of what ought to be."[44]

I argue that there are two types of theory in landscape planning: Substantive and procedural.[45] Substantive theories of landscape planning permit better understanding of the landscape as the interface between human and natural processes. These theories are descriptive and predictive. They originate from the social and natural sciences, as well as the humanities, including such areas as anthropology, biology, ecology, geology, geography, history, and photography. When we seek to understand the landscape as a reflection of culture, we turn to the works of J. B. Jackson, Yi-Fu Tuan, John Stilgoe, Martha Strawn, Denis Wood, Neil Evernden, Cotton Mather, and the like.[46] When we want to understand aquatic systems, we turn to a limnologist and hydrologist. In contrast, procedural theories of landscape planning focus on methodological issues: Ideology, purposes, and principles of the process of landscape planning. They explicate the functional relationships that permit the application of the knowledge of human and natural processes in resolving human use and conflict in the landscape. McHarg's suitability approach remains the most prominent one.

In landscape planning, therefore, we draw upon substantive theories for information. But we use procedural theories as a framework to organize the information in a format that readily permits the use of that information in addressing landscape planning problems. In essence, an underlying duality exists in landscape planning. Herein lie its strengths and weaknesses. On the one hand, the effectiveness in utilizing information from substantive theories will depend largely on how the information is organized and presented to landscape planners and designers. When differences exist in the way landscape planners and those from other disciplines who develop these substantive theories understand reality, differing emphasis in the interpretation of the pertinent information may likely occur. This is one of the reasons that a bonding between ecologists and landscape architects and planners is taking place in landscape ecology, in an effort to overcome misinterpretation by understanding the landscape from the same perspective. On the other hand, it is only after we landscape architects and planners acknowledge that multiplicity and plurality are intrinsic features of landscape planning that we can *condition* ourselves to take advantage of the rich source of information that is offered us by substantive theorists. The key to conditioning is *interpretation.* By this, I mean there must be a conscious effort to understand information in terms of *relationships.* Indeed, this is the essence of ecology: To know and understand reality in terms of relationships.

Adopting ecology as a way of knowing has many profound consequences for landscape planning. It enables landscape architects and planners to inquire into the nature of scientific and cultural information that is provided to them. It forces them to ask such questions as: What does this information mean in terms of the inhabitants of a place, the local character, and the social heritage of the region?[47] Moreover, it expands the consciousness of landscape planners to a higher level, which enables them to appreciate and understand better the intricate web of interactions between human and natural processes. People, a rock outcrop, grasses, and wildflowers all become understood as integral and interdependent parts of a larger system, at varying scales. In ecological thinking and understanding, the distinction between "I" and "They" breaks down.

Ecological thinking presumes there are limits to which landscape planners and designers can understand the intricacies of human and natural processes. It follows that landscape planning and design should always be viewed as a participatory process, involving the inhabitants of a place in a meaningful way. Landscape plans and designs, whenever they are developed, become the byproduct of the process. Such plans and designs are more likely to express the intricacies of interrelationship between people and the landscape. Thus, participation becomes a central feature of the landscape planning process. As Stephen Kaplan pointed out: "Participatory design [and planning] fosters a better understanding of 'community' and is in itself a reflection of ecological processes evolving towards higher forms."[48] Fortunately, many landscape planners and designers already embrace the involvement of people in their works, and they should continue to do so.

Gathering, Amaranth Seed 2   9/23/81   —Alan Gussow

Amaranth, an ancient crop of the Aztecs, is a beautiful, lush, and nutritional grain plant. When drying the heads of the seeds, the artist discovered seductive rhythms that prompted this drawing, "Gathering Amaranth Seed 2," by Alan Gussow, 1981. Gussow conceived of and directed the Artist-in-Residence Program of the National Park Service beginning in 1968. Collection of the artist.

Landscape planners and designers will continue to be technical experts, a role in which they have excelled. But another crucial and complementary role is needed—that of a mediator of human and natural processes. A mediator reconciles, finds, and negotiates compromises for conflicting parties. In landscape planning and design, the parties are people and the landscape. To be effective mediators, to represent the land, we must know the world around us in terms of relationships.[49] This will enable us to ask the right questions, thereby extending the latitude of objective possibilities. Both roles will become more important in the future as landscape architects and planners are increasingly called upon to provide realistic and intelligent options about reconciling human use and conflicts in the landscape. The fundamental mission of landscape architects and planners will continue to be *caretakers of life and land.*

NOTES

1. Scarfo 1991, p. 5.

2. In the literature, the term "landscape ecological planning" is associated with planning that is informed by landscape ecology, a subdisciplinary area within the science of ecology. I use the same term in a generic way to emphasize the important role that ecology plays in understanding the landscape and in informing the theory and practice of landscape planning.

3. Toth 1990, p. 2.

4. Quoted in Steiner 1991b, p. 520.

5. Quoted in MacKaye 1940, p. 340.

6. Steiner 1991a, p. 4.

7. These phases were used by Galloway and Mahayni (1977) to explain developments in the planning profession, which in many ways are similar to those in the subfield of landscape planning. They extensively discussed the difficulties in adopting Kuhn's framework in exploring the evolution of an applied field such as planning and concluded that it was a useful framework. Also, Rosenberg (1986) used Kuhn's theory as a way to focus thinking and research in landscape architecture during the 1980s.

8. Kuhn 1962 asserted that scientific communities pass through many phases: (1) A period in which there is no consensus on a central body of ideas or "paradigm" to guide the community, (2) a period in which there is some agreement on a paradigm, (3) a period in which the paradigm constitutes the basis for research and problem solving in the community, (4) a period of anomaly in which there is an awareness of phenomena or things the paradigm cannot explain or resolve, and (5) a period of paradigm crises in which attempts are made to formulate alternative paradigms.

9. Unlike the natural and physical sciences, the knowledge base used in the discipline of landscape architecture is drawn from the natural, physical, and social sciences as well as from the creative arts. The artistic nature of the landscape literature may help to explain the discrepancies between the phases of paradigm development proposed by Kuhn and those I have identified for landscape planning.

10. Kuhn 1962, p. 4.

11. Wood 1992, p. 16.

12. Marsh 1864.

13. Powell 1879, p. viii.

14. Howard 1898.

15. Kuhn 1962, p. 15.

16. Geddes 1968, p. 351.

17. Steiner 1983, p. 298.

18. The concept of ecological succession was first described by Europeans (especially Eugenius Warming) in 1895. But the pioneering work in the field was the singular effort of Frederick Clements and Herbert Gleason. See Odum 1989, p. 187.

19. Steiner, Young, and Zube, 1988, p. 32. Also, see Grese 1992.

20. Kuhn 1962, p. 15.
21. MacKaye 1928, p. 147.
22. MacKaye 1940, p. 351.
23. Leopold 1949, p. 145.
24. Graham 1944.
25. Vogt 1948.
26. Steinitz, Parker, and Jordan 1976, pp. 444–55.
27. Kuhn 1962, p. 17.
28. Thomas 1956.
29. Hills 1961. One of the first comprehensive documentations of the method's application was a land-use study conducted by the Chester County Planning Commission, Pennsylvania. Toth 1990, p. 6.
30. Lewis 1964, pp. 100–107. Philip Lewis's 1969 study of the Upper Mississippi River was another significant piece of work in landscape planning during the mid-1960s.
31. McHarg 1969, p. 103.
32. Kuhn 1962, p. 23.
33. McHarg and Sutton 1975, p. 81.
34. Lee discussed nine efforts in using concepts about ecosystem structure and processes, and compared them with the application of the McHarg method in Toronto's Central Waterfront Planning Study. Lee 1982, pp. 147–167.
35. Berger and Sinton 1985, p. 24.
36. Zube has addressed this issue in many of his writings; see, for example, Zube 1986.
37. McHarg 1981, pp. 112–13.
38. Berger and Sinton 1985, p. xvii; Ndubisi 1991.
39. Spirn 1988b, p. 108.
40. Thorne and Huang 1991, p. 62.
41. Zonneveld 1990, p. 5.
42. Rosenberg 1986, p. 76. In addition, Rosenberg argues that a shift is taking place in the profession of landscape architecture from people being stewards or caretakers of the land to one in which stewardship and partnership are inherent parts of the environmental continuum. See, also, Sally Schauman's essay in this book.
43. Interview with Bruce Ferguson, professor of landscape architecture, University of Georgia, 29 January 1993.
44. Zube 1986, p. 375.
45. Faludi (1973) made a similar distinction in the city planning profession.
46. Evernden (1992) is an especially important work on this matter.
47. Interview with Bob Scarfo, then associate professor of landscape architecture, University of Maryland, College Park, 3 February 1993.
48. Kaplan 1983, pp. 311–32.
49. See, especially, Wood 1995.

REFERENCES

Appleton, J. 1975. *The Experience of Place*. London: John Wiley & Sons.

Berger, J. 1976. "The Hazleton Ecological Land Planning Study." *Landscape Planning* 3: 303–35.

Berger, J., and J. Sinton. 1985. *Water, Earth, and Fire: Land Use and Environmental Planning in the New Jersey Pine Barrens*. Baltimore: Johns Hopkins University Press.

Evernden, N. 1992. *The Social Creation of Nature*. Baltimore: Johns Hopkins University Press.

Fabos, J. 1973. Model of Landscape Resource Assessment. Part 1 of *The Metropolitan Landscape Planning Model (METLAND)*. Amherst: Massachusetts Agricultural Experiment Station, The University of Massachusetts. Research Bulletin.

———. 1989. "Landscape Planning." Pp. 157–59 in *American Landscape Architecture: Designers and Places*, ed. W. H. Tishler. Washington, D.C.: The Preservation Press.

Faludi, A. 1973. *Planning Theory*. New York: Pergamon Press.

Forman, R. T., and M. Godron. 1986. *Landscape Ecology*. New York: John Wiley & Sons.

Galloway, T. D., and R. G. Mahayni. 1977. "Planning Theory in Retrospect. The Process of Paradigm Change." *Journal of the American Institute of Planners* 43: 399–402.

Geddes, P. 1968. *Cities in Evolution*. New York: Howard Fertig.

Glikson, A. 1971. *The Ecological Basis of Planning*. The Hague, Netherlands: Matinus Nijhoff.

Graham, E. H. 1944. *Natural Principles of Land Use*. New York: Greenwood Press.

Grese, R. E. 1992. *Jens Jensen: Maker of Natural Parks and Gardens*. Baltimore: Johns Hopkins University Press.

Hills, A. 1961. *The Ecological Basis for Land-Use Planning*. Toronto: Ontario Department of Lands and Forests, Research Report No. 26.

Hough, M. 1984. *City Form and Natural Processes*. New York: Van Nostrand Reinhold.

Howard, E. 1898. *Garden Cities of To-Morrow*. 1965. Reprint, ed. J. Osborn. Cambridge, Mass.: MIT Press.

Juneja, N. 1974. *Medford*. Philadelphia: Center for Ecological Planning Research, University of Pennsylvania.

Kuhn, T. S. 1962. *The Structure of Scientific Revolutions*. Chicago: University of Chicago Press.

Kaplan, S. 1983. "A Model of Person-Environment Compatibility." *Environment and Behavior* 15: 311–32.

Lee, B. J. 1982. "An Ecological Comparison of the McHarg Method with Other Planning Initiatives in the Great Lake Basin." *Landscape Planning* 9: 147–69.

Leopold, A. 1949. *A Sand County Almanac*. New York: Oxford University Press.

Lewis, P. 1964. "Quality Corridors for Wisconsin." *Landscape Architecture* 54: 100–107.

———. 1969. *Regional Design for Human Impact: Upper Mississippi River Comprehensive Basin Study*. Madison: Environmental Awareness Center, University of Wisconsin.

Litton, R. B. 1972. "Aesthetic Dimensions of the Landscape." Pp. 262–91 in *Natural Environments: Studies in Theoretical and Applied Analysis*, ed. J. V. Krutilla. Baltimore: Johns Hopkins University Press.

Lyle, J. T. 1985. *Design for Human Ecosystems*. New York: Van Nostrand Reinhold.

MacKaye, B. 1928. *The New Exploration*. New York: Harcourt, Brace.

———. 1940. "Regional Planning and Ecology." *Ecological Monographs* 10: 349–53.

Marsh, G. P. 1864. *Man and Nature, or Physical Geography as Modified by Human Action*. New York: Charles Scribner.

McHarg, I. 1969. *Design with Nature*. Garden City, N.Y.: Doubleday/Natural History Press. 1992. Reprint, New York: John Wiley & Sons.

———. 1981. "Human Ecological Planning at Pennsylvania." *Landscape Planning* 8: 109–20.

McHarg, I., and J. Sutton. 1975. "Ecological Plumbing for the Texas Coastal Plain." *Landscape Architecture* 65: 78–89.

Mumford, L. 1931. *The Brown Decades*. New York: Harcourt, Brace.

Ndubisi, F. 1982. *Community Planning for North Amerindian Subcultures: A Phenomenological Approach*. Master's thesis, Landscape Architecture, University of Guelph, Canada.

———. 1991. "Culturally Responsive Planning: Implications from a Value Study of a Native Canadian Community." *Journal of Planning Education and Research* 11: 51–65.

Newton, N. 1971. *Design on the Land*. Cambridge, Mass.: Belknap Press of Harvard University.

Odum, E. P. 1969. "The Strategy of Ecosystem Development." *Science* 164: 262–70.

———. 1989. *Ecology and Our Endangered Life-Support Systems*. Sunderland, Mass.: Sinauer Associates, Inc.

Powell, J. W. 1879. *Report of the Lands of the Arid Region of the United States*. Washington: U.S. Government Printing Press.

Rosenberg, A. M. 1986. "An Emerging Paradigm for Landscape Architecture." *Landscape Journal* 5: 75–82.

Scarfo, B. 1991. "Aesthetic Carrying Capacity." Unpublished paper, University of Maryland, College Park.

Spirn, A. W. 1984. *The Granite Garden: Urban Nature and Human Design*. New York: Basic Books.

———. 1988a. "Nature, Form, and Meaning." *Landscape Journal* 7: 85–207.

———. 1988b. "The Poetics of City and Nature: Towards a New Aesthetic for Urban Design." *Landscape Journal* 7: 108–26.

Steiner, F. 1983. "Regional Planning in the United States: Historic and Contemporary Examples." *Landscape Planning* 10: 297–315.

———. 1991a. *The Living Landscape: An Ecological Approach to Landscape Planning*. New York: McGraw-Hill, Inc.

———. 1991b. "Landscape Planning: A Method Applied to a Growth Management Example." *Environmental Management* 15: 519–29.

Steiner, F., G. Young, and E. Zube. 1988. "Ecological Planning: Retrospect and Prospect." *Landscape Journal* 7: 31–39.

Steinitz, C. 1967. *Computers and Regional Planning: The DELMARVA Study*. Cambridge, Mass.: Graduate School of Design, Harvard University.

Steinitz, C., Enviromedia Inc., and Roger Associates Inc. 1970. *Natural Resource Protection*. Minneapolis–Saint Paul: The Metropolitan Council of the Twin Cities.

Steinitz, C., P. Parker, and L. Jordan. 1976. "Hand-drawn Overlays: Their History and Prospective Uses." *Landscape Architecture* 66: 444–55.

Thomas, W., ed. 1956. *Man's Role in Changing the Face of the Earth.* Chicago: University of Chicago Press.

Thorne, J., and C. Huang. 1991. "Toward a Landscape Ecological Aesthetics: Methodologies for Designers and Planners." *Landscape and Urban Planning* 21: 61–80.

Toth, R. E. 1990. *The Contribution of Landscape Planning to Environmental Protection: An Overview of Activities in the United States.* Paper presented at the International Landscape Planning Conference, University of Hannover, Germany.

Tyrwhitt, J. 1950. "Surveys for Planning." *Town and Country Planning Textbook,* ed. APRR. London: The Architectural Press.

Vogt, W. 1948. *Road to Survival.* New York: William Sloane Associates, Inc.

Wallace, McHarg, Roberts and Todd. 1971–74. *Woodlands New Community.* 4 volumes. Philadelphia.

Wood, C. A. 1992. "The Extended Garden Metaphor: Increasing Public Awareness of the Profession of Landscape Architecture." Master's thesis, Landscape Architecture, University of Georgia, Athens.

Wood, D. 1995. "The Spell of the Land." Pp. 3–13 in *Landscape in America,* ed. George F. Thompson. Austin: University of Texas Press.

Zonneveld, I. S. 1990. "Scope and Concepts of Landscape Ecology as an Emerging Science." Pp. 3–20 in *Changing Landscapes: An Ecological Perspective,* ed. R. T. Forman and I. S. Zonnefeld. New York: Springer-Verlag.

Zube, E. 1986. "Landscape Planning Education in America: Retrospect and Prospect." *Landscape and Urban Planning* 13: 367–78.

2

THE EXPANDED FIELD OF LANDSCAPE ARCHITECTURE

ELIZABETH K. MEYER

Aesthetics and science. Art and ecology. Culture and nature. Architecture and landscape. City and country. Public and private. Reason and emotion. Male and female. Man and woman. Man and nature.

Why do landscape architects so frequently describe the world and their work in pairs of terms? Either-or. This or that. One or the other. Perhaps this tendency to rely on pairs, on binary terms, reflects an essential attribute of the activities of the landscape architect who is involved in shaping and forming the land—"nature"—to accommodate human use and to embody cultural values. Or is this trait an attribute of a larger societal norm? What does it mean to structure the world into binaries?

Philosophers and cultural critics such as Jacques Derrida, Gilles Deleuze, and Alice Jardine have identified binary thinking as a tool for controlling power and making natural hierarchical relationships. For example, the group in power sees the world as including it alone; all others are described as "not like us" and not accorded positive attributes. Recent challenges to binary thinking, because of the false dichotomies and hierarchies that it poses, have led many scholars to reassess the prior histories of their fields and assumptions of their methodologies. Has binary thinking blinded us from seeing complex webs of interrelationships? What of the minor characters or figures in the binary set? Have their stories been told? Or have they been spoken for by the dominant group and in terms of its negative or "other"?

BINARY SETS: MAN-NATURE, CULTURE-NATURE

These philosophical debates have significant implications for landscape architecture because of the frequency of categories such as culture and nature, art and ecology, and man and nature in the literature of the field. The implications are ethical and aesthetic. First, the continuation of the culture-nature and man-nature hierarchies by designers when they describe the theoretical and formal attributes of their work perpetuates a separation of human life from other forms of life, vegetal and animal. This separation places people outside the ecosystems of which they are a part and reinforces a land ethic of either control or ownership instead of partnership and inter-relationship. Additionally, this artificial separation denies the cultural basis and historical contingencies of our constructs of nature and science.

Second, the juxtaposition of man with nature introduces a gendered nuance to this binary that associates culture with the male and nature with the female. This pairing of nature with woman and the female has been associated with various land ethics, ranging from reverence to abuse. Why would nature be managed differently if conceptualized as female? Some feminist scholars have called our attention to the "woman-nature connection" and the "universal devaluation of women" in modern Western societies.[1] These societies share a dominant way of thinking that makes a distinction between nature and culture—"culture being minimally defined as the transcendence, by means of systems of thought and technology, of the natural givens of existence."[2] These conceptual frameworks associate woman with something "culture devalues"—nature. Simone de Beauvoir is credited with noticing the association of women and nature "by virtue of being 'other' to western culture."[3]

The nature-culture distinction and the "woman-nature connection" that were "created by patriarchal and patricentric societies to debase women" have also served to legitimize the destruction of natural resources necessary to support capitalism's urban, industrial society.[4] Environmental historians Carolyn Merchant and Janet Biehl, along with other ecofeminists, identify the rise of capitalist economies with the increasing separation of culture and nature, man and nature. They find that the integration of morality, ethics, religion, and practice that existed in precapitalist, preindustrial communities gave way to a separation of the inhabitants from the land. Nonhuman nature was disenchanted and reduced to "a mere resource for exploitation."[5]

Hence, a number of discourses emerge concurrent with the emergence of the modern capitalist state that serve to devalue nature-woman and to legitimize the land's destruction and later, paradoxically, its preservation. This vacillation between abuse of the landscape and reverence of nature—and the ensuing inability to strike a middle ground—is exposed in concepts of gender affiliation that are themselves "complex metaphors for ambivalence about human action, in, on, and as part of the natural world."[6] These ambivalences are especially pronounced in North America, as Frederick Turner, Leo Marx, Denis Cosgrove, and James Machor have so eloquently and astutely pointed out.

BINARY SET: ARCHITECTURE-LANDSCAPE

Within the discourses of modern architecture, the binary pair architecture-landscape has relegated the landscape to what is *not architecture*. The biases of modern architectural history are critical to landscape architects because much of the history of landscape architecture is written by architectural historians. Within many of these histories, the landscape is unstructured, informal, irregular, wild—a counterpoint to the pure geometry of a built object. When architectural historian Sigfried Giedion writes about "the juxtaposition of nature and human dwelling" as a constituent fact of architecture, he defines architecture and nature in binary terms that are juxtaposed as opposites.[7] Architecture is the positive object, and nature is opposed to it, negative. More recently, town planners Andres Duany and Elizabeth Plater-Zyberk have exposed their sympathies toward one aspect of the modern architectural project—its tendency to see the land as chaotic, wild, or disorganized. Their site descriptions for an exhibition of their town design work are revealing; *distorted, radical discontinuities,* and *awkward* are the words used to describe adjacent wetlands, a river and its flood plain, and landforms.[8] Here, the landscape is compared to the structure and order of Duany and Plater-Zyberk's typical organizing device, the grid of blocks and streets. Landscape is not grid; thus, it is informal, wild, unstructured.

In other architectural paradigms, the landscape is not wild, but mute—a backdrop, a soft frame or a tabula rasa, an invisible background awaiting a building's design to establish place and order. For instance, Henry Russell Hitchcock, a prominent historian of modern architecture, advocated a minimal approach to the design of the modern house's garden. For Hitchcock, the open ground plan surrounding the house should be the result of a conservation project—"the preservation of all possible values previously in existence in the landscape setting with the adoption of only the simplest and most practical provision for specific human needs."[9] This matrix of trees and grass is, again, the neutral background upon which the dwelling is figured. Le Corbusier's perspectives from the 1920s and 1930s also relegate landscape to a frame for the architectural object, although this is a vertical frame, a picturesque vision. Rarely in modern architectural history is the land conceptualized as a site with its own attributes and structure. Hydrological order, topographic form, geological structure, and plant ecology are unseen, rendered invisible. As such the language of the modern landscape has been mute to many historians, theoreticians, and practitioners of architecture and landscape architecture.

Le Corbusier's modern landscape is frequently relegated to the role of scenographic backdrop for architecture. In this drawing entitled "Une ville contemporaine," the landscape is reduced to a vertical screen that frames and distances the view from the terrace. From Oeuvre Complete 1910–1929.

LANDSCAPE ARCHITECTURE AS MODERN OTHER

Whether discussing land ethics (the culture-nature/man-nature divide) or land aesthetics (the architecture-landscape divide), the landscape in nineteenth- and twentieth-century Western societies occupied a secondary role to culture and architecture. By identifying the landscape and nature as the *minor* character in a binary set and noting the gender associations that land-

1922 UNE VILLE CONTEMPORAINE

scape and nature have assumed in these roles, I describe the landscape as an "other," a concept articulated by de Beauvoir in *The Second Sex* and later developed by various poststructuralist and feminist theorists. From these sources, *other* has come to be understood as signifying what is "outside the conceptual system"; the female other is characterized as what is "the negative, the inessential, or the abnormal to the male."[10]

More precisely and surprisingly, the landscape, land, and nature have been designated as female or feminine "others." Not only are they outside the realm of culture and "mankind," they are also characterized by traits employed to describe and marginalize women. What do these gender associations mean for designers and historians of the landscape? According to Leo Marx, "The backlash against architectural modernism, as expressed by Mumford, replays a deeply rooted American conflict of ideas. It can be traced to the nineteenth-century opposition between the dominant culture (with its patriarchal view that natural beauty is a lesser, soft, 'feminine' concern and its uncritical commitment to technological progress) and the adversary culture (with its belief in the need for a greater harmony between the man-made and the natural, as exemplified by the Jeffersonian ideal of a society of the middle landscape)."[11]

For Marx, the conflation of nature/landscape/woman/feminine is critical both to modernization's unquestioning acceptance of unbridled technological progress—which is predicated on the consumption of natural resources—and to our cultural modernity's commitment to abstraction—which eschews *real* landscapes. While this conflation may be a necessary component of the constituent facts of modern art and architecture, the ideological biases of these dominant discourses tend to suffocate the emergence of an alternative, minor voice of modernism—that of landscape architecture.

The female role ascribed to the landscape, which is explicit in Marx's historical exegesis, and its role as "other," which is implicit in the works and writings of Duany and Plater-Zyberk, Hitchcock, and Giedion, raises the implication of architecture's male affiliation. To paraphrase Sherry Ortner, is landscape to architecture as nature is to culture and female is to male?[12] Is the invisibility of the landscape in the discourses of modern art and architecture a subset of a broader societal devaluation of women and nature relative to men and culture? Can landscape architecture be described as the female other to architecture's transcendent male subject? Has this relationship—which is not a natural given, but a conceptual category constructed by society and embodying social values—not only shaped the received history of modern architecture, but also misrepresented the history of modern landscape architecture?

What is critical to our understanding of landscape architecture is how pervasive this way of thinking was during the very time that landscape architecture emerged as a distinct profession in the United States after the Civil War. The struggle to find the middle ground—Marx's middle landscape—is rife with ambivalences and encumbered by ideological categories. And, for better or worse, the new field of landscape architecture that was borne out of this struggle did not develop a parallel body of history and criticism. For the most part, nineteenth-century landscape architects were makers, not writers; pragmatists, not idealists. They relied on the writing of art and architectural historians to chronicle their achievements. Thus, the industrial societies that were inventing new forms of constructed landscapes depended on writings that tended to view the world through binaries composed of dominant and muted pairs—such as culture and nature, man and woman. These binaries were incapable of describing and interpreting what is unique to the modern built landscape—its investigation of new systems of order through the particulars of its unique medium and materials.

IMPLICATIONS FOR THE HISTORY, THEORY, AND PRACTICE OF LANDSCAPE ARCHITECTURE

I wish to argue for a definition of landscape architecture as a hybrid activity that is not easily described using binary pairs as opposing conditions. Reliance on these outmoded ways of thinking and speaking limits our ability to see, listen, and create. Regarding the woman-nature connection and the man-nature hierarchy, this questioning of binaries is inextricable from our discussion of the landscape as "other." If we think of continuums or hybrids—of spaces in between—instead of opposing dualities, we do not have "others." If we do not have "others," we do not inherently value one term over another.[13]

As soon as landscape architecture is conceptualized as a field that operates "in between" so many previously antithetical terms and concerns, a range of new practices can evolve. This concept of landscape architecture as a hybrid between architecture and landscape, culture and nature, and art and ecology can empower scholars, students, teachers, and practitioners to avoid the destructive polarization that tore the field apart during the late 1970s and

1980s. ("Should I become a landscape artist or an ecological planner, a designer or an environmentalist?") By eschewing the simplistic thinking and ideological biases of binary thinking, landscape architecture can emerge from its dependence on the dominant discourses of art and architectural historiography to tell its own story. By replacing this binary way of thinking with other conceptual strategies, landscape architecture can foster a land ethic and an aesthetic predicated upon a continuum between human nature and nonhuman nature, upon a recognition that the land is a cultural and physical product and that people are living organisms.

LANDSCAPE ARCHITECTURE IN AN EXPANDED FIELD

Landscape architecture must be allowed to speak a language that, first, avoids binaries and operates in the spaces between the boundaries of culture and nature, man and woman, architecture and landscape; and, second, allows us to question the very premises upon which our knowledge of landscape architecture is based. Once we "split open the closure of binary oppositions" that have so blinded late-twentieth-century historians and designers from seeing the "spaces in between," alternative ways of seeing, describing, and evaluating the landscape are revealed.[14]

This rediscovery of the space between the binaries—the space of hybrids, relationships, and tensions—allows us to see the received histories of the modern landscape as the ideologically motivated social constructs that they are. Instead of preserving the marginalized, nonessential surfaces of modernity's "other," the detached vertical picture plane (landscape as sylvan backdrop), we shall recover the vital, spatial, material, and temporal medium of landscape architecture—postmodernity's ground, if you will. The gap between man and nature will be replaced with the continuum of human nature and nonhuman nature. Landscape as a visual image will be replaced by site as a spatial and temporal terrain.

THE REPRESSED FIGURES OF THE MODERN LANDSCAPE

Three new figures emerge within the binary set figure and ground (object and field, mass and space) that so limited landscape architecture's role in the modern architectural project. In addition to the ubiquitous image of early-twentieth-century modernism (the landscape as horizontal background matrix for

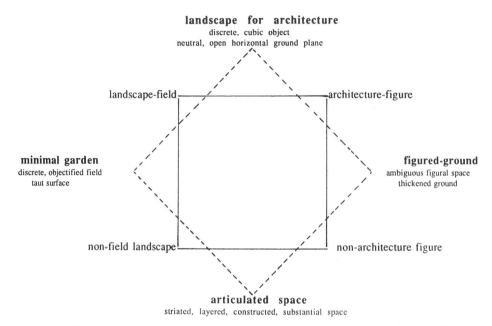

My version of a Klein group diagram describes an expanded spatial field for landscape architecture. In addition, in the landscape for architecture—*a neutral field for the cubic, object buildings of modern architecture*—*three new categories for describing landscapes emerge.* Figured-ground, articulated space, and the minimal garden *describe how the land and plants structure and define space independent of building massing. In between the emphatic black masses and white spaces of a figure-ground diagram emerge as a multitude of spaces.*

the object building), this expanded field includes the *figured ground,* the *articulated space,* and the *minimal garden,* or garden without walls. These three concepts are depicted in my version of a Klein group diagram, which charts their nonhierarchical relationship to one another in the expanded field of landscape architecture. Art historian Rosalind Krauss's use of this diagram to describe how sculpture expanded its field in the 1960s has allowed many landscape architects to reconsider the relationship between landscape and sculpture.[15]

I employ a different version of the diagram here to reconsider the relationship between landscape and architecture, the unseen and the seen, the void and the mass. The *figured ground* is that undulating body between the figural object and neutral field, between mass and void. It finds structure in the ground, its topographic and geological structure. The *articulated space* is the space between figural space framed by buildings and open space, homogeneous and undefined. This is the realm of the spatiality of plants, hedges, hedgerows, allées, bosques, orchards, and forests; it is a space of ambiguity, layering, and change. The *minimal garden,* also called the garden without walls, relies on patterning the ground plane to create a visible landscape. The surface—what is usually undefined—is transformed into a horizontal object that defines an implied space above it—like a Persian rug on a floor.

In addition to these three categories of the modern landscape that operate within a spatial field related to architectural scale and concerns, other possibilities exist for situating modern landscape architecture within its own concerns, concepts, and materials. A second expanded field of concern revolves around the binary set of man and nature, or man-made and natural. Within this field, the *landscape cyborg*—a hybrid of human and nonhuman natural processes, of the mechanical and the organic—can occupy the conceptual space between oppositional pairs such as man-made and natural, man and nature, engineering and natural processes.

The Figured Ground

The *figured ground* does not exist without a design intervention; it is not synonymous with an existing landform. Rather it is the product of the act of inscribing human nature's activities on the land, whose structure preexists the intervention and is reinforced or reconfigured by the intervention. This concept restores the earth's undulating corporealness. In lieu of an ideal, abstract, horizontal landscape surface—the background matrix of modern architecture—we recover a particular topography that has an underlying deep structure, or geomorphology.

Prospect Park in Brooklyn, New York, one of Calvert Vaux and Frederick Law Olmsted's urban parks, exemplifies this concept. This 400-plus-acre park is usually described as possessing "pastoral" and "picturesque" scenery. These two characters, so popular in nineteenth-century landscape aesthetics, represent specific visual attributes. The pastoral was seen to be related to the beautiful—to what is smooth, regular, open, and apprehended in a glance. The park's Long Meadow is a pastoral scene. A picturesque landscape was seen to be varied, irregular, intricate, and complex. Prospect Park's Ravine, for example, has picturesque scenery. But how did Vaux and Olmsted determine where these characters should be located? What were their codes for composing or assembling these characters, the Pastoral and the Picturesque?

The archival record of letters and official reports provides clues to this question. Vaux insisted that the Park Commission change the boundaries of the park to include Litchfield Villa, the land for Prospect Lake, and the Friends Cemetery. These parcels consolidated the parkland to the west of Flatbush Avenue and expanded the types of landforms to be located in

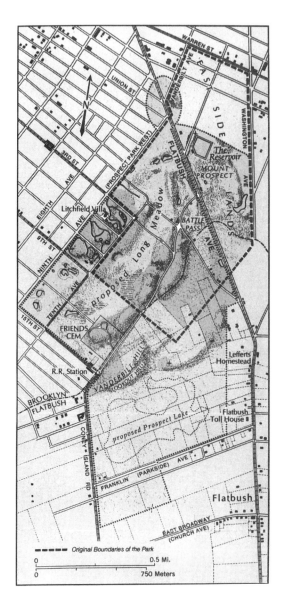

Calvert Vaux's proposal to reconfigure the boundaries of Prospect Park resulted in the inclusion of flatlands to the south, a glacial outwash plain and hilly terrain to the west, and part of the Harbor Hill moraine, which increased the diversity of landscape types in the park. From the Greensward Foundation and Friends of Prospect Park brochure, Prospect Park and the Brooklyn Botanic Garden.

the park. Specifically, the reconfigured park boundaries included three types of glaciated landforms—the rolling meadow along the north boundary enframed by eskers found and supplemented by the designers; the steep and intricate slopes of the Harbor Hill moraine's slopes and ravines (part of an east-west ridge running along Long Island that marks the

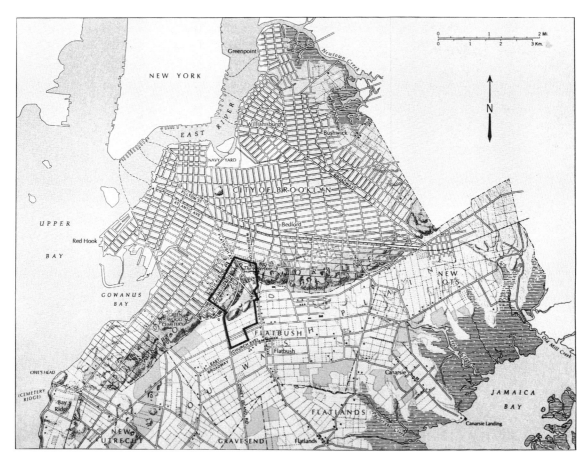

This map situates Prospect Park within the glacial terrain of Brooklyn. The park straddles the boundary between the hilly moraine that runs east-west through the center of Long Island marking the southern extent of the Wisconsonian glacier and the flat expanse of the outwash plain that reaches south to the Atlantic Ocean. The geomorphologic structure of the site establishes a spatial armature for the park's landscape types, the Pastoral (Long Meadow), the Picturesque (the Hills and Ravine), and the Sublime (proposed views of Manhattan and the Atlantic from an unrealized lookout tower). The land is figure, not background. From the Greensward Foundation and Friends of Prospect Park brochure, Prospect Park and the Brooklyn Botanic Garden.

southern extent of the Wisconsonian glacier); and, to the south, the vast, flat outwash plain reaching toward the Atlantic Ocean. These three glacial formations establish the armature for the park—a structure that Vaux and Olmsted reinforced through the disposition of plants and promenades around and across these distinct landforms. Long Meadow, the Ravine and Lookout Hill, and Prospect Lake are characterized as the Beautiful (or Pastoral) and the Picturesque, but they are configured by the uneven advances and retreat of the Wisconsonian glacier across this terrain.

A site plan of this park made without contour lines or hatchures ignores the undulating, sculpted glacial landform. The ground is silent. The landscape is romantic, natural, irregular, invisible, passive, feminine. A site plan of this park that depicts landforms and the park's landscape history, including its geological history (i.e., what preceded human nature's design intervention), allows the ground to speak. This is a formal language of glacial geomorphology: Drumlins, moraines, eskers, kettles, and outwash plains supplemented by designers for human use. The ground is figured. A site emerges from the frame of a landscape.

Articulated Space

The second site of repression for the modern landscape is spatial. Site plans that depict buildings and landscapes frequently rely on figure-ground techniques to differentiate between mass and void, solid and open. One spatial construct that characterizes the modern city is figural mass sited in open space, wherein the figure is a building and the ground is the surrounding, undifferentiated space of the landscape. Alternatively, the traditional city— and, today, some versions of contemporary urbanism—reverses the figure-ground relationship. The space or landscape is given boundaries and shape; it is a figure such as a plaza, square, court, or garden. The ground is solid mass—the street wall of the city or the density of a bosque or plantation. Both models repress the spaces of the landscape in that they render it either amorphous or totally dependent on the building for its shape and structure.

Two inconsistencies within this binary way of thinking come to mind. The first is revealed by reviewing an influential article by Colin Rowe on

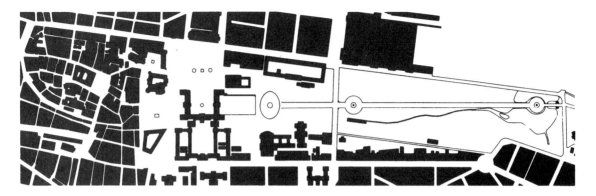

This figure-ground drawing by Wayne Copper represents the built world as mass and void, solid and open. I argue that its value as an analytical tool is limited to a coarse grain of study. Regardless of whether the spatial model relies on object buildings or figural space, figure-ground diagrams fail to represent the spatiality of trees, landforms, and other "in-between" conditions. They render the world black or white, either-or. From Cornell Journal of Architecture 2.

architectural transparency in which he defined a spatial model between the two I just outlined—a spatiality of overlaps, double readings, thickened spaces, layered planes, and opaque transparencies that creates formal analogies between cubism and certain modern buildings.[16] While this description is focused on Le Corbusier's buildings of the 1930s, it could also be applied to the spatial qualities of garden designs of the 1930s by landscape architect James Rose.

The second inconsistency revolves around the notion of a forest or bosque as a solid mass. Perhaps they are such masses in selected rendering techniques or in especially dense rain forests, but the spatiality of a grove of trees is neither solid nor void, neither figure nor field; it exists in an extraordinary realm between the two that changes in layering, densities, and transparencies from year to year and from season to season. The provocative *Pencil Points* articles of the 1930s by Rose suggest that landscape design is unavoidably a spatial enterprise and that the spatiality of plants, their transparencies and layered planes, was reminiscent of the attributes of constructivist sculpture such as Gabo's.[17] Rose's refusal as a student to develop his design projects through plan drawings and his alternative experiments with model making as a design tool are manifestations

In the 1950s, James Rose experimented with representational modes that would convey the layered and transparent spaces created by trees. Rather than depicting trees as opaque solids, he suggested their translucence—and their articulated spatial characteristics—with line and tone drawings. From Rose, Creative Gardens, 1958.

Plant Forms

of his commitment to exploring the space-making opportunities of landscape materials.

This spatiality between the built object and the figural void is a realm I call *articulated space*. Landscapes that display this type of spatiality are those in which the primary material of subdivision is vegetal—trees, shrubs, and vines. Gardens by Rose and his contemporaries, Garrett Eckbo and Dan Kiley, are poorly served by diagrams that reduce the world to black and white. The layered spaces of their gardens are gray zones—neither open nor enclosed. They are stratified, "constructed, substantial and articulate"[18]—with many of the characteristics attributed to phenomenal transparency by Rowe during the 1950s. Only in these experiments in landscape design do the transparencies take on a temporal and spatial quality.

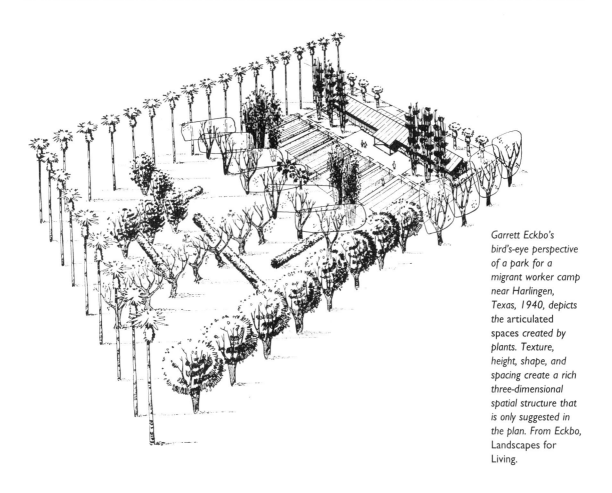

Garrett Eckbo's bird's-eye perspective of a park for a migrant worker camp near Harlingen, Texas, 1940, depicts the articulated spaces created by plants. Texture, height, shape, and spacing create a rich three-dimensional spatial structure that is only suggested in the plan. From Eckbo, Landscapes for Living.

The spatiality of plants is subtle and changing; planting design speaks another language than does architectural design because of the flux inherent in organic materials. Instead of adjectives such as soft, wild, irregular, and feminine, which assume a counterpoint to the hard masculine forms and surfaces of architecture, one can rediscover descriptions that emanate from the process of plant growth and form, its cyclicality and seasonality, its emergence and decline. The veils, screens, scrims, walls, and edges of vegetation are present in the faint veil of spring buds in a canopy; the translucent film of backlit, lime-green spring leaves; the dense, opaque, yet shimmering mass of summer foliage; the exuberant color fields of forests in autumn; and the dendritic network of winter's branches edging but connecting spaces on either side. This is a spatiality unique to landscape architecture. The recovery of this alternative spatiality may seem relatively insignificant if it merely offers us another formal device, a language internal to the conceptualization of landscapes. But I suggest that this spatiality—a mode of representation—has serious consequences for social spaces and for the way we live our lives.

A close look at the incomplete, yet ambitious, Garden City fragment that we know as Radburn near Fairlawn, New Jersey—designed by Clarence Stein and Henry Wright in 1929—illuminates the inextricability of formal space and social space. Standard histories tell us about Radburn's innovations—the superblock, the cul-de-sac, and the continuous internal

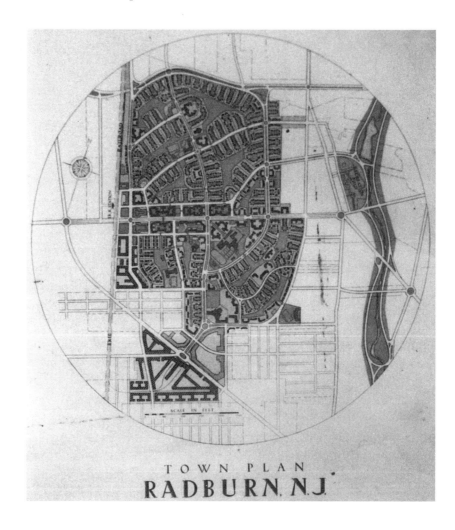

This town plan of Radburn, New Jersey, relies on tone to convey differences in use (i.e., between private yards and the community park), but it does not depict spatial conditions in the landscape. Only the buildings are figured. From Loeb Library Vertical Files, courtesy of Harvard University.

TOWN PLAN
RADBURN. N.J.

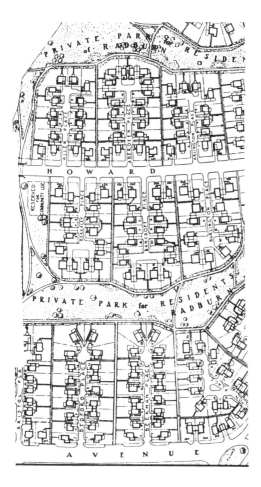

This site plan of a section of Radburn reveals the articulated spaces within the areas that the town plan depicted as open, amorphous, and undifferentiated space. Hedges line the boundary between the park and individual yards, creating semi-enclosed gardens for each house. The social spaces of this articulated spatial structure are different from that of a residential complex with no subdivision between park and yard. From Cautley 1930, Landscape Architecture Magazine 21(1).

block of open space. And yet few of the histories chronicle the contributions of one of the project's collaborators: Marjorie Sewell Cautley, a landscape designer educated at Cornell University who designed the planting plans. The failure of most site plans to depict the trees and the shrubs at Radburn represses more than a particular type of spatiality. It misrepresents the social spaces of the neighborhood that are dependent on the shape, height, location, and species of plant for their degree of separation or connection and their consequent use as public or private spaces. The rear of an individual home at Radburn opened onto a small garden plot defined by hedges that separated the garden from its adjacent neighbor and from the public path running down the middle of the block. These gardens mediated between the porch and the public path, spatially and functionally. These spaces are neither contested, as are the "public open spaces" of many twentieth-century housing projects, nor are they sequestered private enclaves. They are transitional spaces between the enclosure of the private home and the exposure of the public walk. Neither enclosed nor exposed, neither public nor private, they are new spaces of encounter and communicativeness—the products of hybrid parents, the garden and the city. Without site plans that include plants, both the social space and formal space of a project are misrepresented and misunderstood.

The Minimal Garden/Gardens Without Walls

The third quadrant of this expanded field, the *garden without walls* or the *minimal garden,* is frequently associated with the post-1980 design work of Peter Walker and Martha Schwartz and their colleagues and former students. Burnett Park in Fort Worth, Texas, and the temporary Necco garden in Cambridge, Massachusetts, are examples of this category of built landscape.[19] Characterized by a taut, horizontal surface objectified through geometry, seriality, flatness, and gesture, the minimal garden is a self-conscious critique of modern architecture's invisible ground, the undifferentiated landscape of the modern city and suburb. This hardened surface is generally a flat plane given shape through a nonhierarchical, repetitive geometric pattern. The minimal garden can be situated between the neutral tabula rasa or the modern architectural project, a horizontal plane without shape, and the field of objects, the repetitive, point-grid of built elements that marks place within the unshaped landscape. The ordered surfaces of the minimal garden are bounded by the repetitive marks on the land, not by vertical planes.

Yet this concept is not merely critical; it is also constructive, looking to its own time for references and associations, to the seriality of mass production as well as minimal art, instead of retreating to the walled garden enclosure with its figural spaces. Herein lies the invention of this concept. Without resorting to the devices of architecture—the enclosing wall—the minimal garden creates a space that hovers above its ordered and bounded geometry. Like the figured ground, the minimal garden relies on landform to structure the built landscape. Like the articulated space, the minimal garden employs geometry to subdivide and striate the land. This concept—a garden without walls, independent of a surrounding architecture for its boundaries—successfully expands the spatial field of modern landscape architecture.

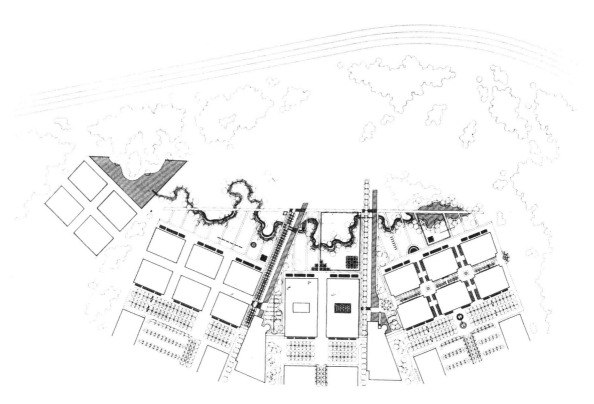

The office of Peter Walker and Martha Schwartz's corporate headquarters for IBM in Southlake-Westlake, Texas, relies on the principles of seriality, flatness, and gesture to create a minimal garden of three parterres. This garden relies on the taut grading of the ground plane, repetitive marks on that surface, and the gestural strokes of water and walk for its spatial structure. In other words, the garden is defined by the space suggested by its horizontal rather than its vertical surfaces; it is a garden without walls. From "Peter Walker: Landscape as Art" Process Architecture 85(1989).

This quaternary field describes languages, codes, and principles for defining a site's preexisting structure and latent character (the figured ground) as well as creating spatial subdivisions and structure independent of the architectural object (articulated space and the minimal garden) and Euclidean geometry. Each concept confronts the limitations of the binary relationships that revolve around architecture and landscape, object and field, figure and ground. They recover the spaces between those binaries that are figured by landform and plant form. They try to rescue the landscape from its "other" role in relation to architecture. This expanded field reestablishes landscape's subjectivity.

The Landscape Hybrid or Cyborg

My initial diagram on page 52 expands the restrictive frame of figure and ground—concepts that tie the landscape into a dependent relationship with architecture. The second restrictive frame to deconstruct is the originary pair, man and nature or man-made and natural. In place of this either-or relationship, I offer a both-and relationship that can be described by the hybrid of human nature and nonhuman nature.[20] This construct establishes a continuum within the world of living organisms—plant and animal—and natural systems. It places people and their actions within the nonhuman natural world, thus rejecting the subject-object relationship of man and nature. The construct "human nature and nonhuman nature" also eschews the gender affiliations attached to culture and nature, and man and nature, that were so pervasive in much of the writing about modern design.

The construct provides a location for what is now called ecological systems design. One precursor to this genre was the Olmsted firm's Boston park system, a seven-mile-long spine designed and assembled during the 1880s and 1890s to connect Franklin Park and the Arnold Arboretum to the Fens along the Riverway and continuing into the city along Commonwealth Avenue toward the Public Garden and the Common. The Emerald Necklace is a compelling model because it is a constructed park system connecting found and made landscapes that were prototypic and, even then, rapidly disappearing. A virtual natural history museum of New England's landscapes can be experienced along this necklace, which connects an upland woodland to a tidal estuary. Yet the firm's primary motivation for the project was the restoration of a tidal marsh for the purposes of controlling floods and improving water quality. Mid-nineteenth-century filling of the Muddy River for city blocks in the Back Bay neighborhood had resulted in frequent flooding and stench. The constructed water systems within the park confound even the most discerning eye—they are a hybrid of machine and organism, a nineteenth-century landscape cyborg, perhaps. Partly a found stream, partly a constructed riverway, partly a storm sewer, partly a constructed wetland, and partly an urban circulation system, this landscape was problematic even to its designers. In an official report about the Fens, Olmsted expressed his desire that Bostonians would come to accept the Fens's salt marsh: It "would be novel, certainly, in labored urban grounds, and there may be a momentary question of its dignity and appropriateness. . . .; but [it] is a direct development of the original conditions of the locality in adaptation to

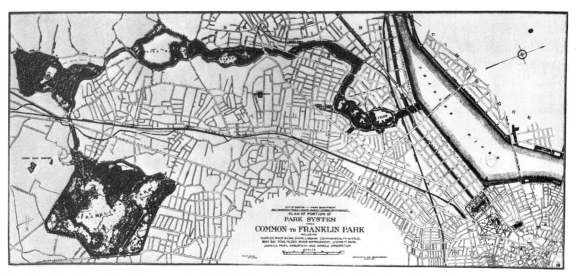

The "Plan of Park System from Common to Franklin Park" (better known as the Emerald Necklace in Boston) is contingent on both the Muddy River drainage system and the location of prototypical regional landscapes along its route. The alignment structures a seven-mile sequence of found artifacts—fens, freshwater stream, kettles, kames, drumlins, meadows, and woods—into an urban park system. The park's shape is not amorphous; it is a hybrid of natural and cultural systems. Courtesy of Olmsted National Historic Site, Brookline, Massachusetts.

This 1904 photograph supports Olmsted's contention that the Fens would not be appreciated by most Boston residents as it did not conform to well-loved landscape characteristics such as the Pastoral or the Picturesque. Rather, the Fens's spaces and systems were formed both to accommodate the nonhuman and natural processes of drainage, filtration, and collection of water to embody cultural concerns over the rapid loss of such landscapes due to the human processes of urbanization, industrialization, and modernization. From Loeb Library Visual Resources lantern slide collection, courtesy of Harvard University.

the needs of a dense community. So regarded, it will be found to be, in the artistic sense of the word, natural, and possibly to suggest a modest poetic sentiment more grateful to town-weary minds than an elaborate garden-like work would have yielded."[21]

Olmsted was concerned that the Fens did not meet the public's expectations for a park landscape, because it was neither pastoral nor picturesque nor gardenesque. Instead, it was a child of civil engineering and landscape architecture, an unusual entity that harnessed and structured natural systems into a new typology of urban infrastructure and aesthetics. Its innovations and dependence on the ecosystems above and below on the waterway were lost to the engineers who later built the Charles River dam in 1910. By then, the Fens was understood only in visual terms and considered a homely landscape at that. The function of the Fens—its life as a brackish, tidal estuary ecosystem—was not understood, and so it was destroyed when the Charles River was transformed into a freshwater impoundment. To this day, the Emerald Necklace is described as irregular, informal, wild, or picturesque in character. For those with no eye for geomorphology and those who view nature as chaos or disorder, the invention and the structure behind this project is invisible.

This space between man-made and natural, machine and organism, the landscape cyborg, has many nooks and crannies for further exploration and interpretation. As final examples, let us review two parks that reject the static conception of the natural and the visual construct of the landscape for the temporal, productive role of sites. They are Rem Koolhaas and the Office for Metropolitan Architecture's (OMA) project for the Parc de la Villette in Paris, France, and C. van Eesteren and A. W. Bos's park in Amsterdam, Bos Park. Like the Emerald Necklace a century ago, La Villette and Bos Park express a "systems aesthetic"—an aesthetic that is concerned with the relationships between things, not the things themselves.

Bos Park is an organism/machine for draining the polder and creating habitable parkland. In the 1930s, 186 miles of underground pipes were laid within the waterlogged parcel in order to drain away enough water to plant wet-tolerant trees and shrubs. The vegetation, in turn, absorbed additional moisture, allowing the parcel to be used as a productive, recreational park.[22] The park continues to evolve, thus defying a static conception of park as a fixed visual image. Furthermore, the park is an organism/machine for producing plants for the city's parks and squares and for harvesting lumber for profit—its vegetation and forests are managed, not preserved. The park is not

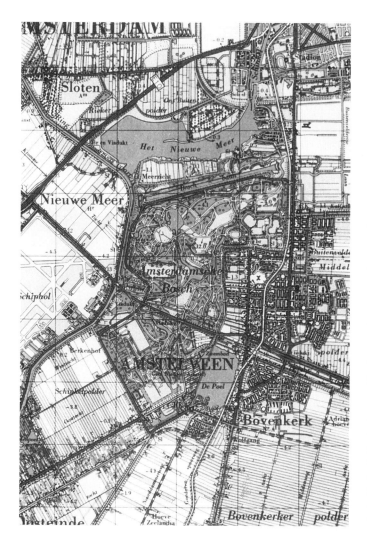

This map of suburban Amsterdam, The Netherlands, situates Bos Park within the spatial structure of a polder landscape. The park site is constructed ground, land taken back from the sea. In the 1930s, the dense plantation of trees absorbed moisture from the soil and prepared the park for more intensive human use. Today, the forest continues to produce and function—trees are harvested, and the park's structure is a dynamic interaction of human and nonhuman processes. From Pusey Library Map Collection, courtesy of Harvard University.

a static, idealized scene—a universal conception of the pastoral. It is a changing, evolving, and productive site that is dependent upon the care of human-nature.

OMA's second-prize scheme for the Parc de la Villette competition, which lost out to Bernard Tschumi's entry, arranges built and vegetal material within the same repetitive structure. Their form and structure is not one of contrast, built versus vegetal, but of similarity. This repetition of alternating built and vegetal strips calls into question the oppositional nature of nat-

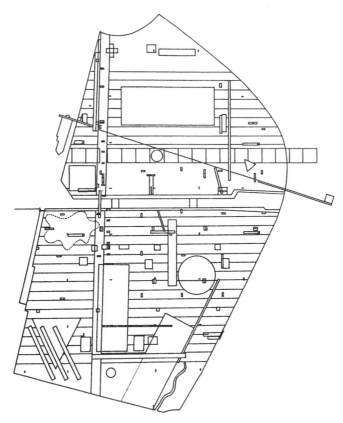

Left: *The Parc de la Villette Competition entry from the Office for Metropolitan Architecture.* Right: *The Site Plan Section-Elevations of Linear Fores, Paris, France. OMA's second-prize proposal employs a nonhierarchical site planning strategy that does not rely on binary opposites such as architecture and nature, artificial and natural. Instead, nature is conceived as a building material. The sections and elevations through the strips explain the growing conditions and building requirements of certain plant associations. The park is open-ended in its form as it is conceived as a strategy for growth, both human and nonhuman, cultural and natural.* From Lucan, OMA–Rem Koolhaas Architecture 170–1990, *1991.*

uralness and artificiality. In fact, the largest block of trees is described as a "forest machine or at least a forest building"—a place replete with "a number of devices to arouse the maximum of sylvan sensations and associations."[23] This confusion of categories, wherein the vegetal can be artificial or human-made and the built can be scattered or natural, refers back to the traditions of nineteenth-century park and promenade design and addresses the 1982 competition brief's call for "the contradictory requirement that the park be at once thoroughly natural and cultural."[24] One Parisian architectural critic, Françoise Choay, who favored Koolhaas's scheme over Tschumi's in the competition jury process, describes it as follows: "Greenery is used extensively. It is treated not only as a building material but almost mechani-

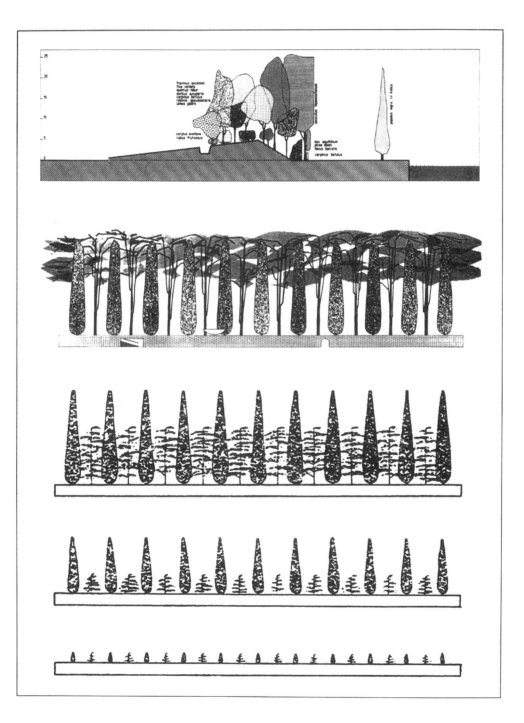

cally: it symbolizes artificiality as it is made part of the general evolving system (this is achieved in part by using different kinds of vegetal earth). This dominant artificial-looking material is in humorous contrast to an almost vegetal urban furniture: Vegetal here not being related to any formal resemblance but to modes of distribution."[25]

While Choay, the architectural historian, is limited in her descriptive vocabulary of landscapes, she avoids the simplifications of formal and informal, architectural and natural, by considering the "modes of distribution"—the ways in which materials and elements are arranged—rather than the things themselves. This critic understands that the relationship between things or objects can be the basis for interpretation and evaluation. Choay's innuendo in the closing paragraph of her essay—that Koolhaas's scheme was given second place in what is, arguably, the most important public space competition of the late twentieth century because the jury of architects feared the strategy of in-betweens, fitting neither one clear category nor another—suggests that the reluctance to drop our set binary ways of thinking is not a historical phenomenon but a contemporary anachronism.

LANDSCAPE ARCHITECTURAL THEORY

I am particularly interested in defining and establishing a theory for the built landscape between the dominant binary categories of many texts on modern design. In particular, I realize that we must alter the marginal role landscape architecture has been assigned in the histories of modernity. As a field that built physical critiques of, and in, the American city that embodied broader society's unquestioning acceptance of industrialization and technological progress, landscape architecture has not fit within the descriptive, evaluative, and interpretive categories of mainstream modernism—historical or theoretical. As such, its contributions to culture and society have either not been recognized or have been misinterpreted and maligned. Landscape architects are only now coming to terms with this deficit and its implications for designers and planners.

My research methods and interpretive strategies for theory-making as a feminist landscape architect can be characterized as follows:

1. Interpretations of built works and treatises should be based on primary experiences that are mediated through the knowledge of historical situa-

tions. This primary experience has two forms—visiting a site; and studying historical plans, maps, treatises, journals, letters, photographs, and the like.

For example, to understand the topographic form and hydrologic systems that structure the Emerald Necklace park system, a student of the Olmsted firm's project must study more than the 1894 plan. That engraving depicts streets, water bodies, plantations of trees, and meadows, but no topography. The site appears flat. The shapes and locations of the various "beads" along the Necklace seem arbitrary—or informal and unstructured. After studying the landforms of the park system through grading plans of the period and contemporary U.S. Geological Survey (USGS) maps of Boston, one discerns repeated landforms, such as drumlins and eskers, that characterized this glaciated terrain. The alignment of the Necklace is not irregular; it maximizes the diversity of landscape types that characterize New England. The alignment of the Necklace and the undulations of the land within its boundaries speak of the structure of the land.

A walk along the seven-mile transect from Franklin Park, the country park, to the Public Garden and the Boston Common is an excellent way to assemble the information found in nineteenth-century maps, plans, and reports into a coherent spatial narrative. This walk, too, must be mediated by comparing historic photographs with contemporary appearances, because the growth and decline of vegetation, and the modification of adjacent roadways, have altered the connections between the "beads."

2. We should be suspect of generalizations that "transcend the boundaries of culture and region."[26] Instead, theoretical work should be contingent, particular, and situated. Grounding in the immediate, the particular, and the circumstantial—the attributes of situational criticism—is an essential characteristic of landscape architectural design and theory. Landscape theory must rely on the specific, not the general; and like situational and feminist criticism landscape architectural design and theory must be based on observation, on what is known through experience, on the immediate and the sensory—what is known by all the senses, not only the eye. Thus, landscape architectural theory is situational; it is explicitly historical, contingent, pragmatic, and ad hoc.[27] It is not about idealist or absolute universals. It finds meaning, form, and structure in the site as it is. The landscape does not sit silent awaiting the arrival of an architectural subject. The site—the land—speaks prior to the act of design.

Earlier I described Prospect Park as a landscape design that applied the abstract conceptual language of nineteenth-century aesthetic theory—the Beautiful or Pastoral, the Picturesque, and the Sublime—to the particular conditions of a tract of land in Brooklyn. The circumstances of the site—its location at the boundary between glaciated and nonglaciated landforms—suggested the most fitting place for each of the aesthetic characters to be developed.

Bos Park in Amsterdam provides another example of how built landscapes should be situated prior to, and through, theoretical interpretation. The location of Bos Park on a polder encourages us to look closely at the section of the park. Height above sea level is the critical dimension in the design; the section, not the plan, is key in describing the structure of the existing land and the design response to it.

3. We should be skeptical of discourses that assign a gender affiliation to the landscape—implicitly or explicitly. The implicit affiliations are manifest as "female"—the "other" who is seen but not heard. Hitchcock's writing on the modern garden, noted earlier, is an example of this. The ideal modern house is surrounded by sylvan nature that merely frames the building. Nature is the neutral backdrop. The explicit affiliations are manifest as "feminine"—that which is irrational, wild, chaotic, emotional, natural. The site descriptions of Duany and Plater-Zyberk are examples of this, as any landscape element that alters the town plan grid is considered awkward or distorting. There are not two structures on the site, only one—that of Euclidean geometry.

4. While the deconstruction of the discourses that relegate landscape to a silent female or irrational feminine role in modernism is necessary, it is not enough. We need to reconstruct the unheard languages of the modern landscape as a means to reinvigorate contemporary design practice. The work of a feminist design critic is reconstructive, not destructive. This reconstruction assumes a multilayered fabric that weaves together threads from primary sources and documents written by landscape architects and about landscape architecture with the concurrent history of ecological ideas, cultural and historical geography, design and planning criticism, and site interpretation.[28]

We must do more than note how badly served landscape architecture is by descriptions that rely solely on architectural categories and concepts. Scholars' research into the history of modern landscape architecture must question what has been lost when landscape design components are overlooked. As noted in the earlier interpretation of Radburn, by ignoring the project's planting plan and the contributions of Cautley, the social spaces of the neighborhood were misunderstood by historians and practitioners. The role of trees and hedges as spatial subdivisions between the public and private realms was ignored, and the result was that the many projects that supposedly emulated Radburn were characterized by amorphous open space. Contemporary residential life, as well as an accurate history, suffered from this incomplete reading.

5. Finally, landscape architectural history has been, for the most part, a masculine discourse focusing primarily on the works of great landscape architects—mostly men. The history of modernity has especially concentrated on the autonomy of these artistic works, their formal attributes, and their plan configurations. This historiography must be enhanced and challenged, for it denies the conditions of practice, conceptualization, and experience. This challenge exposes landscape history as a fiction that has been written through a particular lens or sensibility that has ideological implications.[29] By challenging the "formulation of the crucial questions of the discipline as a whole," I am following in the footsteps of scholars such as Griselda Pollock and Linda Nochlin, whose writings have enriched the histories of modern art.[30] To paraphrase Pollock, a dual role for feminist landscape architectural history and theory—"recovery of women producers" and "deconstruction of the discourses and practices of [architectural] history itself"—is a positive act of construction, not destruction.[31]

For landscape architectural history and theory, this translates into more than research on the many women designers whose careers were ignored by such scholars as landscape historian Norman Newton. Scholars must also reconsider the methodologies of prior histories to ascertain whether or not they precluded some works from entering into the canon. Scholars and students must determine whether a history comprised of monographs on individual designers and their works allows for the consideration of the complexity of collaborative work in a corporate practice. How does one chronicle the works of Sasaki Associates, the SWA Group, or EDAW, for instance—three firms whose employees move in and out of the practice over time? We must discuss whether landscape architecture's quest for status as a profession and discipline on par with that of architecture resulted in the repression of more horticulturally focused designs and designers. We should

wonder about the lack of contextual site plans and urban plans in our histories, which limit our ability to interpret built landscapes as more than great
works or objects. Shouldn't landscape architectural history and theory
attempt to uncover the interrelationships between a project and its surroundings? If we believe it is important for students to know something
about the history of architecture as well as landscape architecture, shouldn't
they also know something about the emergence of ecological thinking, especially during the nineteenth and early twentieth centuries?

One goal of scholarship, therefore, is to construct legitimate alternatives to the limiting binary terms that modern society has adopted to
describe relationships between landscape and architecture, nature and culture, female and male, nature and man. In place of such oppositional binaries, we need conceptual quaternary fields such as those I have proposed
for figure and field, man and nature. These expanded fields are defined by
concepts—such as the figured ground, articulated space, the minimal garden, and landscapes for architecture—with complex, not simple, relationships to one another. The scholar can develop theories for site description
and interpretation that occupy the space between nature and culture, landscape and architecture, man-made and natural, and that are along the spatial continuum that unites, not the solid line that divides, concepts in
binary opposites.

This realm of inclusions will reposition the landscape from "other" to
"ground." Andreas Huyssen's essay "Mapping the Postmodern" may offer
direction here. He proposes that "in an important sector of our culture there
has been an important shift in sensibilities, practices and discourse formations which distinguishes a postmodern set of assumptions, experiences and
propositions from that of the preceding period." He continues by arguing
that postmodernism has not "generated genuinely new aesthetic forms," but
rather has continued to employ modernity's forms "reinscrib[ing] them into
an altered cultural context." Huyssen lists the environment and ecology—
along with the culture of women, minorities, and non-Westerners—as the
grounds upon which modernity's forms are reinscribed.[32] Huyssen's procedure for reinscription connotes an image of intersections, overlaps, hybrids,
and cyborgs that are created only by acknowledging that two terms or elements can relate to one another without implied hierarchies or domi-
nances—without "others." Instead of a static, visual landscape that is out
there, irrational, irregular, and open, we have a spatial, temporal, and eco-

logical site that is present before an artist or a designer begins to work. The designer, then, allows the site to speak more clearly through the design interventions he or she makes. The site and the designer are collaborators.

Let us think then of landscape architecture as a modern "other" and a postmodern "ground." Let us propose that landscape architectural history and theory should be about the cultural, geomorphological, and ecological history of the preexisting site as well as the history of the design project and its designer. Let us propose that landscape architectural history and theory should be about the intersection of a site's preexisting form and structure with the proposed design form and structure. The intersection of geometry and geomorphology, of past site and present project, requires a dialogue between the site as a speaking figure and the designer's markings on that site. Landscape design is not about monologues. Our concern for the many layers of form that are inscribed on a site often requires a "double voiced discourse, containing dominant and muted story, what Gilbert and Gubar call a palimpsest."[33] This double-voiced discourse is predicated on a *systems aesthetic*, not an object aesthetic; it is about the relationship between things, not the things alone.

Relationships between things. Hybrids. Continuums. Cyborgs. Now we are able to circle back to the proper place of landscape architecture. Perhaps Ortner's description of women's intermediate position between nature and culture can act as an analog for landscape architecture's position within the fields, theories, and practices of design and planning as well as within the conceptual frameworks of social and political life: "Shifting our image of the culture/nature relationship once again, we may envision culture in this case as a small clearing within the forest of the larger natural system. From this point of view, that which is intermediate between culture and nature is located on the continuous periphery of culture's clearings; and though it may thus appear to stand above and below (and beside) culture, it is simply outside and around it."[34]

Landscape architecture is not a practice that can be adequately described as either this or that. Art or science. Culture or nature. Man or nature. Architecture or landscape. Our built works on the land, like the theories we construct, are human interpretations of ourselves and the natural world. If nature is a cultural construct, one that evolves as our society changes, shouldn't the field that is most concerned with shaping the land develop a shared language that reflects these hybrid relationships? Why should we continue to rely on conceptual design categories that inadequately convey what is unique to our field—the systems, structures, and spaces of the land, of plants, of soils, of the seasons—and what is characteristic of postmodernity, our culture—the shifting of nature, the landscape, and ecological thinking from a marginal to a central concern?

NOTES

The author extends thanks to three groups for their comments and criticisms on the various guises of this paper (lectures, drafts, and class discussions): The convenors of and participants in the 1992 Edge Too conference in Melbourne, Australia, "The Culture of Landscape Architecture"; Frederick R. Steiner and George F. Thompson for their thoughtful and exacting editorial advice; and the students and faculty of Harvard University's Graduate School of Design, who were the earliest audience for my thoughts about the theoretical constructs of modern landscape architecture.

1. Ortner 1974, pp. 67–87. Note that Marx (1991) and Cosgrove (1984) also discuss the import of speculation—land as a commodity—in early capitalist America. Both men see speculation as engendering a detached relationship between people and the land, a detachment that considers the land a commodity to be bought and sold for profit—with a short-term rate of return. This fosters a land ethic that is incompatible with long-term economic and cultural sustainability.

2. Ibid., p. 84.

3. Biehl 1991, p. 14.

4. Ibid. See also Merchant 1980, p. 193, and Merchant 1989.

5. Biehl 1991, p. 21.

6. Flax 1990, p. 50.

7. Giedion 1969, p. 18. Giedion attributes LeVau and LeNôtre's Versailles with embodying this "important constituent fact." There he sees, "for the first time, a great dwelling complex (equal to the size of a small town) was placed in direct contact with nature" (pp. 21, 138).

8. The exhibition took place at Harvard University's Graduate School of Design in the fall of 1990.

9. Hitchcock 1937, p. 15.

10. Humm 1990, p. 156.

11. Marx 1991, p. 74.

12. Ortner 1974, pp. 67–87.

13. Jardine 1985, p. 71.

14. Moi 1991, p. 108.

15. Krauss 1985, pp. 283–84.

16. Rowe and Slutzky 1976, pp. 159–84.

17. Rose 1938, p. 642; and Rose 1939, pp. 227–30.

18. Rowe and Slutzky 1976, p. 175.

19. Walker and Deino 1990, pp. 120–29.

20. While the initial source for this nomenclature may be different, my first exposure to this terminology was in Carolyn Merchant's writings, in particular *Ecological Revolutions* (1989) and *The Death of Nature* (1980).

21. Olmsted, "Report of the Landscape Architect Advisory," in City Document no. 15–1880, p. 12, as cited in Zaitzevsky 1982, p. 57.

22. Polano 1991, pp. 507–9. See, also, Meto J. Vroom's essay in this book; James Corner discusses this project as well in his essay.

23. Barzilay and Hayward 1984, p. 45

24. Choay 1985, p. 213

25. Ibid., pp. 213–14.

26. See Nicholson 1990, p. 5.

27. These are characteristics of postmodern philosophy as exemplified in the writings of Richard Rorty and Jean François Lyotard. Nicholson 1990, p. 5; and Fraser and Nicholson 1990, p. 21.

28. See Worster 1977 and Cosgrove 1984.

29. Kolodny 1985, p. 153. She continues: "We must re-examine not only our aesthetics but, as well, the inherent biases and assumptions informing the critical methods which (in part) shape our aesthetic responses" (p. 157).

30. My position here has been influenced by Pollock 1988a, p. 2. This particular quote from Pollock refers to a statement made by Linda Nochlin.

31. Pollock 1988b, p. 55.

32. Huyssen 1986, p. 181.

33. Showalter 1985, p. 266.

34. Ortner 1974, p. 85.

REFERENCES

Barzilay, Marianne, and Catherine Hayward. 1984. *L'Invention du Parc: Parc de la Villette.* Paris: Graphite Editions.

Biehl, Janet. 1991. *Rethinking Ecofeminist Politics.* Boston: South End Press.

Cautley, Marjorie Sewell. 1930. "Planting at Radburn." *Landscape Architecture* 21(October): 23–29.

Choay, Françoise. 1985. "Critique." *Princeton Journal of Architecture* 2: 211–20.

Cosgrove, Denis. 1984. *Social Formation and Symbolic Landscape.* Totowa, N.J.: Barnes and Noble.

Duany, Andres, and Elizabeth Plater-Zyberk. 1991. *Towns and Town Making Principles.* New York: Rizzoli.

Flax, Janet. 1990. "Postmodernism and Gender Relations in Feminist Theory." Pp. 39–62 in *Feminism/Postmodernism,* ed. Linda J. Nicholson. New York and London: Routledge.

Fraser, Nancy, and Linda J. Nicholson. 1990. "Social Criticism without Philosophy: An Encounter between Feminism and Postmodernism." Pp. 19–38 in *Feminism/Postmodernism,* ed. Linda J. Nicholson. New York and London: Routledge.

Giedion, Sigfried. 1941. *Space, Time and Architecture.* 1969. Reprint, Cambridge, Mass.: Harvard University Press.

Haraway, Donna. 1990. "A Manifesto for Cyborgs: Science, Technology and Social Feminism in the 1980s." Pp. 190–233 in *Feminism/Postmodernism,* ed. Linda Nicholson. New York and London: Routledge.

Hitchcock, Henry Russell 1937. "Gardens in Relation to Modern Architecture." Pp. 15–20 in *Contemporary Landscape Architecture and Its Sources.* San Francisco: Museum of Modern Art.

Humm, Maggie. 1990. *The Dictionary of Feminist Theory.* Columbus: Ohio State University.

Huyssen, Andreas. 1986. "Mapping the Postmodern." Pp. 178–221 in *After the Great Divide: Modernism, Mass Culture, Postmodernism.* Bloomington: Indiana University Press.

Jardine, Alice. 1985. *Gynesis: Configurations of Women and Modernity.* Ithaca: Cornell University Press.

Kolodny, Annette. 1985. "Dancing through the Minefield. Some Observations on the Theory, Practice and Politics of a Feminist Literary Criticism" [1980]. Pp. 144–67 in *The New Feminist Criticism,* ed. Elaine Showalter. New York: Pantheon Books.

Krauss, Rosalind. 1985. "Sculpture in the Expanded Field" [1978]. Pp. 276–90 in *The Originality of the Avant-Garde and Other Modernist Myths.* Cambridge, Mass.: MIT Press.

Marx, Leo. 1964. *The Machine in the Garden: Technology and the Pastoral Ideal.* London: Oxford University Press.

———. 1991. "The American Ideology of Space." Pp. 62–78 in *Denatured Visions: Landscape and Culture in the Twentieth Century,* ed. Stuart Wrede and William Howard Adams. New York: Museum of Modern Art.

Merchant, Carolyn. 1980. *The Death of Nature.* San Francisco: Harper and Row.

———. 1989. *Ecological Revolutions: Nature, Gender and Science in New England.* Chapel Hill: University of North Carolina Press.

Moi, Toril. 1991. *Sexual/Textual Politics: Feminist Literary Theory.* 1985. Reprint, London: Routledge.

Nicholson, Linda. 1990. "Feminism as against Epistemology: Introduction." Pp. 1–16 in *Feminism/Postmodernism,* ed. Linda Nicholson. New York and London: Routledge.

Olmsted, Frederick Law. 1880. "Report of the Landscape Architect Advisory," in City Document no. 15–1880, p. 12. As cited in Zaitzevsky 1982.

Ortner, Sherry. 1974. "Is Female to Male as Nature Is to Culture?" Pp. 67–87, in *Woman, Culture and Society,* ed. Michelle Zimbalist Rosaldo and Louise Lamphere. Stanford, Calif.: Stanford University Press.

Polano, Sergio. 1991. "The Bos Park, Amsterdam and Urban Development in Holland." Pp. 507–9 in *The Architecture of Western Gardens: A Design History from the Renaissance to the Present Day,* ed. Monique Mosser and Georges Teyssot. Cambridge, Mass.: MIT Press.

Pollock, Griselda. 1988a. "Feminist Interventions in the Histories of Art: An Introduction."
Pp. 1–17 in *Vision and Difference: Femininity, Feminism and Histories of Art*. London and
New York: Routledge.

———. 1988b. "Modernity and the Spaces of Femininity." Pp. 50–90 in *Vision and Difference:
Femininity, Feminism and Histories of Art*. London and New York: Routledge.

Rose, James. 1938. "Freedom in the Garden: A Contemporary Approach to Landscape
Design." *Pencil Points* 19(10): 639–43.

———. 1939. "Plant Forms and Space: Materials Create Volume by Definition of Space."
Pencil Points 20(4): 227–36.

Rowe, Colin, and Robert Slutzky. 1976. "Transparency: Literal and Phenomenal." Pp. 159–83
in *Mathematics of the Ideal Villa*. Cambridge, Mass.: MIT Press.

Showalter, Elaine. 1985. "Feminist Criticism in the Wilderness." Pp. 243–70 in *The New
Feminist Criticism*, ed. Elaine Showalter. New York: Pantheon Books.

Walker, Peter, and Cathy Deino. 1990. "Minimalist Gardens without Walls." Pp. 120–29 in
The Meaning of Gardens: Idea, Place, Action, ed. Mark Francis and Randy Hester.
Cambridge, Mass.: MIT Press.

Worster, Donald. 1977. *Nature's Economy: A History of Ecological Ideas*. Cambridge:
Cambridge University Press.

Zaitzevsky, Cynthia. 1982. *Frederick Law Olmsted and the Boston Park System*. Cambridge,
Mass.: Belknap Press of Harvard University Press.

Max Ernst. The Bewildered Planet (La planète confuse). *1942. Oil on canvas, 119 × 140 cm. Collection of the Tel Aviv Museum. ©1995 Artists Rights Society (ARS), New York/SPADEM/ADAGP, Paris.*

3

ECOLOGY AND LANDSCAPE AS AGENTS OF CREATIVITY

JAMES CORNER

Unchanged within to see all changed without,
Is a blank lot and hard to bear, no doubt.
SAMUEL TAYLOR COLERIDGE[1]

The existence of which we are most assured and which we know best
is unquestionably our own, for of every other object we have notions
which may be considered external and superficial, whereas, of
ourselves, our perception is internal and profound. What, then,
do we find?
HENRI BERGSON[2]

The processes of which ecology and creativity speak are fundamental to the work of landscape architecture. Whether biological or imaginative, evolutionary or metaphorical, such processes are active, dynamic, and complex, each tending toward the increased differentiation, freedom, and richness of a diversely interacting whole. There is no end, no grand scheme for these agents of change, just a cumulative directionality toward further becoming. It is in this productive and active sense that ecology and creativity speak not of fixed and rigid realities but of movement, passage, genesis, and autonomy, of *propulsive life unfolding in time.*

It is odd, then, that while ecology and creativity have each received increasing attention over the years, there remains ambiguity over their content and relationship toward one another, especially with respect to their agency in the evolving of life and consciousness. It is striking, for example, that the possibilities for a vibrant exchange between ecology, creativity, and the design of landscape have barely been recognized beyond mechanical and prescriptive methods. Moreover, landscape architecture's appropriation of ecology and creativity—and the manner in which they are understood and used—has rarely led to the production of work that is equal in effect and magnitude to the transformative phenomena these topics represent. Contemporary landscape architecture has drawn more from objectivist and instrumental models of ecology (the emotional rhetoric of some environmentalists notwithstanding), while design creativity has all too frequently been reduced to dimensions of environmental problem solving (know-how) and aesthetic appearance (scenery). This lack of inventiveness is both surprising and difficult for many landscape architects, especially those who originally entered the field believing that ecology and artistic creativity might *together* help develop new and alternative forms of landscape. This failing points to a relationship between ecology, creativity, and landscape that is either incongruous and impossible to reconcile or (and more likely) to a potential relationship that has not yet been developed—a potential that might inform more meaningful and imaginative cultural practices than the merely ameliorative, compensatory, aesthetic, or commodity oriented.

My concern in this essay is to outline the grounds that are necessary for this potential to appear. I argue that ecology, creativity, and landscape architecture must be considered in terms other or greater than those of visual appearance, resource value, habitat structure, or instrumentality. Instead, these somewhat restrictive traditional views might be complemented by an understanding of how ecology, creativity, and landscape architecture are metaphorical and ideological representations; they are cultural images, or *ideas*. Far from being inactive, however, these ideas have profound agency in the world, effecting change in a variety of material, ideological, and experiential ways. These cultural ideas and practices interact with the nonhuman world in such a way as simultaneously to derive *from* while being constitutive *of* nature, human dwelling, and the modes of relationship therein. What is important and significant here is how ecology and landscape architectural design might invent alternative forms of *relationship* between people, place, and cosmos. Thus, the landscape architectural project becomes more about the invention of new forms and programs than the merely corrective measures of restoration.

If one were to conceive of landscape architecture as an active agent in the play of evolutionary intervention, how would one have to construe ecology and creativity in design practice? In what ways would they have to be appropriated for landscape architecture to function as a significant evolutionary agent—one that might develop greater diversity and reciprocity between the cultural world and unmediated Nature? Of what would such a creative ecology consist?

THE ECOLOGICAL IDEA

Ecology has assumed a heightened level of significance in social and intellectual affairs during the past few decades. This emergence is due, in large part, to an increased awareness of local and global environmental decline, a view that continues to be shaped through vivid media coverage and well-organized ecological activism.[3] The lesson of ecology has been to show how all life upon the planet is so deeply bound into dynamic, complex, and indeterminate networks of relationships that to speak of nature as a linear mechanism, as if it were a great machine that can be either intrinsically or extrinsically controlled and repaired, is simply erroneous and reductive. The ecological view, with its emphasis on temporal, interactive processes, has been further reinforced by new scientific findings of nonlinearity, complexity, and chaos dynamics. While ecology speaks of a "harmony of nature," writes ecologist Daniel Botkin, it is a harmony that is at the same time "discordant, created from the simultaneous movements of many tones, the combination of many processes flowing at the same time along various scales, leading not to a simple melody but to a symphony at some times harsh and at some times pleasing."[4]

While the full measure of these and other emerging views of ecology remains to be realized, the idea of ecology has diversified to such a point that it can no longer be used with unambiguous clarity. Today, one may observe that "ecology" is appropriated as much by corporate and media industries as by environmentalists, land-artists, or politicians. Although ecology has generally been understood as providing a scientific account of natural processes and their interrelationships, the fact that it also both describes and constructs various ideological positions to be taken with regard to nature points to a greater significance. Ecology is never ideologically (or imaginatively) neutral, despite claims of its objectivity. It is not without values, images, and effects. Instead, ecology is a social construction, one that can initiate, inform, and lend legitimacy to particular viewpoints (from "green politics" to nationalism to feminism, for example). Ecology constructs particular "ideas" in the imagination of its advocates; it conjures up particular ways of seeing and relating to Nature—views that range from the extremely rational to the most mystical and religious.

It is, therefore, necessary to distinguish two "natures": The first, "nature," refers to the *concept* of nature, the cultural construction that enables a people to speak of and understand the natural world, and that is so bound into ecological language; the second, "Nature," refers to the amorphous and unmediated flux that is the "actual" cosmos, that which always escapes or exceeds human understanding.

The development of the ecological idea of nature in the cultural imagination—how one conceives of, relates to, and intervenes in Nature—is a radically different kind of reflection than what is found in current instrumentalist (or problem solving) approaches toward ecology in landscape architectural design and planning, wherein "ecology," "nature," "landscape," and "environment" form the primary foci of attention, considered as separate from and external to culture. By "culture," I refer to more than just the behavioral and statistical characteristics of a human group (something that human ecology claims to describe), and to invoke, instead, the image of an unfolding and multivariate artifact, a dynamic entity constructed from the vocabularies, attitudes, customs, beliefs, social forms, and material characteristics of a particular society. Culture is a thick and active archaeology, akin to a deep field that is capable of further moral, intellectual, and social cultivation. Thus, people can only ever *know* what they have made (their language, representations, and artifacts). "Because for thousands of years we have been looking at the world with moral, aesthetic, and religious claims," writes Nietzsche, "with blind inclination, passion, or fear, and have indulged ourselves in the bad habits of illogical thought, this world has gradually *become* so strangely colorful, frightful, profound, soulful; it has acquired color but we have been the painters: the human intellect allowed appearance to appear, and projected its mistaken conceptions onto things."[5] For Nietzsche, the cultural world (like nature) is the result of an accumulation of "errors and fantasies," an accrual that is nothing less than "a treasure: for the *value* of our humanity rests upon it."[6] It is this dynamic, representational, and "erring" characteristic of culture, then, that descriptive and instrumentalist ecology fails to recognize, although it is itself a constituent part and product of the cultural milieu (and is, therefore, just as fictional). In other words, many landscape architects and planners who are advocates of ecological views often fail to understand how the metaphorical characteristics of ecology inform and construct particular realities. Moreover, the sheer diversity of ways in which different social groups represent, speak of, experience, and relate to Nature embodies a richness—a treasure of fictions—that a strictly scientistic ecology (ironically) cannot embrace—nor even acknowledge—its own image within that richness.

THE AMBIGUITIES OF ECOLOGY
WITHIN LANDSCAPE ARCHITECTURE

Ecology has been particularly influential in landscape architecture and planning, especially since the publication of Aldo Leopold's *A Sand County Almanac* (1949), Rachel Carson's *Silent Spring* (1962), and Ian McHarg's *Design with Nature* (1969). Earlier American naturalists such as George Perkins Marsh, Henry David Thoreau, Ralph Waldo Emerson, John Muir, and, later, Lawrence Henderson had no doubt partly influenced some late-nineteenth- and early-twentieth-century landscape architects—most notably Frederick Law Olmsted, Charles Eliot, Jens Jensen, and Warren Manning. The cumulative result over the past century, but especially since the original Earth Day, has been the establishment of ecology as a central part of landscape architectural education and practice.

Whereas ecology has changed and enriched the field of landscape architecture substantially, it has also displaced some of landscape architecture's more traditional aspects and prompted a somewhat ambiguous and estranged disciplinary identity (the oft-asked question: "Is it art or science?"). A number of schools of landscape architecture, for example, now teach little visual art, design theory, or history, focusing instead upon natural science, environmental management, and techniques of ecological restoration. Although these aspects of landscape study are important, one cannot help but feel a concern for the loss of foundational traditions, especially landscape architecture's agency as a representational and productive art, as a *cultural* project. The subsequent polarization of art from science, planning from design, theory from practice, and the lack of critical reflection within "ecological design" circles are further symptoms of this forgetfulness. While the countertendency to privilege design and form at the exclusion of ecological ideas has proven to be retrogressive and productive of environments more like entertainment landscapes than significant places for dwelling, the appropriation of ecology within landscape architecture has yet to precipitate inventive and animistic forms of creativity. This failure is evidenced most embarrassingly in the prosaic and often trivial nature of much contemporary built work, whether it claims to be "ecological" in its design or not.

Moreover, it is ironic that the lively and spontaneous morphogenesis characteristics of evolutionary creation—the active life processes of which ecology speaks—are rarely paralleled in the modern landscape architect's limited capacity to transfigure and transmute.[7] This lack of imaginative depth and actual agency is compounded by often uncritical, reductive, and sometimes even exclusionary views of what is considered to be "natural." For example, the popular conception of ecological design as reconstructing "native" environments is not only founded upon illusory and contradictory ideas about a noncultural "nature," but also displays a remarkably nonecological intolerance of alternative viewpoints and processes of transmutation (terms such as *foreign* and *exotic* betray an exclusivity and privileging of the *natives*).

Given the increased marginalization of contemporary landscape architecture, it would seem promising for landscape architects to look to ecology less for techniques of description and prescription (and even less for its apparent legitimizing of images of "naturalness") and more for its ideational, representational, and material implications with respect to cultural process and evolutionary transformation. After all, as social ecologist John Clark argues, "The flowering of the human spirit and personality is a continuation of natural evolution. Liberation of the human imagination from the deadening effects of mechanization and commodification is one of the most pressing ecological issues."[8] It is ironic that the emancipation of human creativity through the imaginative appropriation of ecological ideas and metaphors has been largely neglected by contemporary landscape architects (and especially those who wave the flag of ecology), even though the deeper traditions of landscape architecture are founded upon such existential objectives. The garden, for example, was historically developed as a place of both connectivity *and* differentiation between people and the world of Nature. Here, the exchange that occurs through cultivation (of food, body, spirit, and physical and psychological relationship) literally unites and distinguishes human life and Nature. The persistent archetype of the garden portends an ecological consciousness that is simultaneously useful and symbolic, one that is rooted not in an external world of nature but within a particular culture's mode of *relating* to Nature. The same power of relationship is encoded not only in the construction of physical places, but also in maps, images, and other place-forming texts.

The difficulty for many landscape architects today lies in a forgetfulness of (and perhaps, too, a skepticism toward) the power that symbolic representation can have in forging cultural relationships, both between one another and between one and Nature. This loss of traditional focus is compounded, in part, by the privileging of a scientistic ecology (utilized in highly rationalized descriptive and prescriptive ways) over phenomenological forms of ecological consciousness (which are all too often wrongly belittled by scientistic ecologists as having naive or trivial goals with respect to the massive technoeconomic scale of the ecological "crisis"). The popular notion that subjectivity, poetry, and art are welcome in the private domains of the gallery or the library but are no match for the power of "rational" instrumentality in "solving" the real problems of the world is to understand these problems in terms that are somehow *external* to the world of symbolic communication and cultural values.[9] This use of ecology as a rational instrument in landscape architectural design and planning not only externalizes the "problem," but also promotes human domination over the nonhuman world—a world that is either rendered mute and inert or deified as a privileged domain over culture. This continual emphasis upon rational prowess—often at the exclusion of phenomenological wonderment, doubt, and humility—also fails to recognize the very minor degree to which the combined landscape architectural constructions around the world have affected the global environment, especially when compared to the scale of industrialization, deforestation, and toxic waste. In contrast, the impact that gardens, parks, and public spaces (and also maps, images, and words) have had on the formation of cultural and existential values has historically proven to be immeasurable. Landscape architecture's focus of concern simply can never be that of the external environment alone but must always entail profoundly cultural interests and ideas.

Clearly, the point remains that, although ecology has surfaced in modern landscape architectural discourse (as in public life in general), a culturally animate ecology—one that is distinct from a purely "scientistic" ecology—has yet to emerge. That such an urgent development might derive from, and contribute to, more animistic types of creativity than current frames of instrumentalism would allow points to a necessary dialogue between the scientific and artistic worlds. Such an emphasis asks that ecology inform and embrace those poetic activities that create meaningful relationships between people, place, and earth. An eco-imaginative landscape/architecture would be creative insofar as it reveals, liberates, enriches, and diversifies both biological and cultural life. How, then, might the ecological idea precipitate imaginative and "world-enlarging" forms of creative endeavor? In turn, how might landscape architectural creativity (informed through its representational traditions) enrich and inform the ecological idea in the imagination and material practices of a people?

MODERNITY AND ENVIRONMENT

Prior to any further discussion of the above themes, it might be helpful to outline some of the central characteristics of modernity (the Western cultural paradigm that stems from development during the late sixteenth century). To discuss the significance of ecology and creativity outside this context is to overlook their relationship within a larger cultural sphere. Of particular importance is an appreciation for how an all-pervasive belief in human "progress" underlies much of what is troublesome in our current age.

The widespread faith in the capacity of technology to make a more perfect world in the future first arose during the sixteenth and seventeenth centuries, when new advances in science (from Copernicus, Galileo, and Descartes, to Newton and Bacon) and the rise of capitalist market economies inspired many Enlightenment intellectuals to assume that people could master nature. With progressive optimism, it was believed that all disease and poverty could be eradicated while material standards of living could be improved. The many successes of modern science during the past three hundred years (especially in medicine and communications) have continued to foster the expectation that further advances in technology will continue to solve all of humankind's problems. That this same science has also led to the development of "darker" technologies, such as nuclear weaponry and the production of toxic waste, has proven to be increasingly troubling. Similarly, more apparently benign experiments such as *Biosphere* II, in Arizona, point to a future in which people might live in their own self-manufactured environments, in which the threats (and marvels) of nature are not allowed to intrude (or appear)—except, of course and inevitably, by accident.

Clearly, it is fair to observe that advances in technology and productivity have not led to an equivalent growth in either moral or ecological consciousness.[10] A corresponding decline of the sacred and the spiritual has only compounded the deterioration of ethical measures in society, especially in terms of establishing the limits for technological inventiveness. This detachment of cultural value from the autonomous, free-wheeling development of a limitless technology is exacerbated by the rise of global, market-based economies, which are governed solely by the capitalist maxims of profit and gain, often at the expense of other people, nations, or life-forms. In turn, the rise of a hierarchical and bureaucratic society—with dominant groups limiting the freedoms of others—has led to radical inequalities, cultural estrangements, and gross reductions in both the cultural and natural spheres. The subsequent loss of alterity and difference portends an increasingly homogeneous and impoverished life-world—one that might have the busy appearance of pluralism, but only as media image and rarely as a co-presence of radically "other" realities. In sum, the belief in human progress and mastery over Nature, for all of its good intentions and successes, has at the same time promoted an often brutally mechanistic, materialistic, and impersonal world, a domain in which the potential creativity of both Nature and culture is diminished to dull equations of utility, production, commodity, and consumption.

The fallacies of progressivist and objectivist practices are sustained in large measure by another primary characteristic of the modern paradigm: The tendency to construct binary oppositions, as in the polarization of the human and social world from the natural world.[11] This dualism parallels the dichotomy between subject and object, wherein concepts such as "environment" are conceived as things that are external to humankind. The severing of reality into opposites is again an outcome of Enlightenment (particularly Cartesian) thinking, in which the objective and subjective worlds were absolutely distinguished and separated, and the incommensurability between the artists' "sensibility" and the scientists' "rationality" first arose. The tension within contemporary landscape architecture between the rational, analytical, and objective "planners" (who put such great emphasis upon a linear process of data accumulation, logical determinism, and large-scale engineering) and the emotional, intuitive, mystical "artists" (who put such great emphasis on subjectivity, emotive experience, and aesthetic appearance) is but one fallacious outcome of this larger, dualistic paradigm.[12]

Although it may be characterized as a "gentle" profession, landscape architecture remains caught within the technoeconomic, progressivist, and dualistic characteristics of modernity. While modern landscape architecture's contribution to resource management, scenic preservation, zoological and commercial theme-park design, and corporate image building has certainly lessened the damage done to the environment, its tendency to conceive and present the landscape as an object—whether aesthetically, ecologically, or instrumentally—has, at the same time, led to further *devaluation* of the environment in cultural terms (the landscape now qualified as resource, as commodity, as compensation, or as system). If landscape architecture is to concern itself with the "ecological crisis" and other difficulties of human life upon the earth, then it must recognize expeditiously how the root cause of environmental (and spiritual) decline is buried in the complex foundations of modern culture, particularly its political-economic practices, its social institutions, and the psychology and intolerance of much of its citizenry.

CONSERVATIONIST/RESOURCIST AND RESTORATIVE ECOLOGY

From within this modern cultural paradigm, two dominant streams of ecological practices of landscape architecture have emerged: One conservationist/resourcist, which espouses the view that further ecological information and knowledge will enable progressive kinds of management and control of ecosystems; and the other restorative, which espouses the view that ecological knowledge may be used to "heal" and reconstruct "natural systems."

In the conservationist/resourcist view of ecology, the landscape is composed of various resources that have particular value to people—such as forestry production, mining, agriculture, built development, recreation, and tourism. Scenery, too, is considered a resource, as are "heritage areas" and tracts of "wilderness," which are valued as a resource for "future human generations." Through the quantification of economic, ecological, and social values, strategies of landscape conservation are developed as "balances" between human needs and natural life. Ecological concepts provide the land-use manager and planner with rational (and apparently value-neutral) criteria for evaluating the "fit" between proposed land uses and environmental systems. The most popular technique for such evaluation of land is called suitability analysis, developed by McHarg at the University of Pennsylvania during the 1960s. This ecological method allows for the quantification of the various parts that make up a particular ecosystem (or at least those parts that are susceptible to being quantified and mapped); measures the impact for various scenarios of development; and recommends the most appropriate, least disruptive land use.[13] The result is a systematic and rational accounting framework—a resource value matrix—for planning and managing development ("growth").

In his book *Nature's Economy,* Donald Worster recognizes that scientific ecology is used by the conservationist/planner solely to enable a "more careful management of . . . resources, to preserve the biotic capital while maximizing the income."[14] In criticizing this view, environmentalist author Neil Evernden argues that the use of ecology in resourcist planning is simply the means by which people may achieve "the maximum utilization of the earth as raw material in the support of one species . . . [even though] environmentalism has typically been a revolt against the presumption that this is indeed a suitable goal."[15] For all its good intentions, a major consequence of the resourcist project is the inevitable reduction of other life-forms and processes of Nature's creation to objectified factors of utility—a devaluation that is often compounded by (and, also, constitutive of) an emotional detachment, or distance, between people and the earth. "In reducing the living world to ingredients that could be easily measured and graphed," observes Worster, "the ecologist was also in danger of removing all the residual emotional impediments to unrestrained development."[16] "To describe a tree as an oxygen-producing device or bog as a filtering agent is [a violence] that is debasing to being itself,"[17] writes Evernden. Both Worster and Evernden conclude that resourcist views of ecology effectively neutralize the wonders of creation; that the objectivist, instrumental manner of manipulating the world leads only to the domestication of all that is genuinely wild, self-determining, and free. "In combating exploitation, [resourcist] environmentalists have [merely] tutored the developer in the art of careful exploitation," Evernden notes.[18] Through such practices, ecology simply promotes an analytic and detached instrumentality, one that facilitates an apparently "harmless" human control over an objectified and inert natural "reserve." In other words, progressivist ecology merely conditions a particular way of seeing that effectively severs the subject from the object. It is this culturally per-petuated relationship to landscape, this continual objectification, that pro-hibits a more empathetic reciprocity between people and the world. While Evernden's remarks may upset professional land-planners whose practices are founded upon objective, ameliorative, and "rational" means, he points directly to the root source of continued environmental decline: *The will to manage and control something that is "out there," not within.*

The second approach toward ecology in landscape architecture is the restorative. Here, the emphasis is on the acquisition of technical knowledge and skill with respect to the physical reconstruction of landscapes or, at a larger scale, regional ecosystems. The belief is that the refinement of more ecologically sensitive techniques of land development will minimize damage to local and regional habitats. Ecology is employed by the restorationist to provide a scientific account of natural cycles and flows of energy, thereby explaining the network of interdependencies that comprise a particular ecosystem. Furthermore, ecology provides the restorationist with a palette of native and successional plant materials and planting patterns, allowing for the re-creation of a precultural, "naturalistic" landscape aesthetic. There is little room for cultural, social, and programmatic innovation in restorative work; the primary focus of attention is the natural world and the techniques necessary to recreate it (token gestures toward local heritage notwithstand-ing). Of course, as restoration is essentially an ideological project—derived from a particular cultural idea of "nature"—it can never escape its inherent cultural status. Unfortunately, restorationists are often as uncritical of this inescapable metaphoricity as they are unaware of the ease with which romantic ideals of "nativeness" can degenerate into exclusionary and "purist" nationalistic attitudes (as most extremely evidenced in fascist Germany in the 1930s and 1940s).[19]

So despising of modern cultural life are some restorationists that a rad-ically ecocentric ideology has emerged in one extreme wing of the environ-mentalist circle. Although the ecocentric impulse is rarely as fierce in land-scape architecture as it can be in some environmental groups, there remains a strong sentiment that urbanity, art, and cultural life in general are grossly inferior to the life of unmediated Nature, a Nature that finds its finest, most creative expression in evolutionary history and wilderness areas (blind though these groups often are to the fact that such views of "untouched nature" are themselves cultural images). Modern dualism and hierarchy (this time, Nature over culture) are not overcome in the ecocentric model, but simply reinforced. It is a model (or an "ethic") that is seriously flawed in its often mystical, antirational, and romantic views of nature—views that privilege ideas of harmony, mutuality, interconnectedness, and stability, while overlooking equally natural phenomena such as competition, exclusion, exploitation, disease, and species extinction.

In both conservationist/resourcist and restorative/ecocentric practices, ecology remains entrenched within the same modern paradigm that many argue is the structural cause of environmental and social decline. Whereas one position utilizes ecology to facilitate further control over the human environment, the other uses it to provide rhetorical force to emotional feelings about the primacy of Nature and the errors of anthropocentricity. In both cases, only the symptoms of ecological distress are dealt with, while causal cultural foundations—the social structures that underlie dualism, alienation, domination, and estrangement—are ignored and unchanged, if not actually upheld. In their dualistic objectifying of the world, both ecological resourcism and restoration are ameliorative at best, and facilitating of exploitation and exclusionism at worst. Unwittingly, landscape architecture, like the multifaceted environmental movement generally, merely replicates and sustains the shortcomings of modernity. Whether the locus of environmental concern be nature or culture, the problem is the belief in a controlling instrumentality and a failure to recognize bioecological constructions as cultural "errors and fantasies"—as treasured fictions that have profound agency in the unfolding of life-worlds.

RADICAL ECOLOGY

In response to the apparent failing of conventional frames of ecology and environmentalism, other, more radical ecological positions have emerged in recent years.[20] They are radical because their work focuses not on Nature but on the sphere of culture. They are also critical of progressivist ecology and its largely technocratic "solutions" to environmental "problems," believing them to be piecemeal approaches toward the manifestations—rather than the foundational social causes—of ecological distress. Philosophical critiques of anthropocentrism, biocentrism, rationalism, objectivism, patriarchism, dualism, hierarchy, moral rights, and ethics form the ground of the debate, with groups such as the "deep ecologists," the "ecofeminists," and the "social ecologists" at odds with one another over foundational principles. That these debates have occurred infrequently in landscape architectural discourse is profoundly unfortunate, as it will only be through a more sophisticated understanding of ecology—one that transcends its status as a descriptive and analytical natural science and recognizes its metaphoricity as a cultural construction—that ecology's significance for a more creative and meaningful landscape architecture might be realized.

Of the various radical ecologies, the one that appears to be of particular interest for landscape architecture is social ecology.[21] This approach targets the technoeconomic aspects of the modern cultural paradigm and is especially critical of social practices of domination, commodification, and instrumentality. In the development of a "new liberatory project," social ecologists believe that the greatest potential for cultural reformation lies within the power of human imagination and creativity, although they insist as well on the parallel development of alternative social structures (political, institutional, ideological, ethical, and habitual) to those that sustain the modern paradigm.[22]

While social ecology seeks an "ethics of complementarity"—structured through a nonhierarchical politics of freedom, mutualism, and self-determination—its advocates are simultaneously aware of the difficulties of trying to promote change in cultural life without resorting to enforcement or dualism. Instead, some social ecologists believe that political, economic, and institutional change may best be effected less through instrumental means than through the reinvigoration of the cultural imagination. They call for a new kind of social "vision," a "new animism" in which human societies would see the world with new eyes—with wonderment, respect, and reverence. In social ecology, the ecological idea transcends its strictly scientific characteristics and assumes social, psychological, poetic, and imaginative dimensions.

In shying away from solitary or mystical subjectivity, however, social ecology seeks to construct a dialectical synthesis between rational thought, spontaneous imagination, and spiritual development—a dialogue that social ecologist Clark describes as "a more profound inquiry into the nature of our embodiedness—as thinking, feeling humans, and as thinking, feeling earth. [Social ecology] directs us in the dialectic of being in its many dimensions. To the erotics of reason. To the logic of the passions. To the politics of the imagination."[23] Moreover, social ecologists see their project as having an evolutionary and moral imperative. They believe that humanity has developed evolutionarily as "nature rendered self-conscious," as nature reflecting upon itself. It is, therefore, an ecological and moral responsibility for human creativity to, as Coleridge so beautifully wrote, "body forth the form of things unknown";[24] to promote a diversity of evolutionary pathways; and to foster an aesthetic appreciation and sense of responsibility toward the fecundity of Natural and cultural evolution. "Evolution" here refers to a propulsive fecundity that is life itself, predicated upon spontaneity, chance, self-determination, and a directionality toward the "actualization of potential."[25] For social ecologists, people must function as "moral agents," creatively intervening in the unfolding of evolution and the increasing of diversity, freedom, and self-reflexivity.[26]

The irony of this moral imperative is hauntingly rational, for, as Erazim Kohak writes: "If there is no God, then everything is not a creation, lovingly created and endowed with purpose and value by its creator. It can only be a cosmic accident, dead matter propelled by blind force, ordered by efficient causality. In such a context, a moral subject, living his life in terms of value and purpose, would indeed be an anomaly."[27] Kohak shows how civilization is simultaneously of Nature and yet radically different from it. It is within the space of this anomalous dialectic that further discussion of ecology and creativity as active agents in the unfolding of evolutionary time must lie, and from within which more critical and active practices of landscape architecture may emerge.

DIALECTICAL ECOLOGY AND LANGUAGE

Human beings, by virtue of their ability to construct a reality through verbal and visual language, are radically different from the wild and indifferent flux that is nature, and different cultures at different times have, of course, related to the same "reality" in significantly dissimilar ways. Cultural "worlds" are composed of linguistic and imagistic structures; they are as much fictional as they are factual, as much symbolic as they are useful. As Nietzsche recognized: "To a world that is *not* our idea, the laws of numbers [and concepts] are completely inapplicable: they are valid in the human world."[28] The only nature that is real for us is constituted through the field of language. Without language there would be no place, only primal habitat; no dwelling, only subsistence. Moreover, not only does language ground and orient a culture, but it also facilitates moral reflection upon human existence and the existence of others.

The capacity of the human mind to comprehend and reflect upon the comprehensibility of the cosmos was "the most significant fact" of any for Aristotle, and this correspondence underlay the Greek formulation of the word *logos,* which referred to the "natural" symmetry of mind and Nature and to the forging of that relation through language.[29] Of course, the word *ecology* carries with it the union of *oikos* with *logos,* which allows it to be loosely translated as the "relations of home." In tracing this etymology, Robert Pogue Harrison writes: "The word ecology names far more than the science that studies ecosystems; it names the universal manner of being in the world. . . . *We dwell not in nature but in the relation to nature. We do not inhabit the earth but inhabit the excess of the earth*"[30] (emphasis added). This relation—or network of relations—is something that people make; it is an excess (of which landscape architecture is a part) within which a culture dwells. As such, human dwelling is always an estranged construction, one that can be as destructive and parasitic as it can be reciprocal and symbiotic. This view is echoed by Charles Bergman's claim: "Extinction . . . may always have been with us, but endangered species are a modern invention, a uniquely modern contribution to science and culture. They are one of the unhappy consequences of the way we have come to know animals, the dark side of our relation with nature."[31] Consequently, "even though it is the demise of earthly forests that elicit our concern," writes Evernden, "we must bear in mind that as culture-dwellers we do not so much live in forests of trees as much as in forests of words. And the source of the blight that afflicts the earth's forests must be sought in the word forests—that is, in the world we articulate, and which confirms us as agents of that earthly malaise."[32]

The realization that nature and culture are constructions, woven together as a network of relationships, has led some to argue that any development of social behavior belongs to a critical revitalization of the powers of signification—to the poetics of world making and transfiguration. Clark, for example, writes of the need to "delve more deeply into those inseparable dimensions of body and mind that dualism has so fatefully divided. As we explore such realities as thought, idea, image, sign, symbol, signifier and language on the one hand, and feeling, emotion, disposition, instinct, passion, and desire on the other, the interconnection between the two realms will become increasingly apparent."[33] Evidently, the locus of such an enterprise is the liminal space between signifier and signified, mind and matter, intellect and body.

People are caught, then, in this place between recognizing themselves as part of Nature and being separate from it. This double sense arises through the acknowledging of "otherness," or the copresence of what is not of culture and what will always exceed cultural definition. This is the wild in its most autonomous and unmediated form. As a radical "other," the wild is unrepresentable, unnameable; and although it can never be captured as a presence, it is at the same time not exactly nothing. The poet Wallace Stevens perhaps best captures this sense in the last few lines of "The Snow Man":

> For the listener who listens in the snow,
> And, nothing himself, beholds
> Nothing that is not there and the nothing that is.[34]

The nonabsent absence of the "other" escapes being seen or said, and yet it remains the original source of all saying, the first inspiration. All people have likely experienced this at one time or another, especially as young children staring with wonder at the world, or, perhaps, during times of hallucination or of religious and holy encounter.[35] Such "happenings," in turn, precipitate wonder, reflection, language, and ideas, enabling reality to "appear" (partially) and be shared among members of a community. With time, the surrounding of this (partial) reality with words and concepts attributes an everyday status to things, a familiarity.

The difficulty arises when the wonderful original disappears behind an excessively habitual, meaningless language—one in which the signifier has thickened to a "crust," denying the fullness of what is signified to present itself fully as other. Such paralysis occurs when the habits and conventions of cultural signification become so prosaic, so hardened, so total as absolute presence, that one can simply no longer see the self-contained mystery and potential of beings and things in themselves. Banished, also, is the unruly wildness and freedom of the nonhuman other—of what is, in fact, the very source of evolutionary life and human creativity. One need only consider how the engineering of the gene—that last bastion of nonhuman, indeterminate, and wild freedom—is close to being fully mapped, colonized, and manipulated. Our modern-day "wilderness areas" are no refuge either, as they, too, have been charted, mapped, photographed, painted, managed, and "set aside" as a cultural resource. All of creation is apparently becoming less wild and more domesticated, possessed, inert, and drained of all that prompts wonderment and reflection. Habitual modes of knowing and speaking, when hardened and blinkered, simply exclude the otherness that is internal to things, denying them the possibility of becoming, of further emerging and fulfilling their potential. The contemporary denial of others is of consequence for both biological evolution as well as for the development of human consciousness and moral reflectivity.[36]

In evolutionary terms, the calcification of life occurs when transmutation slows or ceases, when life stops. In linguistic and cultural terms, this atrophy translates to the deadening of poetic metaphor, to the failure to recognize that metaphor and image are not secondary representations of a deeper, external truth, but are constitutive of a cultural reality and ever capable of inventing truth. This atrophy of the imagination has arisen in large part because of the predominance of empiricist and objective logic, inherited from the promotion of rationality during the Enlightenment. Here, one simply cannot see beyond "X is equal to what is." Creative development in both Natural evolution and the human imagination, however, entails the realization of potential—the bringing forth of latent and previously unknown events and meanings. In the creative process of becoming, "X is equal to what is and what is not (yet)." The revitalization of wonderment and poetic value in human relations with Nature is, therefore, dependent on the ability to strip away the crust of habit and convention that prohibits fresh sight and relationship. One must get behind the veneer of language in order to discover aspects of the unknown within what is already familiar. Such transfiguration is a process of finding and then founding *alternative* worlds. I can think of no greater raison d'être for the landscape architectural project.

In describing the capacity of human thought, George Steiner writes that "ours is the ability, the need, to gainsay or 'unsay' the world, to image it and speak it otherwise."[37] Through the *disappearance* of the distinct and separate form of things there is enabled the *appearance* of a radically new form of experience and knowing. One must first shed the conventional view that language merely describes an external, detached reality, and realize instead that both the signified field and the things signified are combined inextricably in mutually constitutive processes of ever-becoming. Nature as an autonomous, free, irreducible, and animate "other" must be enabled to engage with, and have presence for, people, thereby continually challenging human concepts and ways of knowing. As Merleau-Ponty outlines: "It is essential for the thing and the world to present themselves as 'open,' to project us beyond their predetermined manifestations and constantly to promise us other things to see."[38] This view may entail as much terror and fear as it does harmony and mutuality (which, of course, was the idea of the Sublime in landscape and art during the eighteenth century, and which underlay Otto's ideas of the Holy in the twentieth century). Current attempts to control Nature, to leave it alone, or to conflate it with culture fail to recognize the inevitable anomalous dialectic of human existence.

The emancipation of both nature and the human imagination depends, therefore, first on the capacity to "unsay" the world and, second, on the ability to image it differently so that wonder might be brought into appearance. This transformation and enrichment of meaning belongs to the poetic—to the capacity of the visionary to change vocabularies and break convention so that hidden potentials are made actual. As Joel Kovel recognizes: "We cannot collapse the human and Natural worlds one into the other, except as a wishful illusion. We have only the choice as to how Nature is to be signified: As an inert other, or as [the poet William] Blake fully expressed, an entity transfigured with spirit."[39] Culture evolves through metaphor and the release of more edifying relationships between things. Poetic transfiguration enables an unfolding of things previously unforeseen, raising people to a perception of the wonderful and the infinite. The aim is one of ever-increasing wholeness, richness, and fullness of differentiation and subjectivity.

The idea that the poetic language of images and likenesses can expand—both imaginatively and literally—the internal structures of the world underlies the writings of the chemist-turned-poet Gaston Bachelard, who believed that poetic image could be "a synthesizing force for human existence."[40] In warning against the studying of matter as an object (as in the scientific experiment), Bachelard insisted instead on the development of a deeply sensual knowledge of the world, derived from how one lives or experiences it. He spoke, also, of the "reverberancy" with which poetic images resonate with human feelings and imagination, describing their constitutive power in forging renewed relations between things. Through his description of "poetic reverie," Bachelard's work shows how the joining of substances with adjectives can derive from matter a spirit—a truth. Hence, one might speak of "humid fire," "milky water," or "night as nocturnal matter."

BEWILDERMENT, WONDER, AND INDETERMINATION

These ideas about imaginative renewal through fresh and resonant association were particularly well understood by the Surrealists. Artists such as Breton, Miró, Magritte, Tanguy, and Ernst sought to find correspondences between Natural life and human life through the workings of the psyche and the imagination.[41] In Max Ernst's work, sun, sky, universe, earth, vegetable, animal, serpent, mineral, and human are woven together in ways that are both familiar and radically new. They are uncanny in that their oddness, their strange and bewildering quality, prompts both wonder and imaginative recognition—they evoke *relationship*. The Cartesian dualities of people and Nature, matter and thought, subject and object, male and female are conflated into fantastic worlds of mutuality, paradox, and difference. In describing certain poetic procedures such as "overpainting," "frottage," and "loplop," Ernst insisted upon the "bewitching" of reason, taste, and objectivity. In fact, one of the key procedures in Surrealist transformation was "the exploitation of the fortuitous meeting of two distant realities on an inappropriate plane . . . or, to use a shorter term, *the cultivation of a systematic bewildering*."[42]

Bewilderment is simply a prerequisite for another form of seeing; it is an unsettled appearance that allows for the double presence of human and other. That the poet or the artist are the seers and makers of such works derives from the traditions of *mimesis* and *poesis*, activities that entail the actualization of potential, the bringing forth of something previously unknown, or even nonexistent. The development of techniques of collage and montage simply represents the deep (natural?) human desire to realize new and latent visions—new connections and possibilities for relationship between things.[43] Furthermore, the parallels between the vocabularies of ecology and collage are striking—terms such as *indeterminacy, inclusivity, overlay, rupture, simultaneity, stochastic event, instability, association, collusion,* and other morphological processes speak of an ever-renewing "unity through diversity." Similarities between ecology and creative transmutation are indicative of an alternative kind of landscape architecture, one in which calcified conventions about how people live and relate to land, nature, and place are challenged and the multivariate wonders of life are once again released through invention.

These forms of ecological creativity would appear to follow from Henri Bergson's remark in *Creative Evolution* that "the role of life is to inject some

Max Ernst. The Ways of Leaves (Les moeurs des feuilles). *Histoire naturelle, sheet 18. Frottage: Pencil, watercolor, and gouache on paper, 42.7 × 26 cm. Private collection. ©1995 Artists Rights Society (ARS), New York/SPADEM/ADAGP, Paris.*

Max Ernst. Speech of the Bird Woman. *1920. Collage and gouache, 7¼ × 4¼ in. E. W. Cornfeld Collection, Bern. ©1995 Artists Rights Society (ARS), NewYork/SPADEM/ADAGP, Paris.*

indetermination into matter."[44] Bergson speaks of the infinite creativity of biological and imaginative *life*. In his refusal to reduce nature to a physical, "knowable" object, he describes a need to liberate life so that its fullest potentials may come into appearance. Bergson's is a creative evolution of indeterminate unfolding, a process in which "matter is the deposit of life, the static residues of actions done, choices made in the past. Living memory is the past felt in the actualities of realities, of change."[45] Such an interrelational view directs us toward more "heterotopic" kinds of activity and space than singular, "utopic" acts. Whereas heterotopia's ad hoc inclusivity and openendedness portends a disturbing and bewildering prospect, it also systematically denies singularity, totality, determinacy, and hierarchy. As a "structured heterogeneity," such a complex field is neither chaotic nor ordered, but free and organic. Thus, a truly ecological landscape architecture might be less about the construction of finished and complete works, and more about the design of "processes," "strategies," "agencies," and "scaffoldings"—catalytic frameworks that might enable a diversity of relationships to create, emerge, network, interconnect, and differentiate.[46]

The aim for the design of these strategic grounds would be not to celebrate differentiation and pluralism in a representational way, but rather to construct enabling relationships between the freedoms of life (in terms of unpredictability, contingency, and change) and the presence of formal coherency and structural/material precision. This double aim underlies—in part—the work of Rem Koolhaas and is particularly well exemplified in his unbuilt proposal for the Parc de la Villette, Paris, in which the delineation and "equipping" of a "strategic field" with "social instruments" was planned to optimize physical, spatial, and material identity while allowing for an almost infinite range of programmatic events, combinations, improvisations, differentiations, and adjacencies.[47] As Sanford Kwinter describes: "All of Koolhaas's recent work is *evolved*—rather than designed—within the hypermodern event-space of complex, sensitive, dynamical indeterminacy and change. . . . [The design principles display] a very clear orientation toward evolutionary, time-based processes, dynamic geometric *structurations*—not structures per se, but forms that follow and fill the wake of concrete yet unpredeterminable events. . . . This is because, instead of designing artificial environments, [Koolhaas] deploys richly imbricated systems of interacting elements that set in motion rather artificial ecologies that, in turn, take on a genuine self-organizing life of their own."[48] The resultant "image" of such designs may not be one that is currently thought to be ecological in appearance (which, as I have argued, remains fallaciously bound up with ideas of untouched and native "nature"), but its strategic organicism—its deployment as an active agent, a metabolic urbanism—aspires to nothing less than the injection of indetermination, diversification, and freedom into both the social and Natural worlds—values that are surely central to any ecological, moral, and poetic notions about evolutionary and creative life. Other pro-

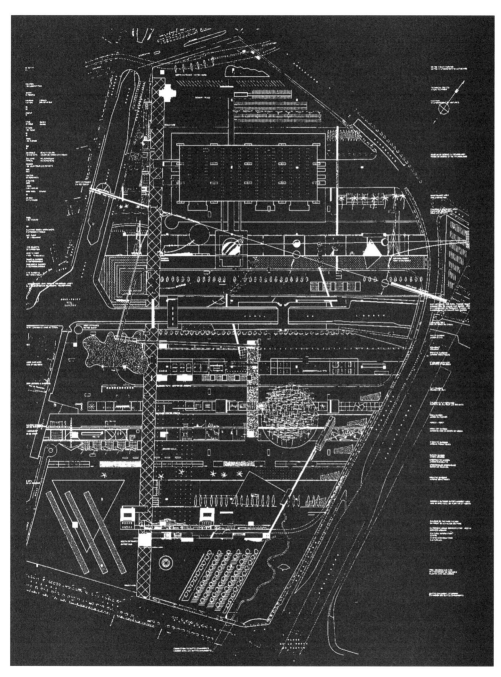

Rem Koolhaas—OMA (Office for Metropolitan Architecture). Plan for the Parc de la Villette, Paris (unbuilt proposal). 1982–1983. Reprinted with permission of OMA.

Rem Koolhaas—OMA. Parc de la Villette, Paris; detail from model (unbuilt proposal). 1982–1983. Reprinted with permission of OMA.

Rem Koolhaas—OMA. Planometric demonstration, Parc de la Villette, Paris (unbuilt proposal). 1982–1983. Drawing by Alex Wall. Reprinted with permission of OMA.

jects by Koolhaas, such as Yokohama Harbor, further demonstrate the oneiric lyricism of programmatic strategies that remain open-ended and promote new life-forms and sets of events.

CODA

My purpose in this essay is to present a number of theoretical bases that might allow for a more animate appropriation of ecology in landscape architectural practice. These bases have little to do with the object-centered advocacy of Nature ("environment") or culture ("art") and point instead toward the highly interactive processes and relationships that are *life* itself—life as both a specific and autonomous system of networks, forces, combinations, unfoldings, events, and transformations. What is important in this view is how creative practices of ecology and landscape architecture construct—or, more precisely, *enable*—alternative forms of relationship and hybridization between people, place, material, and Earth. Echoing evolutionary principles, these enabling strategies function less as instruments and ameliorants and more as agents, as processes, as active imbroglios and ever-emerging networks of potential. Obviously, I am speaking here of a landscape architecture that has yet to appear fully, one that is less preoccupied with ameliorative, stylistic, or pictorial concerns and more actively engaged with imaginative, enabling, and diversifying practices—*practices of the wild.*[49]

How may the pulsing flow and flux of wild life, its autonomous status as "other," and its reflective and moral sense be channeled, liberated, and expressed through an ecology and landscape of creative agents? The answers, I believe, lie within the powers of both Natural and cultural agencies in the evolving of landscapes that precipitate (and are caught within) processes of indetermination and diversification; landscapes that engage, enable, diversify, trick, emancipate, and elude—put simply, landscapes that function as actants, as continual transformations and encounters that actively resist closure and representation.[50]

NOTES

1. Coleridge 1845, p. 223.
2. Bergson 1944, p. 3.
3. Wilson 1992.
4. Botkin 1990, p. 25.
5. Nietzsche 1984, pp. 23–24.
6. Ibid., p. 24.
7. The relationship between biological, evolutionary processes and the human imagination is discussed beautifully in Cobb 1977. Creativity and evolution is also implicit in Bergson 1944.
8. Clark 1993, p. 351.
9. Corner 1991, pp. 125–31.
10. Habermas 1983; Goin 1996.
11. Although the tendency to speak of a duality between nature and culture has persisted throughout modernity, the truth of this belief has been challenged by Latour 1993, who argues that the social and natural worlds are inextricably interrelated. See, also, Elizabeth K. Meyer's essay in this book.
12. Corner 1990.
13. McHarg 1969.

14. Worster 1979, p. 315.

15. Evernden 1993, p. 22.

16. Worster 1979, p. 304.

17. Evernden 1993, p. 23.

18. Ibid., p. 23.

19. Groening and Wolschke-Buhlman 1992 and 1994; Sorvig 1994; and MacKenzie 1987.

20. Zimmerman et al. 1993; Merchant 1992; Oelschlaeger 1991, pp. 281–319.

21. Zimmerman et al. 1993, pp. 345–437.

22. Bookchin 1993 and 1991.

23. Clark 1993, p. 352.

24. Coleridge 1845. Quoted in Cobb 1977, p. 15.

25. Bookchin 1990, pp. 12–48.

26. For more on the idea of agency see Haraway 1991, Latour 1993, and Rose 1994.

27. Kohak 1984, p. 5.

28. Nietzsche 1984, p. 27.

29. Biehl 1993, p. 375.

30. Harrison 1992, p. 201.

31. Bergman 1990, pp. 1–2.

32. Evernden 1993, pp. 145–46.

33. Clark 1993, p. 352.

34. Stevens 1981, p. 10.

35. Evernden 1992, pp. 107–24; Cobb 1977, p. 30; Taylor 1990; and Vanderbilt 1993.

36. Evernden 1992, pp. 116–24; Oelschlaeger 1991, pp. 320–53; and Bergman 1990.

37. Steiner 1984, p. 398.

38. Merleau-Ponty 1962, p. 384.

39. Kovel 1993, pp. 413–14.

40. Bachelard 1987, p. 107.

41. The importance of the psyche for how people relate to Nature is discussed most profoundly in Jung 1973. Of particular relevance is Jung's discussion of "synchronicity," which, like Bachelard's ideas of "reverberation," describes correspondences between Natural life and human life, especially as apprehended in the unconscious imagination.

42. Spies 1991, p. 43.

43. Corner 1992, pp. 265–75.

44. Bergson 1944, p. 139.

45. Ibid., p. xiv.

46. Haraway 1991, Latour 1993, Rose 1994.

47. Koolhaas and Mau 1995, pp. 894–939; Lucan 1991, pp. 86–95.

48. Kwinter 1993, pp. 84–85. See, also, Koolhaas and Mau 1995.

49. Snyder 1990.

50. Corner 1996.

REFERENCES

Bachelard, Gaston. 1987. *On Poetic Imagination and Reverie.* Rev. ed. Translated by Colette Gaudin. Dallas: Spring Publications.

Bergman, Charles. 1990. *Wild Echoes.* New York: McGraw-Hill.

Bergson, Henri. 1944. *Creative Evolution.* Translated by Arthur Mitchell. New York: Modern Library.

Biehl, Janet. 1993. "Dialectics in the Ethics of Social Ecology." Pp. 374–89 in *Environmental Philosophy,* ed. Michael Zimmerman, et al. Englewood Cliffs, N.J.: Prentice Hall.

Bookchin, Murray. 1990. *The Philosophy of Social Ecology.* Montreal: Black Rose Books.

———. 1991. *The Ecology of Freedom.* Rev. ed. Montreal: Black Rose Books.

———. 1993. "What Is Social Ecology?" Pp. 354–73 in *Environmental Philosophy,* ed. Michael Zimmerman, et al. Englewood Cliffs, N.J.: Prentice Hall.

Botkin, Daniel. 1990. *Discordant Harmonies: A New Ecology for the Twenty-First Century.* Oxford: Oxford University Press.

Carson, Rachel. 1962. *Silent Spring.* Boston: Houghton Mifflin.

Clark, John. 1993. "Social Ecology: Introduction." Pp. 345–53 in *Environmental Philosophy,* ed. Michael Zimmerman, et al. Englewood Cliffs, N.J.: Prentice Hall.

Cobb, Edith. 1977. *The Ecology of Imagination in Childhood.* New York: Columbia University Press.

Coleridge, Samuel Taylor. 1845. *The Works of Samuel Taylor Coleridge, Prose and Verse.* Philadelphia: Thomas Cowperthwait.

Collingwood, R. G. 1960. *The Idea of Nature.* London: Oxford University Press.

Corner, James. 1990. "A Discourse on Theory I: Sounding the Depths—Origins, Theory, and Representation." *Landscape Journal* 9(2): 60–78.

———. 1991. "A Discourse on Theory II: Three Tyrannies of Contemporary Theory and the Alternative of Hermeneutics." *Landscape Journal* 10(2): 115–33.

———. 1992. "Representation and Landscape: Drawing and Making in the Landscape Medium." *Word and Image* 8(3): 243–75.

———. 1996. "Aqueous Agents: The (Re)Presentation of Water in the Work of George Hargreaves." *Process Architecture* 128: 46–61.

Evernden, Neil. 1992. *The Social Creation of Nature.* Baltimore: Johns Hopkins University Press.

———. 1993. *The Natural Alien: Humankind and Environment.* 2d ed. Toronto: University of Toronto Press.

Goin, Peter. 1996. *Humanature.* Austin: University of Texas Press.

Groening, Gert, and Joachim Wolschke-Buhlman. 1992. "Some Notes on the Mania for Native Plants in Germany." *Landscape Journal* 11(2): 116–26.

———. 1994. "Response: If the Shoe Fits, Wear It!" *Landscape Journal* 13(1): 62–63.

Habermas, Jurgen. 1983. "Modernity: An Incomplete Project." Pp. 13–15 in *The Anti-Aesthetic,* ed. Hal Foster. Port Townsend, Wash.: Bay Press.

Haraway, Donna. 1991. *Simians, Cyborgs, and Women: The Reinvention of Nature.* New York: Routledge.

Harrison, Robert Pogue. 1992. *Forests: The Shadow of Civilization.* Chicago: University of Chicago Press.

Harvey, David. 1989. *The Condition of Postmodernity.* Oxford: Blackwell.

Jung, C. G. 1973. *Synchronicity: An Acausal Connecting Principle.* Translated by R. Hull. Princeton, N.J.: Princeton University Press.

Kohak, Erazim. 1984. *The Embers and the Stars.* Chicago: University of Chicago Press.

Koolhaas, Rem, and Bruce Mau. 1995. *S, M, L, XL.* New York: Monacelli Press.

Kovel, Joel. 1993. "The Marriage of Radical Ecologies." Pp. 406–17 in *Environmental Philosophy,* ed. Michael Zimmerman, et al. Englewood Cliffs, N.J.: Prentice Hall.

Kwinter, Sanford. 1993. "Rem Koolhaas, OMA: The Reinvention of Geometry." *Assemblage* 18: 83–85.

Latour, Bruno. 1993. *We Have Never Been Modern.* Cambridge, Mass.: Harvard University Press.

Leopold, Aldo. 1949. *A Sand County Almanac.* New York: Oxford University Press.

Lucan, Jacques. 1991. *OMA—Rem Koolhaas.* Princeton, N.J.: Princeton University Press.

MacKenzie, J. 1987. *The Empire of Nature.* Manchester: Manchester University Press.

McHarg, Ian. 1969. *Design with Nature.* Garden City, N.Y.: Doubleday/Natural History Press. 1992. Reprint, New York: John Wiley & Sons.

Merchant, Carolyn. 1992. *Radical Ecology.* New York: Routledge, Chapman & Hall.

Merleau-Ponty, Maurice. 1962. *The Phenomenology of Perception.* Translated by Colin Smith. Suffolk, U.K.: Routledge and Kegan Paul.

Nietzsche, Friedrich. 1984. *Human, All Too Human.* Translated by Marion Faber. Lincoln: University of Nebraska Press.

Oelschlaeger, Max. 1991. *The Idea of Wilderness: From Prehistory to the Age of Ecology.* New Haven: Yale University Press.

Rorty, Richard. 1979. *Philosophy and the Mirror of Nature.* Princeton, N.J.: Princeton University Press.

Rose, Dan. 1994. *Active Ingredients.* Unpublished manuscript, University of Pennsylvania.

Snyder, Gary. 1990. *The Practice of the Wild.* Berkeley, Calif.: North Point Press.

Sorvig, Kim. 1994. "Natives and Nazis: An Imaginary Conspiracy in Ecological Design." *Landscape Journal* 13(1): 58–61.

Spies, Werner. 1991. *Max Ernst: Collages.* Translated by John William Gabriel. New York: Harry N. Abrams.

Steiner, George. 1984. *George Steiner: A Reader.* Oxford: Oxford University Press.

Stevens, Wallace. 1981. *Collected Poems.* New York: Knopf.

Taylor, Mark. 1990. *Tears.* Albany: State University of New York Press.

Vanderbilt, Paul. 1993. *Between the Landscape and Its Other.* Baltimore: Johns Hopkins University Press.

Wilson, Alex. 1992. *The Culture of Nature.* Cambridge, Mass.: Blackwell.

Worster, Donald. 1979. *Nature's Economy: The Roots of Ecology.* New York: Anchor Press.

Zimmerman, Michael E., J. Baird Callicott, George Sessions, Karen J. Warren, and John Clark, eds. 1993. *Environmental Philosophy.* Englewood Cliffs, N.J.: Prentice Hall.

4

LANDSCAPE DESIGN AND NATURE

LAURIE OLIN

A principal issue under consideration in this book is the role of "nature" and its processes in the art of landscape design. In recent years too much has been made of a supposed dichotomy between art and science in landscape architecture, specifically that of ecology as it is taught within the contemporary profession and many graduate programs in Europe and North America. It is my firm belief that any such division or controversy can only take place in the minds of those who are uncomfortable or ignorant of the world that sustains us, for "nature" is the great metaphor that underlies all art. Several questions must be posed and answered briefly, however, before one can give examples that might demonstrate such a position: What is nature? What is art? What is landscape architecture? Only then can one discuss issues of interest within the field, such as how it relates to nature and what this means in terms of form, meaning, and expression.

WHAT IS NATURE?

"Nature" is an idea or the general name we give to life and the cosmos. As society's knowledge and understanding of the physical universe has changed and increased, so, too, have our ideas about life, the world, and its processes. Although some philosophers and theologians have questioned our ability to ever truly know or understand the universe and its events—some even question its existence or verifiability—I happen to believe that the world exists and that life is not a dream. Without commenting upon the possible implications for beliefs that one might be able to sustain vis-à-vis religion, let me say that I accept the findings of modern science—as far as I can understand them—to be the best description to date of what is going on around me. I also know that this body of theory will continue to change and evolve, because it is based upon a current state of description, hypotheses, and imagination.

Next, one can consider the word *nature*. This word can stand for the physical universe in its unity and diversity just referred to. Or it can refer to some *idea* of nature that describes the physical world and its processes as an omnipresent force or presence of actions and events, and, as such, it provides a great bundle of metaphors (frequently of a biological, geological, meteorological, or physiological sort) that underlie all art. This is the "Nature" of seventeenth- and eighteenth-century texts, in which nature seems, on the one hand, to be an anthropomorphic presence, rather like the river gods of antiquity or the paternalistic Jehovah figure of the Hebrews, and, on the other hand, a vaguely ghostlike set of causal forces akin to abstractions derived from technology and its machinery. This meaning of the word is related to the usage of *nature* to connote the intrinsic character, quality, or behavior of some thing, place, person, or creation. One particular aspect of this sense of the word is the idea of "human nature" (of which more later).

Finally, there are the *phenomena* of nature; that is, all of the palpable, physical things of the world—the oceans and mountains, storms and meteors, forests and deserts, animals, fish, insects, molds, breezes, earthquakes, avalanches, fires, diseases, coral reefs, people, cities, giants, midgets, worms, flowers, trees, and stones. There is the incredible plethora of things and events that is celebrated in art from the caves of Lascaux through the sonorous lists of the Old Testament, from the songs of Walt Whitman and Gerard Manley Hopkins to those of Theodore Roethke, from the paintings of Giotto and sculpture of Bernini to the work of Picasso, Frank Stella, and Georgia O'Keeffe. Assuming that Kepler and Heisenberg were trying to understand and describe the world and some of its workings, it is only fair to also point out that so, too, were artists as different as Heironymous Bosch and Rembrandt.

Nature, and frequently those aspects of nature that frame our daily setting or behavior, make up a large portion of the subject(s) of art. Some of the more obvious examples of artists who have depicted and speculated upon the forces of nature and were conversant with studies in science and technology, such as Leonardo and Michelangelo, hardly need defense or a word of explanation in relation to this assertion. Others, who are less popular and more idiosyncratic, or positively delirious, such as the Surrealists, or seemingly in retreat from the direct, immediate world (at least as far as literally representing or describing it goes), such as the abstract expressionists and minimalists of recent decades, need more consideration and explication in this regard. A case has been made for their concern and value in presenting aspects and attitudes to life and our emotional or perceptual relationships to it. Just as science often strives to reveal and understand aspects of the physical world that are invisible to the unassisted eye, so, too, much of art has attempted to portray and bring forward for consideration aspects of the world and the human condition that are neither obvious nor well understood. Part of this legacy has been to explore constantly the boundaries of whatever society perceives to be normal or true. Just as much of life and the world around us is neither good nor bad but just is, so, too, much of art comments upon or reflects these non-human, biophysical phenomena. The majority of all the products of art, however, probably have addressed some aspect of human affairs, and of our interaction with each other or the world, oftentimes with a consideration of values and according to some set of principles. How, then, does a practical art such as landscape architecture, with all its messiness, functional requirements, and a medium that could be said to be nature itself, fit into such a discussion?[1]

Before Earth Day few people in the general populace were familiar with the principles of ecology. So, too, today. Even in the field of landscape architecture, many hold ideas about nature and ecology that are out of date or incorrect. Large numbers of city dwellers are also out of touch with the workings of the world, thinking they are separate from nature somehow, or, when they do think of it, think of it as something alien, something other. But it is not other. Nature is what there is. It is ourselves as well as our setting. Nature is not cute; it is not pretty, handsome, or even beautiful. Those are cultural ideas. Nature is not nasty or vicious either, although it can be dangerous and deadly. It is only wild in that this is what we use the word *wild* to mean. It is a series of things and interactions that are life and the world. It is, ultimately, indifferent.

Recently we have come to believe that nature not only abhors a vacuum, but also that it has no natural and normal stable state. It was Heraclitus who first pointed out what modern science is developing mathematical models to prove: Everything is in flux. Concepts such as those of a "climax" forest must be comprehended more in terms of the original meaning of the word, that of building up to some level of energy or physical complexity, followed by a falling-off or decline, sometimes gradual, sometimes precipitous or catastrophic. At a conference one ecologist after another stood up and delivered papers supporting the not-so-recent theory that the only thing that is constant is change, that the idea of a balance of (or in) nature is a human idea that does not have a basis in the physical world.[2]

This is not so surprising to me. Ever since I was a young boy in Alaska, I have related the notion of stasis with death. The idea of a stable state of anything seems a little naive. Although I was not consciously studying nature or my environment per se while growing up, I was, as is every person who is sentient, to some degree soaking up information about my immediate surroundings. Like most people, from the Archie Bunkers to the Bertrand Russells, I have some sense of what nature is and is not, and of what human nature is. Like most of my fellow landscape architects, however, I have no credentials to talk about nature in terms of scientific knowledge. Nonetheless, I am highly qualified to discuss it in terms of experience, feeling, and spirit. I am keenly interested in the relationship between the phenomena of the physical world and our feelings toward them, of matters of spirit and how cultures (or individuals) express their understanding of humanity and the world in art, religion, and philosophy. What lasts after us? What endures? The physical world as altered, improved, or degraded. What will survive from our brief period in terms of art and thought? This interests me very much. If one were to conceive of cities as analogous to coral reefs—growing, dying, reformulating, as a natural development—then one can begin to see many congruences between culture and nature.

WHAT IS ART?

Art, like nature, is many things. Most certainly it entails different human activities that have evolved and changed in scope and purpose since the dawn of civilization.

Like nature, art—what it is, what its purpose is, what it can do and mean—has been the subject of considerable speculation and debate since classical antiquity. The thorny field of aesthetics, which according to some is the science of sensation and feeling and not merely the consideration of art or the idea (or phenomenon, if it exists) of beauty, is largely the province of philosophers. A daunting area of thought, it is generally useless to those who actually make things. As one wag put it, "Aesthetics is to artists as ornithology is to the birds." Put even more simply, aesthetics is not much help during the act of creation, for it does not tell a designer what to do, or how as yet unknown combinations of things will be, feel, or relate to each other. Aesthetics, like much of traditional science, examines and attempts to explain what is and what has been, but it sheds little light on what could, would, or should be. It is analytical but not synthetic or generative.

When most people think of art they immediately think of drawing, painting, photography, sculpture, music, dance, and literature. Some also include other activities and their products that are in large or some part utilitarian such as architecture and landscape design. Although architecture and more recently landscape gardening have come to be seen as artistic products—as the residue of civilization and creativity—and as such are studied by art historians, landscape, as opposed to gardens, or landscape in the larger sense, is still poorly understood and frequently seen as the province of social historians and human geographers. It would seem that when a landscape of whatever nature is the conscious construction of an individual or a collaboration between individuals—designer, client, patron, builder, the state, or an office—rather than the anonymous accretion of a disparate group unconsciously working together on a composition, we can consider landscape as an art and judge it by whatever criteria we judge artistic endeavors by. In many cases we may find that such works are not very original or interesting; in others we will undoubtedly find brilliant and inspiring works. It would seem that landscape design can achieve works of lasting worth as often as do any of the other compositional arts (as opposed to the performing arts), largely by extending ideas found in the other arts through different means. Similarly, both cinema and photography have come to join the arts in our time by extending particular aspects of traditional fields such as drama and painting through their own means.

For a long time and for many people (even today), a central tenet of the theory of art has been that of mimesis and of progress or development in relationship to the representation of the things of this world—objects, events, motives, or feelings—in short, the consideration of the environment and the human condition, but in terms other than those of science or philosophy. Arthur Danto suggests that if mimesis had not been directed toward *narrative,* it would soon have worn off as a novelty. A recent example he gives of this phenomenon at work is the invention, evolution, and continued life of motion pictures. What this suggests about landscape architecture is worth consideration.[3]

Art has been many things and has served many purposes. Some have related to survival and power, some to cosmology and ethics, some to understanding and self-fulfillment, some to experience and feeling. Magic, religion, government, and the search for self-expression and fulfillment have all been served at one time or another. Now, however, many people within and outside the art world are convinced that an era of great energy, optimism, and innovation in art, namely that of modernism, has come to an end.[4] This mood—or fact, if it is that—has spawned an outburst of reflections and theories about the end of art, the end of history, the death of the avant-garde, and postmodernism and its dilemmas. Certainly we are facing the end of the twentieth century with dwindling prospects and severe societal and environmental problems. To a certain extent this condition has been mirrored by an outpouring of grim and disturbing art, much of which is hateful or worse. In architecture and, to a lesser degree, in landscape architecture experiments expressive of this general mood have been met with mixed reactions both within and outside the fields. It would be just as wrong to dismiss this work out of hand as it would be to embrace it unquestioningly.

Art both reflects and leads. It allows us to explore new avenues for creativity as easily as it can express yearning and nostalgia. Art and, by extension, landscape design (when it is operating at the level of art) can give form to dreams and myths, for better or for worse. Like nature, art does this not by starting over, but by reworking, transforming, extending, and reshaping what is into what will be. There is a recycling of dead matter, of old nutrients and ideas lying on the forest floor of the studio or of society. Some things run amok and die out. Slime molds and dinosaurs become extinct, baroque music is relegated to public radio—maybe the automobile is next. The dominant animal or art form of the next era already exists during the time of what is passing, often without gaining much notice.

WHAT IS LANDSCAPE ARCHITECTURE?

There has been considerable soul-searching among design professionals and academics for some time as to just what constitutes the subject and disciplinary nature of the field. In my view, landscape architecture is simply the design and planning of physical environments. This can range from the development of plans for wildlife refuges or natural system manipulations for various purposes, to urban design plans for all kinds of development, to physical designs for parks, gardens, and estates. It can encompass preservation, conservation, restoration, and the management of existing landscapes. It can include the design and arrangement of significant or minor structures, from highways and water management structures to buildings and urban districts. It is a stupefyingly wide array of activities that virtually no one in the field can master fully, although some have engaged in several of the different aspects over a period of time.

At times it seems as if there are many different subfields of landscape architecture and, thus, that the range of formal expression in such a situation should be large, as broad as nature itself. Despite minor variations of formal structures and compositional strategies in the gardens and built landscapes of different cultures that have emerged around the world, a review of them shows the continuity and tenacious persistence of a handful of design ideas and images of nature and gardens, frequently referred to as styles or typologies. Why is this so? The principal reason for such limitations is strictly cultural. In every society there is a tension between the need and desire for change and experimentation and the need and desire for stability and tradition. Some of the most stubborn and outdated attitudes that we cling to as a society and as professionals are involved with nature and natural systems. There is a desire to see people as separate from nature coupled with a recurring desire to see them come to terms with it. There is, also, a persistent view not only that nature is "other" from us, but also that it is wild, chaotic, and unfathomable, whereas people are orderly and understandable, or at least knowable. One can quarrel with both sides of this equation.

I am a designer who is interested in physical design, which is the making and shaping of phenomenal spaces and objects. I am involved in the design and construction of places for people to live, work, and visit. It is one of the facts of our human situation that there are a great number of things wrong with our physical environment and that many natural systems are under attack or seriously degraded. Indeed, innumerable social—especially urban—environments are in decline, hostile to the life they are intended to nurture. But most of what is wrong with the environment today I can do very little about. The forces that prevail upon the ecosystems and much of the urban infrastructure have next to nothing to do with my work or the work of most of my peers. The problems of the larger environment derive from flagrant abuses of resources, from poor and ignorant government policy, and from systematic problems related to things ranging from packaging policies and dietary habits to the economics of agriculture and the defense and transportation industries. The scale of the problems facing us is beyond the scope of individual site designers. In fact, without a resurgence in serious regional planning at the academic, professional, and governmental level, there is little that the field of landscape architecture can do about our situation.

Everyone I know who may be working on the site design of individual homes or large-scale development has to go through many hoops to protect slopes, maintain water quality, preserve significant vegetation and water bodies, plant sensible things, and meet a series of strict local or regional regulations that are desirable in the interests of both the community's and environment's long-term benefit. This is admirable, but only incrementally beneficial; given the real scale and scope of the problem, it also seems trivial. For all of the sensible land planning and design that private practitioners may enact, poor land and resource planning rushes along at a frightening pace at every bureaucratic level. Recently I drove past an entire mountainside in the Tuscarora Mountains of Pennsylvania that had been clear-cut, leaving several miles of desolation: A landscape of rock piles, mudslides, dead streams—a ruined valley with little future for both natural and human populations, the latter of which were still there at the bottom of the slope. This sort of thing is so pervasive as to be hardly noticeable to most Americans and is often perfectly legal, part of the desperate economic plans of state and federal agencies. For me to do something about this sort of structural problem in our society and the environment I would need to abandon my practice and become a planner or an attorney or enter government. I applaud those who do, and who do so effectively for this purpose, but this is another calling, one for which I am neither suited nor trained.

Landscape design can and should be responsible toward a community and the environment. In a meaningful, albeit fragmentary way, it can help to create an environment that is healthy and functional within a larger framework of natural systems, and it can help us to understand our environment through the use of traditional artistic strategies that have to do with meaning and expression. Landscape architecture is not, however, the activity that will save the planet or society from ourselves. Pogo has the last word on that.

LANDSCAPE DESIGN AND NATURE

We are left, therefore, with a puzzling discipline and a series of riddles. The medium of landscape design is as diverse and simple as life itself. It is sensual and phenomenal; it has form that is both finite and infinite in its variations. Each generation must learn and define nature for itself, much in the same way that every generation of artists must recapitulate the history and meaning of art again for itself. Each one of us must come to some understanding for ourselves of landscape design's properties and processes. We are dealing with what is eternal and at the same time mutable.

Our ability to understand both the world and landscape design is bound up in the emerging science of description—fractals, chaos theory, ecology, nuclear physics, cosmology, biochemistry, revisionist paleontology, and so on. It is no wonder that some of the old answers do not hold true today, or that we are uncomfortable with new findings in both art and science throughout history. What does *landscape* mean? It depends upon one's terms of reference, one's moment in time, one's insight, and the quality of one's travel and education. The process of reference, the norms of meaning, and the range of expressions one can give depends upon one's notions about the problem of "natural" versus "invented" meanings and the limitations of linguistic analogies. Landscapes do not literally "say" anything. They have meaning in other ways.[5]

The most common devices employed in the design and creation of landscapes—of investing them with meaning—are those of metaphor, figural representation, abstract representation, and iconography. Various ideas of nature have been invested into landscape design in the West for more than two thousand years with such devices, and even longer in the East. Can one say that any work of Andre Le Nôtre or Lancelot Brown express any particular human mood? Joy, fear, anger, solemnity, humor? Probably not. Can we say that they express any such emotions on the part of their authors? Again, I think not. What then, if anything, do they express? Have they any meaning or not? If so, what? I believe they do possess meaning, some—but only some—of which is related to feelings that are aroused in us upon experiencing them. One thing that nearly everyone who has ever seen and discussed the work of Le Nôtre, Brown, or Olmsted has mentioned has been nature and the expression (in nonverbal ways) by these designers of views about the nature of Nature.

I am deeply interested in aspects of the environment that might be termed "ordinary" or "common" and the role they play in the creation of landscape works that are exemplary and uncommon—those works that are artful and thoughtful and embody the devices and attributes of the commonplace with respect to form, meaning, and expression. The power of our preconceptions and deeply held views of what is or should be normal are amply demonstrated in elections and social confrontations. Nevertheless, I am taken aback by the hostility, intolerance, and ignorance I encounter when I present schemes that do not seem radical at all. Designers are accustomed to opposition toward their work when it threatens to remove existing buildings or open space. Occasionally we find opposition on the grounds of different social values or taste. The sort of commotion that Stravinsky caused in Paris with the premiere of *The Rite of Spring* hardly seems possible today. What, after all, would shock a modern audience, especially in a landscape design? Designs that somehow seriously offend or challenge ideas of what is normal and acceptable? Designs that are seen as offensive to some perceived natural order, a perversion to be stopped?

Much of the work that my colleagues and I have been engaged in is urban and of a sort that has not consciously taken ecology as a starting point or reference, much less as its subject. We are always concerned with the nature of the place in which we find ourselves. At the same time we have been concerned with the continual transformation of the present in the creation of the ever receding future, and the retrieval or loss of the past. This seems, to me, to be the most *natural* thing in the world for a landscape architect to do.

PRACTICING WHAT ONE PREACHES

Since 1976 I have worked on a series of ongoing experiments with my partners, associates, and employees wherein we attempt to bring ideas concerning nature and cultural responses to it into play in our work. Some of these make more overt and literal references to ecological ideas and principles than others. Large portions of our work do not allude consciously to nature at all; on the other hand, many do. Every one of our projects has, to a greater or lesser degree, employed fairly traditional site analyses that I will not discuss here. Some projects have been developed solely as a response to the site conditions, suggested and shaped by the site and the phenomena of a specific place. There have, however, been many sites that did not necessarily dictate or even hint at what could or should be done there. For me this is neither a good nor bad thing.

Robert Hanna (my former partner), Dennis McGlade (my current partner, who was also a partner in Hanna/Olin), and I spent many years fighting against determinism both in the academy and in practice. It is a deeply held belief of ours that the site (or the data about the site) does not tell us what to do, but informs us of the choices, costs, and alternatives that we might make. We can point to projects that have been driven by the soils or hydrologic problems, of projects that had us bend over backward to preserve existing features such as streams or a woodland, that made us talk architects into moving their buildings to reveal and express landforms or particularly worthy landscape elements.[6] But what of the urban scene with its poor soils and little natural process? What of the landfill, the redundant railroad yard, the roof deck, and the hostile urban corridor and street? What do you do when there is little of natural value to hang your hat on? I am fond of telling my friends in architecture that there is no such thing as a blank slate. There is always something there—a memory, a trace, a hint of context of the greater world and all its machinations. There is always the example of Nature itself with all of its works and examples, principles and methods, things and events.

I believe that no site has all the answers and that the data never really tell one what to do. If so there would be no achievement such as the city of Venice. There is nothing natural about thousands of pilings holding up tons of marble, as one finds in the great churches and piazzas of this wonderful city. For all of the art and science of our own time we have yet to produce an environment as felicitous. Nowhere in all of our ecological planning methods do we have the resilience and sophistication to generate something as contrary and beautiful as this watery realm. In fact, every example of contemporary planning methods would have argued against embarking on such an adventure. One must stand back, therefore, and be cautious about our certainty that we have the best—or most foolproof—methods. As Ian McHarg has said on many occasions, part of the motive behind the development of ecological planning at the University of Pennsylvania has been to produce methods that could be used by people of all abilities, and that such methods would prevent the terrible mistakes and abuses that were and still are so common in planning and design.

Preventing mistakes and producing tools that will prevent harm is not the same thing as working at the cutting edge of a field in terms of what is possible within the medium in the hands of its gifted practitioners. While I would never make claims that I or my firm function in this exalted sphere, I feel comfortable in asserting that we have moved beyond the amateur or beginner status in our field or art. We can point to numerous projects that exemplify McHargian site analysis and response in design gestures. At the same time we can point to many others where ecological methods yielded next to nothing or formed only the jumping-off point in an exploration of what to do.

Our work cannot escape its physical being and shortcomings any more than I can escape my moment and place in contemporary society. While I believe deeply in the inescapable presence and limitations of nature and of natural process, I also have an abiding interest and enthusiasm for the human imagination and spirit that has produced the great gardens and cities, the breathtaking works of art and humble agriculture that pay homage to the earth and its possibilities, to contrary situations such as the cities built in estuaries—Venice, Amsterdam, New York, and Boston— many of whose most salient features would now be illegal under laws based upon articles of faith derived from ecological planning methods. There are, it seems to me, more ways to relate to ecological processes and principles than one might think of when merely examining a site and its constituent parts.

In the gallery of projects that follows, I present examples of other ways of looking to nature beyond particular sites and their features. Each design addresses the issue of nature and ecology in a different way.

Villa Olimpica, Barcelona, Spain

In 1991 Hanna/Olin developed a landscape design for a commercial development on the waterfront in Barcelona that was to form part of the Olympic village scheduled to open the following year. On this occasion a strategy of fairly direct and literal landscape representation was chosen, wherein we employed at least three strategies commonly used in *critical regionalism*.[7] The first was the use of plants and building materials associated with the region and city. Second, we made reference to the region through the use of a metaphor—that of treating the building complex as though it were a landform analogous to that of the Catalan coastal formations, developing parts of the scheme as a transect in accordance with ecological and cultural associations related to particular aspects of the region. Third, we made reference to particular high and low art traditions of the region, especially in painting and tilework.

I tell my clients and students that landscape is a noun and not a verb, that it is not a sauce that can be poured over buildings and urban designs to improve their taste or appearance; rather it is structure, *the* very structure

Villa Olimpica, Olin Partnership. Installation of Mediterranean plants on the hotel roof adjacent to the dining and recreation area. A cliff overlooks the town and sea.

and fabric of a project. In this case the whole idea was literally that of a living skin of plants, animals, and activity spread upon, running over, down, and between the buildings. Upper terraces adjacent to hotel lobbies and restaurants were conceived to be upland plateaus and clifftop ledges with aromatic and herbaceous, sun-loving, Mediterranean plants, inspired by kitchen gardens and agriculture as much as by natural associations. Below is a cooler, shadier stream valley of sorts, with plane trees, willows, and islands. Here one also finds echoes of the Ramblas, Barcelona's most successful and unique public social spaces that have evolved from paths that followed the medieval walls of the city in tree-lined dry streambeds. This space and its water burst out onto the playa, a great sandy beach where a palm-lined promenade links an adjacent new park and marina, developed for the Olympics, to an older part of town. While palms are not common to the region, dates have been grown here since before Hannibal marched his troops through to defeat in Italy. In recent times Mexican fan palms have become a signature of resort life from Algiers to Capri. We included the smaller native Mediterranean fan palm with its imported compatriots on the upper levels, more closely paralleling its place in the local ecology.

While considerable thought went into this simple, almost obvious metaphor, we were not interested in trying to produce a simulation of any particular natural landscape, visually or biologically, for several reasons. First, it would almost certainly be impossible. The site was totally artificial. It was a completely urban environment of roofs, parking garages, shops, and pavements. The buildings were high-style modern in the extreme, designed by Bruce Graham of S.O.M., Chicago, and Frank O. Gehry, Los Angeles; although they would look as marvelous in a natural setting as in an urban one, there was little scope for site work. It was a tight site with only sidewalks and streets around it on three sides and a beach on the remainder. Hence, I declared the buildings themselves to be the site. Second, the pollution from industrial waste in the windborne ocean spray at this location on the harbor is so extreme that we had to rule out using many species of native plants—for example, *Cupressus sempervirens,* one of the quintessential skyline trees of the region. Third, I would have considered it a foolish abandonment of the artistic challenge and obligation facing us. We were being invited to work in the city of Antonio Gaudí, Pablo Picasso, and Joan Miró. It is the city of Adolphense Cerda's brilliant contribution to urban design, the

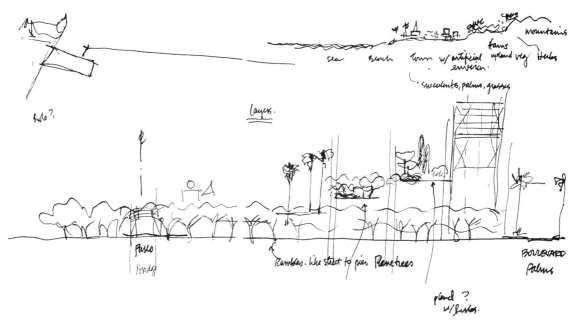

*Villa Olimpica, Olin Partnership. Early sketch by Laurie Olin depicting the analogous
transect of Catalonia and commercial development.*

*Villa Olimpica, Olin Partnership. Cross section of the final design of the transect through the project from the
city to the sea.*

Ensanche plan, and the site of Mies van der Rohe's Barcelona Pavilion. Surely, I thought, one could add something to the mix, no matter how humbly, that might help to carry forward the deep tradition of modern design informed by life and nature. Surely one could imbue these universalist, contemporary, and somewhat placeless building activities—an urban high-rise holiday resort hotel, a pricey shopping complex with cafes, bars, health club, and pool—with a sense of region and particular place.

To do so, the most natural thing in the world was to scrutinize the local environment, both natural and human-made, and develop an abstraction or poetic synthesis to form these new public spaces. Even before coming to Spain I had for years been impressed by the early paintings of Miró that achieve similar ends. Although he was producing paintings, those paintings are very much abstract representations of the Catalan landscape, its vegetation, color, landform, and architecture. I had no intention of attempting to "build" a Miró painting, nor was I about to "build" a *natural* landscape, but rather, like such painters, one that would be artifice, personal as well as regional.

Goldstein Housing, Frankfurt, Germany

Another example of a metaphor regarding nature in our work that eschews mimesis or verisimilitude in the representation of its reference occurs in the Goldstein housing scheme now nearing completion of construction. Done in collaboration with Frank O. Gehry, the project was to provide apartments for low-income families on the urban/suburban fringe of Frankfurt. In addition to a fairly dense number of apartments for the site, the city mandated a certain amount of open space for children's playgrounds, car parks, recycling facilities, and so on. As in most such instrumental plans, there was no indication of any particular physical expression. Although, like most clients, they probably hoped for a certain amount of invention on the part of their designers, I doubt if they envisioned our particular solution.

Gehry and I began with a few simple ideas, which seems to be common to both of us in our separate careers. He gathered the apartments together into bars of several stories like any number of units from the early Seidlung housing exhibitions of the 1920s and 1930s to the suburban condos of today. We began arranging them to create the largest possible social and recreational spaces that seemed possible on the site, just as any student or old pro might. I then pointed to an adjacent forest preserve, now used as a park on

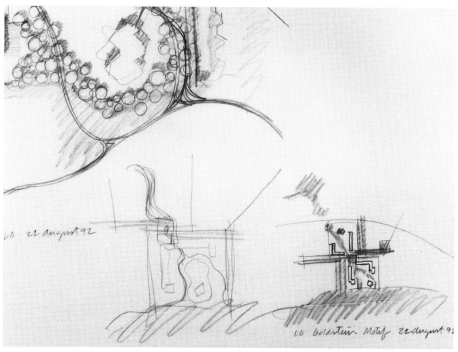

Goldstein Housing, Olin Partnership. Laurie Olin's concept sketch of the site plan depicting the flow of trees making a path and "theater" space. There is a second extension of orchards into the surrounding area.

one side of the development, and a community center with a town square across a street in the other direction. Two things occurred to me simultaneously: Why not run a path through the whole project to connect these two desirable off-site amenities, and why not make it a green route, a river of trees? Then I realized that to do this through each of the two spaces was to render them boringly similar, resulting in little spatial variety and precluding the possibility of achieving any large spaces. I was also concerned about social use and the need to create a series of layers and subspaces within the courtyards, especially if we did create a large one.

Turning from analogies in the natural world to those from the cultural one I hit upon something I had been wanting to try for years, which was to conceive of a park-like space in terms of a theater, specifically an opera house of the Rococo era such as one sees in Bavaria and Austria. Around the periphery we could make a series of small spaces (terraces, places to sit, cook out, or whatever for the units behind), and these terraces and the adjacent

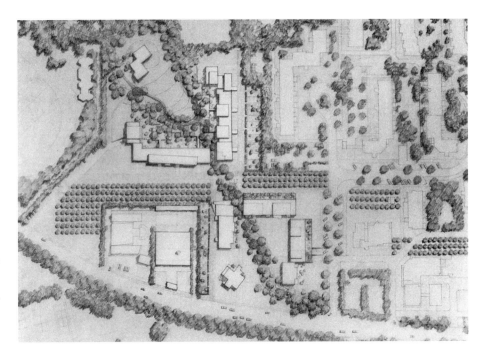

Goldstein Housing, Olin Partnership. Plan of the developed scheme as it was presented to the owner and Frankfurt Planning Office.

houses would all look down like opera boxes into a central green bowl—the orchestra, as it were. The entire ensemble would slope gently down toward a lower place, a stage so to speak, which would help with drainage and community events. Here Gehry could have a more special building for people who want and need more attention, a place for the somewhat constrained architecture to be frisky and to show off a bit.

In very little time the green river came to flow out of the woods on the hill above, around the stone or island of this object building, and on, swirling back together at the far corner, to break through the courtyard building across a transverse path and, gathering strength, to move directly across the second courtyard and out to the road, leading to the town center. Here under the trees and alongside the sunny open spaces we dispersed the children's play facilities and seating. This became the underlying idea for the interior of the development. Outside, to connect it to the surrounding community, which was predominantly orthogonal in nature, we used agricultural forms—the hedgerow and orchard fragments—to organize automobiles, bicycle paths, fire lanes, and pedestrian walkways.

*Goldstein Housing,
Frank O. Gehry.
Model of development
seen from the south
looking toward an
adjacent forest pre-
serve.*

None of this looks like a piece of nature, nor particularly like other open spaces in the area. On the other hand, because of the strong and clear metaphorical structure the parts seem to hang together well without being terribly restrictive or dysfunctional. As in nature, there seems to be a greater group orderliness, despite the jumble of things and people, sizes, shapes, purposes.

Carnegie Mellon Research Institute, Pittsburgh, Pennsylvania

Asked to produce the site design of a portion of a research campus on the banks of the Monongahela River, my partners and I became interested—as often happens—in the history of the site, and explored aspects of its past, developing a scheme for contemporary use that represented some of this history in abstract terms. The device used was taken from the realm of natural process: Deposition and erosion. As a method to promote the development of physical form this is, of course, one of the most common and ubiquitous (in human terms, banal) of natural processes—the slow, steady wearing away of

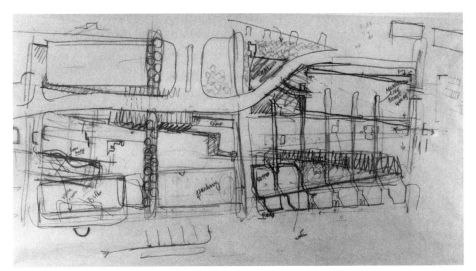

Carnegie Mellon Research Institute, Olin Partnership. An early sketch by Laurie Olin of fault lines, hedgerow, and erosion as organizational devices within the project .

things by some force (water or wind, hooves or feet treading the same spot) and the gradual accretion of things (grains of sand, rock and dust, leaves and detritus, wreckage and dead organisms piling up, one atop another, one cell placed next to another, laying down an ocean floor, building up soil, growing a tree, twig by twig, leaf by leaf). Our project was neither so simple nor so profound, but it produced some relatively fresh and interesting forms.

We began by examining an existing master plan. To us, the scheme seemed both dull and antisocial. It was placeless and would produce the sort of suburban sprawl that has been gobbling up the American countryside and has now turned around and begun to chew up our cities with malls and environments dominated by the automobile. Looked at one way, this scheme was a grotesque caricature of the pastoral dream of eighteenth- and nineteenth-century landscape design, where the buildings sit in parkland settings of trees and grass with undulating paths and bodies of water. The difference in Pittsburgh was that the buildings had grown, the green spaces had shrunk, and automobiles had replaced the herds of livestock to such a degree that it was neither pastoral nor urban. There was a sea of automobiles and asphalt with little wiggly lines of green here and there and a series of suburban office and research buildings with postmodern pretensions fronting onto the river like the country houses of the Veneto of yore. Our response was to see if there was another way to organize this material that would produce a more coherent place of meaning for the community and the research institutions that were to inhabit it, and to render it more particular to region and place.

We initiated a brief inventory and analysis of the site in rapid and sketchy post-McHargian overlays, noting the various events that had shaped the site: Deposition of ancient forests and the creation of shale and coal seams; erosion and creation of the deep river canyon; evolution of modern forests; inhabitation by aboriginal settlers; invasion by Europeans; the French and Indian War; further settlement with property surveys, divisions of land into parcels, and development of early industry; development of roads and the emergence of a steel industry; amalgamation of parcels and creation of the giant Jones and Laughlin steel mill; the deposition of vast quantities of slag and toxic waste, amounting to the rebuilding and growth of the riverbank's site; emergence and evolution of Carnegie Tech (later Carnegie Mellon University) and the University of Pittsburgh on the heights above the site; the demise of the steel industry and demolition of the enormous industrial works on the site; the creation of urban redevelopment parcels and the joint venture between the two universities and the city to create a research park. We plotted all of this, layer upon layer, and then stepped back and looked at it. What would happen, I asked, if we just went ahead and, in our imagination, placed more levels of activity and program on top of all of this and then began to erode it selectively to reveal aspects of these previous events?

I began with a layer of asphalt striped for parking across the entire site and placed the building program in one long continuous strip the length of the site atop this. Then, shifting about along a series of metaphorical fault lines—using some of the historic property lines—I broke this strip up into building-size chunks, as if by an earthquake. Next I imagined a river similar to the Monongahela, scouring along down the center of the parking area, tearing through the asphalt layer, down through the gravel and slag, exposing the ruins and foundations of the rolling mill and earlier structures. It would be old, of course, and native plants would have come into this ravine. Trees would have grown up along the fault lines that had parted the buildings.

This was the genesis of the green river that became the unifying park and social space of the project, and of the hedgerow walkways that connected the

Carnegie Mellon Research Institute, Olin Partnership. One of a series of studies of the central "green river" and hedgerows.

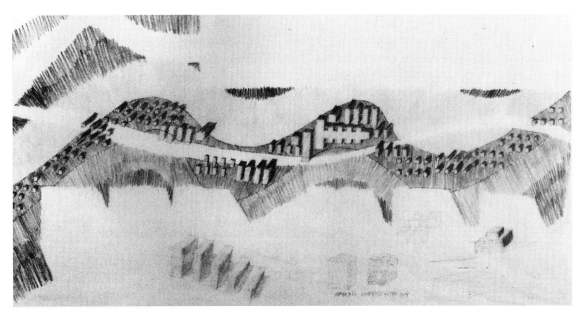

Carnegie Mellon Research Institute, Olin Partnership. One of a series of studies of the central "green river" with its reconstructed ruins of a demolished rolling mill.

parking to the building entries and river walk. The scheme no longer resembled the insipid office park scheme that we found, yet it had all the working parts and provided a story line that enabled us to elaborate the parts in ways that were both site specific and meaningful to the scientists and engineers who formed our client group. I know of no one who thinks that this scheme is particularly natural looking; nevertheless, the forms and parts all result from thinking about the twin natural processes of deposition and erosion.

Rebstock Park, Frankfurt, Germany

In this project (an urban design competition that we produced and won in collaboration with architect Peter Eisenman), the reference to nature and to natural process was not to any particular visual image, order, or structure, but rather to recent studies and theory relating to dynamic processes that take place in nature, and some of the analytical tools and methods that have been developed to describe them, specifically to aspects of chaos theory developed by René Thom and some diagrams that we noticed in *Scientific American* that were used to describe catastrophes.[8] We were not interested in emulating catastrophes or producing chaos—far from it. We were interested in the investigation of alternatives to the two most powerful urban design paradigms that are currently in use, namely that of the contextual (and highly aestheticized or compositional) strategy of the townscape school derived from Camillo Sitte and his followers, such as Gordon Cullen and Fred Koetter; or its opposite, that of modernist (heroic and sculptural) objects floating in space à la Le Corbusier and his followers.[9] Put another way, we were curious to see if there was a choice other than that of the figure-ground duality that has dominated urban design theory and practice for the past generation.

Catastrophe theory focuses upon the description of events, particularly transformational ones, not objects. This interested us because we were looking for a way to take aspects of the context—the adjacent historic city—and to extend and change them qualitatively. A fundamental concept of this theory is that of the *fold*. For Eisenman, this concept enabled an exploration in his buildings of metaphors that relate to ideas of repression and the condition of architecture, society, and the individual—human nature from a particular point of view. For me, it allowed an exploration of intertwining or of *folding* of several elements that I was eager to combine in an urban setting.

First, we placed the fairly conventional program of social housing, offices, shops, and recreation upon the site in a straightforward manner, allowing for traffic and connection to existing uses. Next, we imagined that we could fold the entire site in a manner similar to that described by the mathematics and diagrams of a catastrophic event. These phantom folds acted in extraordinary ways upon the very ordinary bars of the buildings that we had adopted from an adjacent housing project—itself a product of the powerful Seidlung housing movement pioneered by Hans May in Frankfurt

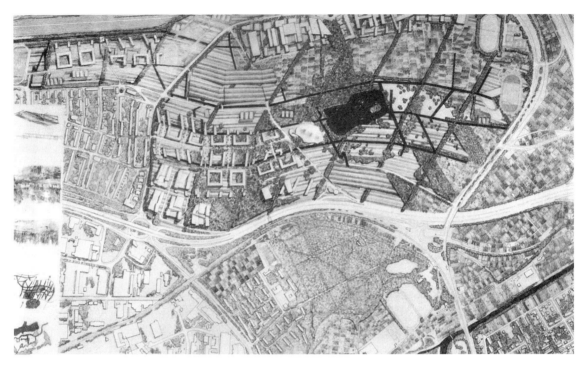

Rebstock Park, Olin Partnership. The plan of the entire site with adjacent context, as submitted for the competition.

between the two world wars. Of course, the floors and rooms inside the buildings were not crushed by this imaginary act, but rather we seized upon the deformed and unusual elements as the opportunity for unique community spaces, as opposed to the individual apartments that tended to be in the normal bits. At the scale of the site, this allowed for the introduction of a larger overall structure that could accommodate both the program elements from the competition, such as the parking of thousands of automobiles for the nearby *Messe* (fairgrounds), and those I wished to introduce. The latter included hedgerows to aid in cold air drainage from the nearby greenbelt, partial reforestation, the creation of a stormwater treatment and recharge system throughout the site that would also double as a network of riparian habitats, and the development of a patchwork of fields of varying size that could be operated agriculturally.

Despite some adventurous grading, the site is no more folded than the buildings. The powerful metaphor of folding, however, has given the entire

Rebstock Park, Olin Partnership. Sketchbook study by Laurie Olin of the western portion of the site with fields, hedgerows, and canals—to be used for recreation, trade-fair parking, agriculture, and stormwater recharge.

project a structure and logic as purposeful, orderly, and rife with chance and coincidence as are many natural environments.[10] There is no chance of this being mistaken for a natural environment, and yet it is deeply inspired by natural processes.

Playa Vista, Los Angeles, California

Finally, I wish to discuss the sort of landscape design that many laypeople and landscape architects think of when the topic of nature and ecology comes up. This is the creation, preservation, and/or restoration of natural areas, areas dominated by and devoted to wild creatures and natural processes. By creation I mean the introduction or encouragement of natural things or areas in places where they do not exist or have been seriously degraded. I am not sure that we really can create natural places or things, although we can help to set them in motion or direct and deflect them. This

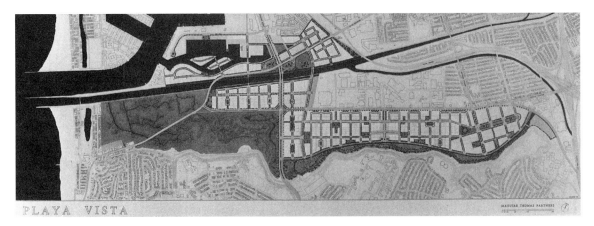

Maya Vista, Olin Partnership. Overall site plan circa 1992. The Pacific Ocean is to the left, Marina del Ray is at the top, and Westchester Bluffs is at the bottom.

is more than merely subscribing to the "only God can make a tree" point of view. The topic is not as simple as it sounds, nor is the work. As articles and interviews in recent issues of *Landscape Architecture* have pointed out, landscape architects—and the profession itself—have much to learn, and the body of knowledge and theory that specifically address this endeavor is recent, still relatively small, and subject to debate.[11]

The Playa Vista project in Los Angeles contains several kinds of open space, some of which are to be highly urban and some of which are to contain truly natural elements that are intended to function as parts of a larger ecosystem. The project is a large urban fragment, and, as such, it both resembles in miniature aspects of the larger urban complex while it connects to, and becomes a working part of, this larger urban fabric. Los Angeles, as is commonly known, is a far-flung city of diffuse and diverse urban fragments and populations. Within its boundaries are numerous skipped over lands, many of which, due to their steep slopes, unstable soils, susceptibility to fire or flood, or owing to blighting industries such as petroleum exploration and extraction, have retained some of their natural characteristics. The Playa Vista site contains three such elements: The Ballona Wetlands, the Westchester Bluffs, and Centinela Creek. It is the intention of the plan that has been developed to reinvigorate, reshape, and, to the degree possible, restore these elements to a functional, natural character.[12]

For the design of the natural areas many scientists have been engaged to carry out the inventory, analysis, and feasibility studies. Another landscape architect, Charles Rapp, at an early stage, worked on aspects of these facilities, largely on how they come in contact with the developed areas and how to accommodate people within them. Both our firm and Rapp's acted as go-betweens for the client-owner with the scientists, engineers, and politicians, a group made up predominantly of lawyers and city planners. Several years after beginning the project a local firm that specializes in wetland restoration produced the final construction documents for the first phase. Some of the scientists are of the new breed of ecologists who have worked on restoration projects around the region and country and are interested in interacting with their material and engaging in what has been called restoration biology. They have as many war stories about their experiments, successes, and failures as do landscape practitioners.

Playa Vista, Olin Partnership. Model of the infrastructure for Phase 1, including streets, street trees, freshwater marsh, and a stream below the bluff.

Of great interest to me was their disinterest in what their work looked like. Several ecologists, such as John Rieger and Sharon Lockhart, pointed out to me that, in their early work, they had tried to make their new and restored habitats look like those they had studied, replicating the forms and varied sizes and mixtures of things that they found in natural situations. They had discovered, however, that many things died, some grew by leaps and bounds in ways they had not anticipated, and that other things just turned up. They found themselves engaged in a sort of wilderness gardening for a few years until the systems and various populations took hold. As a result, they said they now do not bother trying to make a site look "pretty" but lay things out boldly and diagramatically, set out plugs and whips in large masses and fairly mechanical plantings with little or no concern for verisimilitude or a natural feeling. They insist that, after three or four years, one cannot tell the difference between these sites and those that receive a

Playa Vista, Olin Partnership. An early concept sketch, in watercolor, by Laurie Olin of the proposed wetland habitat restoration area, which was presented to the owner-client, agency personnel, and public groups.

high degree of composition and management. As far as the numbers of animals and insects supported, there seems to be no advantage either way, except from the standpoint of human time, labor, and cost. What nature looks like, or is supposed to look like, appears to be our problem, a cultural matter; it has little to do with ecology. This does not mean it is unimportant, for property values matter a lot to citizens, landowners, and municipal tax collectors. It just means that it matters more to us than to the birds.

As Playa Vista stands in 1996, 240 acres of salt water, tidal marsh, and a freshwater marsh are under construction. A freshwater stream modeled after one of the only ones remaining in the Santa Monica Mountains will feed the marsh and three miles of bluff will become even more of a landmark as it is returned to a coastal sage community. Overall, this is an interesting, socially responsible, and rewarding project. The restoration of these three different habitat areas is a vital part of the project and, from a planning and social point of view, one of the most important aspects of the project. From a professional and artistic point of view, however, it is one of the simplest and least interesting. Although it is technically difficult and demands skill, experiment, and expertise—even innovation—this ecological rebuilding is neither philosophically nor compositionally challenging or rewarding. It is an environmental good and, like breathing or the circulation of the blood, is necessary in order that other things may happen. Great pleasure is to be had from the experience of it and its constituent life-forms once it has been achieved, but not so much from its design and creation, largely because we know the answer—how it is supposed to turn out. It will bring us the reassurance of old news about the planet.

NOTES

1. Although it may be commonplace, it is important to reemphasize that our idea of nature has changed over time from one society to another and is changing still, frequently resulting in differing views within any given society. These changing views of nature are inevitably intertwined with our values and concepts of society. Many of the conflicts that torment our nation today, such as the struggle for control of women's bodies, sexuality, and abortion, could be said to stem from these different and changing views. Recently many new books have appeared on the topic of our relationship to nature and our concepts of it, several of which are superb. Certainly one of the best such surveys to date remains that of Clarence Glacken, *Traces on the Rhodian Shore* (1967); also of great value is Neil Evernden's *The Social Construction of Nature* (1992).

2. Stevens 1990, reporting on a symposium at the annual meeting of Ecological Society of America at Snowbird, Utah, July of 1990.

3. Danto actually wrote about something else: The putative end of art, or at least the problems raised by ideas of progress and of the potential for traditional methods of expression to become used up or to metamorphose into other modes. Danto 1990, p. 340.

4. Hughes 1991, pp. 365–425; Danto 1986, pp. 81–115; Danto 1990, pp. 297–312.

5. Thompson 1995 offers excellent interpretations about the *idea* of landscape.

6. Many such Hanna/Olin Ltd. projects have been published: Arco Research Center (the Meadows) in Lynch 1984 and *Landscape Architecture;* Pitney Bowes Headquarters, *Architectural Record;* Codex Corporation Headquarters, *Landscape Architecture, Architecture,* The Li-Wu River Gorge Study, *Landscape Architecture (Taiwan). See* profile of Hanna/Olin Ltd. practice; Steiner and Johnson 1992, pp. 68–77.

7. See Frampton 1983 and Olin 1995 for a discussion of theory and methods in contemporary design.

8. Zeeman 1976, diagram, top of p. 79. See also Gleick 1987.

9. Olin 1992, pp. 25–35 and illus. ff.

10. Gordon Cullen, an English architect and editor of *Architectural Review,* London, published a series of highly influential essays and a book, *Townscape* (1961), that greatly influenced many in my generation, including Fred Koetter, now dean of architecture at Yale. Cullen argued for a contextual and place-based design approach embracing vernacular and eclectic elements: Essentially opposing many tenants of modernism that had been so pervasive in urban design following the polemics of Le Corbusier and the Bauhaus. Critics of Cullen have accused him and his followers of romanticism and of devotion to the picturesque; supporters argue that his beliefs foster a deep concern for humanity and historic continuity that is absent in much of modernism. See also Trancick 1986.

11. See, for example, Lecesse 1992, pp. 54–57; McCormick 1991, pp. 88–91.

12. Although an even larger and more important water course, Ballona Creek, passes through the site, this feature is out of bounds for the time being due to the regional flood control policies of the U.S. Army Corps of Engineers and other agencies. It should be noted, also, that part of the underlying philosophy of the developers, Maguire Thomas Partners, and the design team has been to offer a distinct and responsible alternative to recent development in the region. This entails the creation of density and centrality so as to make walking to work, shops, and school and the use of transit (which is part of the design) feasible within the development, as well as the on-site treatment of waste and sewage. Since the site is more than a thousand acres in size, this is all possible and indeed essential. The project has been under way since the early 1980s and has seen several changes in leadership, ownership, and design professionals. Hanna/Olin became involved in 1985 when the site was owned by the heirs of Howard Hughes and managed by the Summa Corporation. Consultants prior to 1985 included Wallace, McHarg, Roberts and Todd, Welton Beckett and Associates, SWA, and Charles Rapp, for different aspects of the work. From 1985 to 1989, the project was directed by David O'Malley, and the design team consisted of Hanna/Olin Ltd., I. M. Pei & Partners, Allan Jacobs, Warren Travers & Partners, with Lathom and Watkins and Psomas Engineers. From 1989 to 1995 the project was owned by the Summa Corporation, Maguire Thomas Partners, and JBM Realty, with management for development by Maguire Thomas Partners. From 1995 to the time of this writing the pro-

ject has been owned by Maguire Thomas Partners and Dreamworks Studios. The design team since the change in ownership has consisted of The Olin Partnership, formerly Hanna/Olin Ltd., Moore Ruble Yudell, Polyzoides and deBretteville (now Polyzoides and Moule), Legoretta Architectos, Duany Plater-Zyberk, Johnson Fain Periera, Zimmer Gunsel Frasca, Genzler Associates, Johannes Van Tilberg, Hodgetts and Fung, Mark Mack, Allen Fong & Associates, with numerous consultants including Barton-Aschman, Psomas, Latham and Watkins, Daniel Solomon & Partner, and a range of natural scientists.

REFERENCES

Cullen, Gordon. 1961. *Townscape*. New York: Reinhold.

Danto, Arthur C. 1986. "The End of Art." Pp. 81–115 in *The Philosophical Disenfranchisement of Art*. New York: Columbia University Press.

———. 1990. "Bad Aesthetic Times," and "Narratives of the End of Art." Pp. 297–312 and 331–45 in *Encounters and Reflections: Art in the Historical Present*. New York: Farrar, Straus & Giroux.

Evernden, Neil. 1992. *The Social Construction of Nature*. Baltimore: Johns Hopkins University Press.

Frampton, Kenneth. 1983. "Towards a Critical Regionalism: Six Points for an Architecture of Resistance." Pp. 16–30 in *The Anti-Aesthetic: Essays on Postmodern Culture*, ed. Hal Foster. Port Townsend, Wash.: Bay Press.

Glacken, Clarence J. 1967. *Traces on the Rhodian Shore*. Berkeley: University of California Press.

Gleick, James. 1987. *Chaos: Making a New Science*. New York: Penguin Books.

Hughes, Robert. 1991. "The Future That Was." Pp. 365–425 in *The Shock of the New*. New York: Knopf.

Lecesse, Michael. 1992. "I Profess." *Landscape Architecture* 82, no. 1 (January): 54–57.

Lynch, Kevin. 1984. *Site Planning*. 3d ed. Cambridge, Mass.: MIT Press. Pp. 13–28.

McCormick, Kathleen. 1991. "We Don't 'Do' Wetlands." *Landscape Architecture* 81, no. 10 (October): 88–91.

Olin, Laurie. 1992. "Landschaftsgestaltung am Rebstockpark." Pp. 25–35 in *Frankfurt Rebstock Park, Folding in Time, Eisenman Architects, Albert Speer & Partner, Hanna/Olin*, ed. Volker Fischer. Munich: Prestel-Verlag.

———. 1995. "Regionalism and the Practice of Hanna/Olin Ltd." Pp. 243–270 in *Regional Garden Design in the United States*, ed. Therese O'Malley and Marc Treib. Washington, D.C.: Dumbarton Oaks.

Steiner, Frederick and Todd Johnson. 1992. "Perfecting the Ordinary." *Landscape Architecture* 82, no. 3 (March): 68–77.

Stevens, William K. 1990. "New Eye on Nature: The Real Constant is Eternal Turmoil." *New York Times*, 31 July.

Thompson, George F., ed. 1995. *Landscape in America*. Austin: University of Texas Press.

Trancick, Roger. 1986. *Finding Lost Space*. Cambridge, Mass.: MIT Press.

Zeeman, E. C. 1976. "Catastrophe Theory." *Scientific American*, April, pp. 65–83.

GALLERY I

PHOTOGRAPHS BY STEVE MARTINO

A desert rat goes to Hyde Park and Hampton Court in England, November of 1990. Photographs by Steve Martino.

The camera in my brain is just going all the time.

There's so much to absorb.

I can feel the history of the place.

I learned lessons from this trip. The interesting thing about these parks is that the grass is out in the open and the understory plants are all fenced in to keep out people. I thought that was unusual, but practical.

Man, can they grow trees over there.

PART II

PROSPECT

5

LANDSCAPE ARCHITECTURE AND THE CHANGING CITY

MICHAEL LAURIE

Few would disagree that one of the critical issues for the twenty-first century will be the rebuilding of our cities, including the renewal of their degraded natural environments. Where landscape architecture fits in and how it will contribute to our future depends not only on what society decides to do and what priorities it sets, but also on the alternative visions that landscape architecture offers. But one aspect of this dialogue is certain: We must adhere to Aldo Leopold's land ethic, for he was right when he observed: "A thing is right when it tends to preserve the integrity, stability and beauty of the biotic community. It is wrong when it tends otherwise."[1]

After World War II a group of young landscape architects in the United States developed and expanded the scope of professional practice. Garrett Eckbo, John Simonds, and Lawrence Halprin each came to the profession in different ways, and made their respective contributions in practice and in education as they responded to a series of new challenges. The visibility of the work and the literary output of these practitioners brought landscape architecture into the forefront of American life.[2]

Increases in population and standards of living created design opportunities for urban renewal and new developments such as city centers and shopping malls, colleges and schools, parks and playgrounds, corporate headquarters and public housing, and the recycling of old buildings and waterfront areas. New techniques were developed for indoor spaces and roof gardens. A large body of work was produced by Eckbo, Simonds, Halprin, Dan Kiley, and others who joined their ranks from the increasing number of academic programs in landscape architecture throughout the United States and Canada. Their approach to design was characterized by comprehensive site analysis and a clear expression of program requirements. The physical forms that resulted ranged from strong geometry—though rarely symmetry—to more naturalistic effects.

At the end of the period, Ian McHarg at the University of Pennsylvania published *Design with Nature* (1969). The ecological land-use planning he advocated invoked Leopold's concept of right and wrong and a growing concern for environmental protection and conservation of natural resources. He foresaw the wave of environmental legislation enacted during the 1970s and initiated a new realm of landscape architecture practice that centered on environmental impact assessment and ecological planning and design.

Also, during the mid-1960s, there was renewed concern for the under-privileged in a prosperous America. Linked to the civil rights movement was the concept of community participation in decision making. The face-to-face contact between designer and planner and the public led to a more complicated design and planning process, with results that were more attentive to social needs.

The 1960s and 1970s was a golden era in which the scope and content of landscape architecture began to change radically.[3] New positions in the expanded public sector and the increasingly larger private landscape architecture practices provided a wide range of opportunities in urban design, regional planning, environmental impact assessment, and the more traditional area of site planning. Community participation became increasingly common, either as required by law or as seen to be politically correct or advantageous to the implementation of plans and projects.[4]

A second important development related to landscape architecture at this time was the emergence of environmental art and site works. Robert Smithson and Michael Heizer, for example, moved thousands of tons of earth and rock to create large-scale forms with a sense of prehistory in remote, harsh environments of no special beauty in a traditional sense. The Vietnam Veterans Memorial by Maya Lin (1981) and California Scenario by Isamu Noguchi (1982), expressing symbolism in a more conventional setting, were equally impressive and avant-garde.

During the 1980s, the influence on landscape architecture by architectural postmodernism and environmental art began to be apparent in the work of younger professionals, many of whom studied under Peter Walker at the Harvard University Graduate School of Design: Examples include Walker's Tanner Fountain and Burnett Park (1983), Harlequin Plaza by George Hargreaves (1983), and the *Transforming the American Garden* exhibition and catalogue by Michael Van Valkenberg (1986). Paradoxically, this was the same time when Frederick Law Olmsted was rediscovered. The management and restoration plan for Central Park in New York City (1985), for example, was one of the first notable achievements in this passionate endeavor.[5]

Current professional trends and concerns in landscape architecture, as expressed by university curricula, research projects, and professional organizations, reflect interest in and concern for environmental and social values. These are expressed in concepts such as stewardship of public and other lands, resource conservation and protection, open space for recreation, quality of life measures, and professional issues. As a result of the apparent difference between theory and practice, an artificial, harmful, and misleading schism appears to have developed between art and science in landscape architecture. In part, this is due to some overzealous and unrelenting science-biased landscape architects and planners who rightly criticize those colleagues who dismiss science and who seem blind to Leopold's broader vision of an ecological aesthetic. On the other side, art-biased landscape architects have gone overboard in rejecting the picturesque landscape ideal, which has been misrepresented as nature, replacing it in theory and in practice with pretentious, nonsustainable, inhuman landscapes. The reality is that landscape architecture and planning can be an expression of both natural and human processes. They can maintain respect for ecological integrity and the principles of sustainability, and embrace cultural aspirations and social needs that will result in a new aesthetic.

Landscape design and planning in whatever form they are practiced in the twenty-first century will surely benefit from advances in our understanding of the issues that occur at the interface of culture and the landscape. For example, the concept of regionalism, central to geography and planning, has taken on new significance in relation to increasing interest in historic restoration and regional identity. The concept of ecological integrity

An example of a restored land-scape is Wild Cat Creek in Alvarado Park of the East Bay Regional Park District in Richmond, California. Tons of concrete and silt have been removed. A more stable and natural stream bed has been re-created with banks protected by rocks and plants and a series of pools that will prevent erosion and allow steelhead trout to migrate from San Pablo Bay to Tilden Park. The wall on the right of each photograph was built by 1930s Depression-era work crews and is a historic landmark. The project is the result of a collabora-tion between hydrologist David Rosgen and Michael Lamb, a landscape architect with the East Bay Regional Park District. Courtesy of East Bay Regional Park District.

Before restoration

embraces a growing concern for adequate habitat and wildlife conditions to ensure biodiversity, the restoration of degraded landscapes, and the expression of natural processes within towns and cities. The concept of socially informed design and planning is the result of research in environmental psychology, human behavior and cultural variation, and the community participation process. Aesthetics as expressed by environmental artists brings us closer to the real meaning of the idea: Perception with feeling. This suggests that land-scape architecture can and should do more to improve the quality of life.

Practitioners and scholars of landscape architecture should become more informed about natural and built environments. As the urban popula-tion grows worldwide and demands on the planet increase, the importance

After restoration

of landscape architecture and planning becomes central to us all. Implicit in the so-called New World Order is the economic prescription that we do more good with fewer resources.

The restoration of our cities' degraded landscapes and the conservation of our economic and ecological resources require a healing of the unnecessary dichotomy between art and science, research and intuition. Only then will landscape architecture and planning be capable of contributing to new, sustainable, regionally and culturally appropriate forms and to ecologically and socially sound land-use policies and plans. The result will be a new aesthetic with popular appeal.

Its popularity will reflect a renewed understanding or even a discovery by the public of Leopold's land ethic and his requirement for integrity, stability, and beauty in the biotic and human communities. Thus, ecological planning and design are necessarily and holistically interdependent. Sustainability will continue to be a popular rallying cry for this economically sound and environmentally aware movement.

In design and planning, the concept of sustainability rests heavily on accountability to regional factors such as climate, geology, hydrology, history, economics, and myriad cultural processes. But sustainability must also account for potential impacts. On a regional scale the city makes its contribution of wastes, heat, smoke, and other forms of pollution while drawing a variety of resources from environments at home and abroad with cumulative local and global impact, such as rain forest depletion and degraded landscapes that result from inept or irresponsible building, mining, and agricultural practices.[6] Sustainable landscape design and planning seeks to reduce such impacts by minimizing consumption of energy and other natural resources. This can be accomplished, for example, by creating benign microclimates through urban forestry and solar orientation of buildings and by planning communities that facilitate and encourage walking and bicycling rather than the use of automobiles.

Closer to most people's homes, ecology can be applied in two ways to the form of cities. First, we can adapt the ecosystem concept as a theoretical model or metaphor in which the city is seen as a family dwelling with various private and public spaces. Just as an ecosystem embraces change and adapts according to self-sustaining process, the city must likewise change and adapt to new circumstances to remain viable. This occurs in the recycling of warehouses into museums and shopping centers, the conversion of large houses into townhouses and apartments, and the periodic redesign of public gardens, parks, and plazas. A second way involves the redevelopment of city form with respect to natural processes and features. The nineteenth-century plans of Bourneville in England, Boston's Emerald Necklace, and Minneapolis–Saint Paul's park system are excellent examples of this approach. This kind of design applies today to the planning of new suburbs. In retrofitting older urban areas, it is more difficult to reinstate altered or eradicated natural processes. Such processes, however altered, exist and continue to shape the landscape and spirit of a place.

Ecological expressionism emphasizes the importance of a sense of place and it reveals the natural processes of a site. These processes should remind us physically of our home environment. For example, we should seriously consider restoring a few acres of sand dunes at their original site in San Francisco's Golden Gate Park.

The concept of economy is similar in many respects to that of ecological expression, as Henry David Thoreau clearly articulated in *Walden* (1851). If ecology is the study of the house, then economy is the management of the house. Productivity is an essential characteristic of economy *and* a healthy ecosystem. In urban open space, multiple use by different groups at different times of the day and year is an economical and, therefore, productive idea with definite applications for design. Single-purpose places are often wasteful, and likely to be dull.

Another concept congruent with ecology is livability. The livable city has been defined as a city of distinct neighborhoods that possess a sense of pride, place, history, safety, good housing, friendly playgrounds, parks, and open spaces. If we examine the typical hierarchy of open spaces in cities, we will find a few neighborhood parks that contribute to livability and many that do not because their historic functions are less relevant today.

Let us visit Washington Square in San Francisco, redesigned by Douglas Baylis in 1956. An examination of its location, design, and multiple uses suggest criteria for livability. The park is in a high-density area with a mix of age and ethnic groups. The square's configuration is in a hollow that acts through psychological gravity as the meeting point of a social watershed. Streets surround the square and include stops for two major bus routes and several major destinations for people: A church, post office, cafes and restaurants, hardware store, printing and copying franchise, and movie theater. The design is basically a four- or five-acre green. On the edge, or ecotone, linked by a circular path, are seating places, a playground and restroom, and a variety of features that tells us where we are. The square has a varied daily use from organized Chinese exercises in the early morning to generic sunbathing in the afternoon. In summary, the park is a place for all ages. Diversity and productivity and the rich edge are the ecological characteristics. Multiple use is the economic characteristic. Use by locals and visitors results in a highly aesthetic experience, expressive of changes in society, including new work routines and recreational preferences. I liken the future neighborhood park to the mantelpiece in a house, supporting an ever-changing set of objects, invitations, and memorabilia, and capable of being swept clear for special occasions or, alternatively, of including an increasing number of treasures.

Early morning

Washington Square, San Francisco, redesigned by landscape architect Douglas Baylis in 1956, permits a variety of uses throughout the day, week, or year, and as such is a highly productive urban place with metaphorical ecological characteristics. Photographs by Michael Laurie.

Late morning

Sunday afternoon

Annual circus

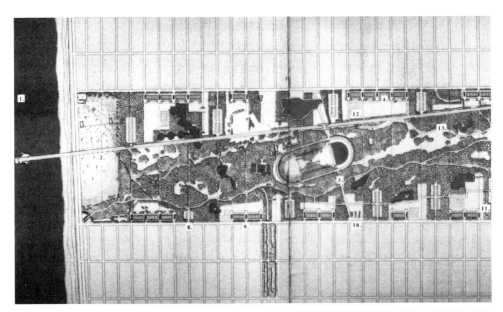

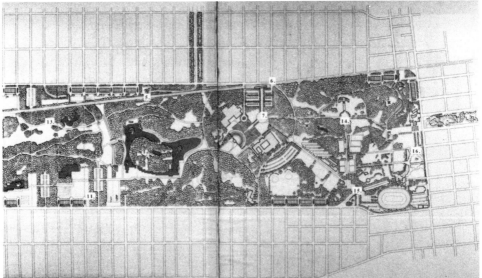

A theoretical renewal plan for Golden Gate Park in San Francisco for the year 2050 involves major replanting and the removal of all automobile traffic. It includes a transit link to downtown. Housing, playing fields, and community gardens are located along the street edges. There is a sewage treatment plant, and a windmill farm is located on restored sand dunes next to the ocean beach. The center portion remains pastoral, providing habitat for wildlife and relatively remote areas for solitude. Paths and bicycle trails connect to adjoining neighborhoods. The park is completely sustainable and self-sufficient in water, power, and sewage treatment. Designed by landscape architecture students Knobbs, Meissner, and Schadt, University of California at Berkeley, 1992. Courtesy of Michael Laurie.

Most large pastoral urban parks of nineteenth-century America have passed through a period of neglect and abuse. Some, however, such as Central Park in New York City, have maintained their strategic importance in contemporary urban life and, as a result, have undergone appropriate but expensive restoration. It is also true that many pastoral parks are no longer the crown jewel of a city's park system they once were and that the large parks that remain in cities of the future may need to be changed, as Anne Spirn suggests, in order to serve new environmental roles.[7] These will include urban forestry, community gardens, microclimate modification, and contemporary forms of recreation. Recognizing an urban park's ecological value is critical.

Aesthetic appreciation of these new urban landscapes will improve our collective sense of nature as process. The designers and planners who cooperate with, and learn from, the people who live in or use such places, and who integrate art and science in their work, will be in a position to create stunning new forms for our cities. Just as Central Park was considered art in the nineteenth century, so, too, can some redesigned urban parks emerge as art in the twenty-first century.

I believe a new theory of landscape architecture that embraces ecology, planning, and design is evolving. Innovative solutions to new or rewritten problems will arise from the designer's integration of meaning, intention, and form, from a response to universal yearnings and current technology, from a concern for economy, environmental protection, and renewal, and from the principles of art and science that are at the root of the discipline and profession. The results may be unfamiliar initially and, in some cases, may not fit well into a mode of practice some have come to regard as fixed. But these changes are necessary if landscape architecture is to develop socially and ecologically as a responsible professional field in the twenty-first century.

NOTES

1. Leopold 1949, p. 240
2. See, especially, Eckbo 1950, Halprin 1963, and Simonds 1961.
3. Membership in the American Society of Landscape Architects grew, for example, from 542 in 1950 to 2,872 in 1970; it has continued to expand to the 1995 figure of about 11,000, with women constituting an increasing percentage of membership.

4. It is interesting to note that, since the 1970s, we have witnessed a demise of modern architecture and the emergence of concepts of postmodernism, including the importance of context (not new to landscape architecture), historical reference, metaphor, and metaphysics.

5. The corporate landscape, historic preservation, and postmodern design as preoccupations of the 1980s seem far removed from the concerns discussed by Albert Fein in his 1972 study of the profession that, in 1996, is being revisited. Fein identified a role for the landscape architect as a peacemaker between the advance of civilization and the conservation of natural resources. See Fein 1972.

6. Especially revealing is Little 1995.

7. Spirn 1984.

REFERENCES

Eckbo, Garrett. 1950. *Landscape for Living*. New York: Architectural Record with Duell, Sloan and Pearce.

Fein, Albert. 1972. "A Study of the Profession of Landscape Architecture." Technical report. McLean, Va.: American Society of Landscape Architects Foundation.

Halprin, Lawrence. 1963. *Cities*. New York: Reinhold.

Leopold, Aldo. 1949. *A Sand County Almanac, and Sketches Here and There*. New York: Oxford University Press.

Little, Charles E. 1995. *The Dying of the Trees: The Pandemic in America's Forests*. New York: Viking.

McHarg, Ian. 1969. *Design with Nature*. Garden City, N.Y.: Doubleday/The Natural History Press. 1992. Reprint, New York: John Wiley & Sons.

Simonds, John. 1961. *Landscape Architecture: The Shaping of Man's Natural Environment*. New York: F. W. Dodge.

Spirn, Anne Whiston. 1984. *The Granite Garden: Urban Nature and Human Design*. New York: Basic Books.

Thoreau, Henry David. [1851] 1878. *Walden*. Boston: J. R. Osgood.

Van Valkenberg, Michael. 1986. *Transforming the American Garden*. Cambridge: Harvard University Press.

6

ECOLOGY AND THE URBAN AESTHETIC

MARK JOHNSON

The relationship between aesthetics and ecology in the urban environment is a curious one. Ecology and urbanity are rarely considered together in the common culture. But within the realms of those who shape the city, and of those who seek to restore the ecology, it is a uniquely pertinent confluence of seemingly opposing thought.

That this matter is of concern within the academy is a welcome sign that the many focal points of landscape architecture may be part of a purposeful composition. While it is expected that there will be a divergent discourse within academia, it is apparent that uncertainties have crept into practice as well. The professional world appears to be preparing, however awkwardly, for a realization that ecology, design, and planning can be part of a synthesis that is central to the discipline of landscape architecture and beneficial to the recipients of landscape architects' work.

It is in the design and building of landscapes that my thoughts are revealed. In sharing them you may think of them as "postcards from the edge," yet it is an edge that I believe may soon look more like the middle of our professional composition.

At Civitas, we think deeply about our work and how it fits into a larger sphere. We believe that landscape architecture is more art than science, that the solution is in the problem, and that many points of view must survive a challenging dialogue before a synthesis is reached. Together with my partner Ann Mullins, former partner Todd Johnson, and a talented staff, our work seeks to avoid stylistic traps. More than from any particular theory or process of design, we feel that built form should be an expression of the personal relationships of the people who create design with the people who will use it. The medium for this connection can take many forms, but it must derive from values that are common, purposeful, evocative, and emotional.

In today's urban society, the forms of modernism are not universal. At best they are deterministic and univalent, precluding the elements of chance and uncertainty that give meaning to the world. As world culture becomes more dependent on technology, the traditional connections of place and identity are decaying into a fragmentation of images and experiences. As designers we must choose whether our purpose is to restore the orders we are losing or to create new orders that give meaning to a more expansive view of the world.

THE CITY AS INFRASTRUCTURE

Since the Renaissance, science has sought to cleanse the city of grime, filth, disease, and death. Engineering emerged as the applied science of clean cities, bringing rigorous, repeatable solutions to sanitation, transportation, and drainage in a quest to improve public health and safety. For centuries the city has been seen as a delivery and disposal system, a network of engineering designed to deliver the services that support commerce and culture. As an extension of the scientific method, the city has an inherent order and logic. The form of the city devolves from the extension of linear constructs, designed to meet singular needs. Bridges are built to cross rivers, sewers are built to drain land, roads are built to provide access. Services are sent and received in efficient, maintainable facilities. Thus, we tend to visualize cities analytically, as networks and layers of interconnected parts and systems.

Over time, Western and particularly American culture has found a measure of beauty in the resulting urban landscape. Just as we value a clean home that is free of mice, we value a clean city that is free of rats. We may not think of a sewer as beautiful, but we have internalized the idea that a controlled, maintained environment is secure from pestilence and, therefore, is better. This underlies our urban aesthetic.

Cleanliness may be next to godliness, but it is also nearly a prerequisite to beauty in the public realm and consciousness. Whether this is a result of some human urge to control, to overcome a fear of disorder, or as a way of confirming the human identity or tilling God's garden is uncertain. Regardless, our cultural need for domestication of the environment is a powerful motivation in defining what we value in the city around us.

THE CITY AS GARDEN

Landscape architecture grew out of this urge. As science and engineering found the means to organize and cleanse the city, architecture and landscape gardening found ways to objectify, compose, and romanticize it. Just as the great portrait artists of the Renaissance illuminated our understanding of the human character, later movements in landscape painting transformed nature from something that was used into something that was looked at. Rembrandt van Rijn elevated the subject of his portraits above their own reality, ennobling them in images that were bigger than life, but still burdened by the realities of life. Joseph M. W. Turner transformed the industrial waterfront into an heroic landscape and venue for nostalgic reflection. These purified images encouraged culture to seek something better than nature. The romantic landscapes of the English garden became the objectified reality of the landscape painting. Lancelot Brown did for the landscape what Rembrandt did for the person, giving us a model of nature made both heroic and domesticated.

The form of the American city derives from our need to protect health and safety, combined with our desire to domesticate the land. Historically, urban design has depleted the ecological resource by displacing natural functions with technology and replacing native landscapes with romantic ones. This raises certain questions: Will our attempt to bring ecology into the city be blocked by an aesthetic heritage that we created ourselves? Are the English garden and the Frederick Law Olmsted designs the most appropriate landscapes today, or are they nearly mythological forms that might be superseded by a new aesthetic? They are probably both. The Olmstedian park and the City Beautiful boulevard are functional, venerated symbols of health and beauty in the city, with apparently wide appeal for a variety of cultural and ethnic groups. Yet there seems to be little room within this conception of the city for nature to be reintegrated into the scene, except in the occasional restoration of riparian areas, as cities seek to preserve or establish greenways and river corridors as open spaces. For any significant change to be made, landscape architects could be at the forefront of change, yet we must look back at our own legacy to understand how that change might be accomplished.

Landscape architecture today works in the shadow of gaps in its history. Significantly, our embrace of the environmental movement during the 1970s detached design education from its traditions, replacing it with inventions. Landscape architects educated during the 1970s and later are deeply affected by this. No greater shift had occurred since the late 1930s, when we embraced modernism, and before that since the mid-nineteenth century, with the advent of the Olmsted era. Note that landscape architecture did not make the shift to modernism at the turn of the twentieth century along with the other fine arts. At that time, architects and landscape architects thought they had already made their discovery, in the design of Central Park, where park and nature could become the centerpiece of the industrial/technological city.

Later, an even more powerful transformation in the role of landscape in the city was represented by Olmsted's design for Riverside, Illinois. Where his prior work created spaces, and places to be within, here he translated the idea of landscape space into the fluid, scenographic landscape backdrop that came to be embraced by the early modern architects, notably by Le Corbusier. Why should landscape architecture change when it had already established the healthful, pastoral context for an architecture and city of the future? The landscape was not just the backdrop of Le Corbusier's renderings; it was the antidote to the modernist's purified concept of city form, and the tragic heroine to the dominant, heroic architecture. Some notable exceptions took place, but few people reinforced the efforts made by Patrick Geddes, Warren Manning, and others to develop a systematic view of the landscape, or by Jens Jensen, Alfred Caldwell, and others to meld local ecological principles with visual principles of design. The overtly romantic imagery of Olmsted, reinforced by H. W. S. Cleveland, George Kessler, Charles Eliot, Marian Coffin, and others, was too strong.

Many permutations of the city-ecology paradox have since been explored. In Olmsted, we see the reformulation of nature into the romantic image preferred by Victorian culture. The landscape is made to relieve its congested urban counterpart. In schemes for ideal cities such as Ebenezer Howard's Garden City, we see the idea of romantic space used as a land-use determinant, the beginning of the planned segregation of use and space that differentiates the city from nature today. Since 1900, the landscape paradigms of the North American city have been ones of juxtaposition of ecology against the city, isolation of landscape from the city, and appropriation of landscape within the city. We have not achieved an integration of nature and city, yet there is a growing concern that ecological processes must be reinstated if we are to sustain and reinvigorate the urban framework.

THE MODERNIST GARDEN

The works of the early modernist landscape architects—especially Garrett Eckbo, who was concerned with the urban environment—emulated the reductive, formal planning of modern architecture and civic infrastructure. These efforts created an abstracted, purified philosophy of design that reduced the landscape aesthetic to a set of descriptive *artistic* norms that could be used in a variety of applications: In essence, an international style for landscape architecture. The works of the 1950s and 1960s provided a landscape architecture of service and the delivery of efficient, reductive spaces that appealed to the timeless aesthetic of the rational and conservative, but not to the emotional. Subsequent developments in theories of design were stalled, especially after the wonderful but pernicious redirection of the field by the environmental movement and the shift of landscape architecture toward ecological planning and analysis, with a consequent attempt in the academy to take our art and turn it into a science. But, for better or for worse, what landscape architects do is not science. Landscape architecture remains an art, and we are left today retracing our steps, seeking still to find our traditions when the world demands that we find invention.

THE CONTEMPORARY CITY

We must consider what the nature of the city is today. Our definition of the city has broadened dramatically since the advent of the automobile, air travel, computers, and communications technology. Where once Chicago was the geographer's idealized urban pattern, urban culture and commerce are now possible in dispersed cities of less than 100,000 in population. Access and ability to pay are still the important variables, however. With today's communications, urban commerce and culture are accessible in relatively remote locations. They can be enjoyed from near or far, as part of the urban milieu or outside of it. The distinctions between urban centers and their surrounding landscapes are no longer based in the distinctions of agriculture, commerce, and transportation. What we once knew as the country is now becoming urban, and, interestingly, what we knew as the city is now becoming suburban. The economics of access have turned the economies of real estate upside down, conspiring with shifting cultural values to draw the population away from urban centers and toward a matrix of multicentered exurbs.

Suddenly, the notion of cities as dense centers and of landscape as an aesthetic backdrop is transforming the substance of entire regions from agriculture into a pervasive domestication. People leaving the city are bringing the domestic, romantic landscape with them. People returning to the city are demanding a return to the City Beautiful, the livable city with beauty, access, and security commensurate to the suburb they are leaving. The North American landscape is experiencing a transformation of similar scale and significance to the shift of the western frontier from grassland and desert to agriculture. The older city is subjected to reinvigoration by a population that desires the ease of access, sense of security, and domesticated realm of the suburb. A melding of the city-suburb and the suburb-city is taking place. The need to consider the impact of this on the local and global ecology should be clear.

The transformation of the city is much more than a landscape issue. The culture of this decentralizing population appears to be changing rapidly as well. To seek an appropriate revision to our urban aesthetic requires an understanding of some of these changes.

The urban condition today is one in which architecture, landscape, and infrastructure are not understood as part of a unified order or cohesive plan. If traditional cities such as Paris or Rome can be identified with predictable forms, nested into a hierarchy, today's North American city is more difficult to characterize because of its lack of hierarchy, its formal disorder, and its emphasis on proximity to access above most other variables. There is no longer a compelling need for a central space, a dominant center, or an axis mundi to organize and orient the population. Even when there are remnants of centers, such as in downtown Denver, they have become specialized. Downtowns are now only one of many possible choices of location in the expanded city. As a result, our cognitive experience of city form is no longer a matter of distance from the center or other landmark. Instead, people live in one area, shop in another, work in another, and recreate in several. Furthermore, each individual uses the city in a completely unique way, sharing the structure but not the particulars of their experience with others. Our patterns of behavior are similar, but the similarity of experiences do not converge to create common values as they did in pre-automobile, traditional cities. Instead we share not our experiences, but the relationships between them. People perceive these relationships largely relative to themselves, seen through the lens of their personal condition, their history and place-reaction, complicating, enriching, and opening up the aesthetic responses and constructs that are possible. Our urban aesthetic is itself a collective of these expectations, responses, and remembrances. One hundred years ago, George Kessler could envision a beautiful city that substantiated the culture's pride and hope for the future. There is no City Beautiful in sight for the twenty-first century because currently there is no way to achieve consensus on the definition of the city, the role that the city should play in our lives, or what elements would make it beautiful.

Today, cities are the afterfact of design. As uncoordinated wholes they confront us daily with myriad random images and experiences. The individual is no longer part of a culture. Instead we are members of the urban cast(e), left to sort for ourselves our experience, identity, and the messages of the city. Each of us takes up a distinct position within the matrix of contemporary urban culture, differentiated from all others by what we see from our vantage point. Each person receives and judges the environment in his or her own way, most of us equipped with little understanding of how our position in the realm relates to any other. We experience the city not as a singular place, but as a cafeteria of images and experiences open to our choosing.

To define the condition I describe as postmodern, or contemporary, has largely been the task of philosophers and anthropologists. Culture was once defined by common traditions and norms, but today it results from common conditions and situations. Since the late 1970s we have seen architecture and, to a lesser extent, landscape architecture respond to a general disenchantment with the reductive forms and empty abstractions of modernism. The so-called postmodern architecture that was popularized by Michael Graves and Robert Venturi attempted to wake up our aesthetic sense by adding familiar, historical architectural symbols to simple modern buildings. We attempted to give meaning through reference to historical symbol, by inventing a semiology to satisfy the emptiness of our cities. The return to the City Beautiful in the last decade, the infection we know as the festival marketplace, and the escape to art and sculpture in landscape architecture are each manifestations of our dissatisfaction with the models of design that we know.

THE CONTEMPORARY ARTS

The visual and performing arts have transformed dramatically in response to cultural change. Early in the twentieth century, the modern revolution in art sought to find new ways of representing the environment. The Russian Constructivists, for example, motivated by an urgency to abandon the bourgeois symbolism of figurative art and isolated by political domination, purified and abstracted traditional design principles to the point that their art became a stimulating but empty vessel, available for a socialist, propagandistic appropriation, in service to the claimed universality of the Bolshevik revolution. Art was exploited by artists themselves and elevated to an inherently valueless plane. With the advent of abstract expressionism later in the century, the transfer of art from objectification to abstraction was complete. The subject of the work mattered little, leaving the art to rest in the relationships of intellectual principles. Art had become a closed circle, a self-referencing code available only to those artists and dilettantes who could interpret it.

By the early 1960s, a countermovement began in art that attempted to restore the meaning and emotional content that this century had taken away. The early earthworks of Robert Smithson, Michael Heizer, and others are used often today as examples of the relationship of art to landscape architecture. A body of work from both artists and landscape architects has resulted. From this a new form of manipulation of the landscape emerged during the 1970s and 1980s, one in which the landscape is mannered to represent sculpture. Works such as Smithson's *Spiral Jetty* and Heizer's *Double Negative* opened the door to enable us to see landscape as a material that is available for a freer manipulation, one that is independent from modernist theory, design tradition, or function. These works are purely visual statements, using geologic materials to reveal the substance of the earth, and sculptural forms as a narrative commentary on the purpose of modern art.

While these artists attacked modernism head-on, another movement addressed the idea of contemporary culture directly. In the late 1970s a number of visual artists became involved in the idea of art as performance. Rather than pursue art as makers of precious artifacts or landscapes, these artists chose to de-objectify and de-value the artifacts of art. They believed that the value of art is in its ability to transfer the intentions and concepts of the artist into the experience and aesthetic of the audience. By taking the object away, art can be elevated to pure expression and emotion residing not in the artist but in the viewer. With this release from objective reality, art can provide each viewer a pure, individual art experience that is personal, emotional, and different from and unobtainable by anyone else. The work of Robert Wilson in opera and Laurie Anderson in music, the vulgar, exploitive work of Carolee Schneeman, and the verbal commentaries of Barbara Kruger and Jenny Holzer are well-known examples of attempts to connect the artist with the viewer in personal, emotional linkages.

THE OPEN-ENDED LANDSCAPE

Parallel trends are at work in landscape architecture today, as designers seek to create environments that restore a sense of place and meaning to individual experience. As in art, the works of the last decade and a half have begun to seek grounding in the ecological, prehistorical, and emotional. Design is becoming more about the personal and less about the analytical. Note, for example, the work of Jones & Jones, a firm that has developed the art of interpreting and presenting ecosystems. Using the zoological and botanical garden as a venue, whole landscape experiences are re-created with a dramatic compression of scales that highlight the distinctions between bioclimatic zones and cultural place. Visitors to these environments are confronted with an unfamiliar reality that causes them to compare their attitudes toward nature with the alternative environment they are experiencing. At the other extreme of scale are the works of landscape architect Gary Dwyer and artist Andy Goldsworthy, whose works mark the landscape with evocative focal points that act as ciphers, giving clues to unfamiliar patterns within nature. Such work makes a connection between the human, ecological, and spiritual; it is more emotional than analytical, more personal than rational, and different for each individual.

The "Visionary and Unbuilt Landscapes" competitions held since 1990 by *Landscape Architecture* magazine are fresh indicators of the designer's willingness to think of landscape as a substance to be expressed, rather than as one to be domesticated. Competition submissions have ranged from landscapes of death and decay, to landscapes that are processes, and even to mobile landscapes. After some three hundred or more years of tradition in landscape design, we may finally see the landscape for what it is and not for what we think it should be.

Landscape architecture has a role in transforming our culture's aesthetic, which must be transformed if we are to embrace ecology within it. The work of landscape architects can evoke and even provoke an awareness of the relationships between culture, beauty, geography, and ecology. With the changes in North American culture, designers now have the opportunity to redirect the urge to purify a landscape. We have the opportunity, even the imperative, to create an open-ended landscape that is structured to express relationships that are encoded with meanings and that are interpretable and accessible to ordinary people.

What my partners and I seek in our work is to connect people with a sense of place by offering an open-ended environment—one that is neither an empty vessel nor one that is a deterministic composition. Chance, accident, and personal experience must remain within the design if people are to find their own value and meaning. We wish to create spaces that will be venerated by virtue of what they mean to the users over time, and not to ourselves. To accomplish this requires that the landscapes we design have multiple meanings, and sufficient substance, to connect with the individual, to stimulate reaction, and to allow for personal interpretation.

To be meaningful, the open-ended landscape must be encoded with the patterns and symbols of human use. It must include the obvious and the familiar, the startling and the unexpected. It must combine the effect of images and the synapses between them. It need not be disorderly, but neither should it be univalent or directive. It must leave a person's position and role open to his or her interpretation; it cannot be predictive of a person's response. Rather than design the landscape as a pictorial image, designers should leave it open to be expressed differently to different viewers, allowing for the choice and chance of use, available for and capable of adaptation to a future we cannot predetermine.

Community College of Aurora, Colorado. The remnant of a historic canal was restored as the central campus space. Natural and cultural history form the context for campus life. Landscape architect: Civitas, Inc. Photograph by Richard Peterson.

Community College of Aurora. The landscape does not dictate. It informs campus life with growth and changes that are rooted in the place. Landscape architect: Civitas, Inc. Photograph by Richard Peterson.

Community College of Aurora. Natural and architectural patterns coexist without transitions. One is not forced to accommodate the other; neither is more significant. Landscape architect: Civitas, Inc. Photograph by Richard Peterson.

Community College of Aurora. The essence of the High Plains landscape is only revealed through contact with life and death. The contrast of culture and nature is celebrated. Landscape architect: Civitas, Inc. Photograph by Richard Peterson.

Aspen/Centennial employee housing. The diversity, vitality, and beauty of the restored native landscape contrasts with the sterility of the domestic landscape. Landscape architect: Civitas, Inc. Photograph by Richard Peterson.

The Green Room, Great West Life Corporation, Denver, Colorado. The garden creates an alternative environment for 1,400 employees. Elements of the garden relate to one another as if in a dance, creating a constantly changing sense of place. Landscape architect: Civitas, Inc./Larry Kirkland Studios. Photograph by Thorney Lieberman.

The Green Room, Great West Life Corporation. Forms, materials, scale, and position each inform the user of the meaning of place. Designer: Civitas, Inc./Larry Kirkland Studios. Photograph by Thorney Lieberman.

The Green Room, Great West Life Corporation. Natural and domestic forms inhabit the space. Materials are used to invoke meaning and reference. Designer: Civitas, Inc./Larry Kirkland Studios. Photograph by Thorney Lieberman.

SUSTAINABILITY

If landscape architects can allow their designs to escape the pictorial, they can begin to invest them with a more open range of content. In the romantic urban landscape of the past, content was limited largely to the materials and forms that support the romantic image. The City Beautiful's landscape expressed dominance over nature, reducing the landscape into subservience to formal order. With the rapid changes in our culture, designers now have the opportunity to change the content of their work to include materials that express the natural landscape of a region rather than to replicate typologies borrowed from elsewhere.

When we review the design efforts at creating sustainable landscapes underway today, differences of emphasis should be noted. For some designers, it is imperative that the processes of nature be emulated, so as to restore natural function to the environment. Clearly this is important, since the function of ecological processes has been displaced by urbanization. These works involve developing new technologies to replace conventional engineering, affecting drainage, wastewater application, biological treatment, soil aeration, and other functions. This emphasis presumes that designers must perform as many urban functions as possible in ways that emulate natural process, in the hope that this will diminish the loss of natural functions. Such work is important, but it will have an incremental effect on the environment, to the extent that designers, governments, and the public adapt to the new, more appropriate techniques. These efforts will get to the heart of the issue of sustainability, by purposefully replacing damaging technologies with more appropriate ones. It is to be hoped that we are advancing. Sustainability is now a central topic at engineering and architecture conferences, as all the design professions get on the bandwagon. The extensive effort toward new technologies and a return to older, nondestructive ones is a positive, substantive sign.

AESTHETICS

As important as the use of sustainable technology is, a more important aspect of sustainability must be addressed by designers, not technicians. Landscape architects need to adopt, or even create, an aesthetic that communicates the value of the ecological processes they are trying to restore. Landscape architects must create an aesthetic that brings the natural landscape into the conventional notions of beauty in the city. Basically, this means initiating a revision of the public taste. If the natural landscape is not always as clean and tidy as we desire our cities to be, then we must find a way of making it beautiful so that people will value, desire, and nurture it. We must overcome our urge to domesticate. We must move beyond Andrew Jackson Downing and the Hudson River School of painters.

Landscape architects need to discover a new way of observation. They should not seek a solution that denies aesthetics for ecology, nor one that appropriates the appearance of the natural to communicate a false sense of ecological actuality. Before the public can incorporate ecology into its urban aesthetic, people must value the presence of natural process in the city, in the same way that a rancher values and protects his well. Without the nour-

ishment of clean water, all shall perish, and one simple ecological recognition becomes a community imperative. We need to find ways of making
people recognize the importance of their well.

Landscape architects can try to educate people directly about the
importance of a healthy environment, in the media and in interpretive
works, but this is not the central province of landscape architecture as project design. Presenting functioning ecological or sustainable solutions to
project design may contribute to society's ecological objectives, but they
may go unnoticed by the public. In North American culture there is a tendency for things that look "natural" in the city to be regarded as either left-
over, underutilized, or unsightly.

In the natural environment a call for aesthetics is a call for conservation. In the city, aesthetics is an active force in shaping both function and
meaning in built form. Here, aesthetics shapes nature itself. While we may
judge natural or rural landscapes from an ecologically correct viewpoint, we
cannot do the same in the city, for it is the summation of innumerable decisions that result in a whole whose ecological correctness has not, and maybe
cannot, be defined.

Is aesthetics relevant to ecology? Most contemporary environmental
design work is partly determined by aesthetics, with emphases on order,
continuity, space cognition, orientation, sensations of beauty and place, and
a sense that care and quality exist. Pride is represented in aesthetics, com-
municating that a place exists within a framework of people and their values. These values have implicit in them statements of control over the
environment. Clean and neat—this is not nature. Alive and healthy, pretty
and fragrant—this is not the death and renewal that nature depends on.
Nurtured and cared for—this speaks of pride and value. If contemporary
values demand domesticated nature, how can ecological values be realized
without offending contemporary sensibilities? How can pride be developed
in doing the right ecological thing, rather than in domesticating a landscape?

The urban landscape need not look ecological to communicate ecological values to people. Ian McHarg has shown that we need to be con-
siderate of natural processes in looking at the land. His approach, though
transformed by his followers, is applied in some form across the continent
with beneficial effect in preserving fragments of regional ecology. As rich
as this thinking is, its impact on the quality of life is arguable. It does not

provide an aesthetic to apply to areas that were lost long ago from the natural to the urban, where no trace of process has been untouched by the engineer. The central question is, How will landscape architects repair the urban environment, its infrastructure, and its psyche in a way that satisfies what is known about ecology and aesthetics?

I believe we cannot change a culture's aesthetic judgment by appealing to its sense of principle. The persistence of the classical, romantic, and nostalgic in the popular taste suggests that designers must find ways of making the ecological landscape refer visually to these known measures of beauty. The landscape of the contemporary city should evoke action and interaction, using the interfaces of nature and built form to reveal and interpret urban life.

The essence of the city can be of an inculturated ecology of person, place, and environment. For the designer the city is an urban ecology demanding expression. Ecology in the city should function with a restorative power, using the interface of nature and built form to reveal and interpret their mutual interdependence. The charge of landscape architecture must be to synthesize both conditions—to respond to the culture with landscapes that are beautiful, encoded with meaning, and built of a substance that brings ecological responsibility into the language of popular culture.

A NEW URBAN AESTHETIC

The ethos of the city must be of landscape—native, domestic, and contrived. The value of personal experience, the invasion of nature into the public realm, and the reconceptualization of aesthetic experience are prerequisite to achieving it. Today's cultural perceptions need not value the unity of romanticism. With our daily barrage of images—a cacophony of eclecticism—we have already altered the basic assumptions of modernism. For the viewer of contemporary culture each image relates to place without needing to become a place, and refers to the past, present, and future without relating to time. Yet people retain a need for substance to underlie and inform their experiences, and they desire an encoded environment they can understand, if only for the comfort of familiarity. But the erosion of common culture and its substitution by the fragmentation of common images undermines any common response and understanding of the substance in the environment around us. To meet this paradox with the substance of nature is to define a new urban aesthetic.

The voices of nature must speak through design as a code to bind our experience with value—not a return to nature, not romantic mimicry, and not visual art. The designer's abstractions are preconceptions that filter out the reality of ecological process and cultural change. An aesthetic that includes cultural disorder and the "accidents" of nature can inform the public of the substance of the human condition and the significance of natural processes that modernism excluded. The values and sense of order within the individual, and not those of the designer, should be both the screen by which images are sorted and the human motive force of the environment.

The knowledge of nature as a force affecting the city is now an imperative for design. Today we seek value, meaning, and substance as fundamental to our urban experience. Human and ecological roles must evolve into a focused relationship. The work of the landscape architect may be pretty, but does it improve the environment for people or for the regional ecology? Designers should strive to make it work for both.

7

BIOREGIONAL PLANNING AND ECOSYSTEM PROTECTION

CLAIR REINIGER

The earth is composed of ecosystems, the borders of which are not represented by political demarcations but follow nature's contours. Areas that are defined by natural boundaries have come to be called bioregions, or life territories, from the Greek *bio* for "life" and Latin *regio* for "territory." The basic root meaning of bioregion has been expanded over the years to mean "part of the earth's surface whose rough boundaries are determined by natural characteristics rather than human dictates, distinguishable from other areas by particular attributes of flora, fauna, water, climate, soils, landforms, and by human settlements and cultures those attributes have given rise to."[1]

The protection and management of natural resources in the United States is largely a compartmentalized bureaucratic activity. This is evident from the multitude of federal agencies responsible for various aspects of resource management, including the Forest Service, Natural Resources Conservation Service, Bureau of Land Management, Environmental Protection Agency, National Park Service, Fish and Wildlife Service, Bureau of Reclamation, Bureau of Indian Affairs, Geological Survey, Army Corps of Engineers, Federal Energy Regulatory Administration, as well as the state agencies with similar overlapping responsibilities.

Each agency is responsible for the preservation and development of only a portion of our nation's natural resources. Few agencies take a bioregional approach. The result is a lack of unified resource management in the United States as well as competition among federal agencies and their state counterparts. Many countries around the world follow the American example.

Bioregional planning is a way of understanding the complexities of ecosystems as they relate to regional culture; it is an integrated approach to resource management as defined by the ecosystem's characteristics. To understand the ecosystem of a bioregion, a Bioregional Resource Inventory is compiled, providing detailed analyses of climate, precipitation, vegetation, soils, geology, animal life, air quality, surface hydrology, groundwater depths, surface-water drainage, topography, land-use patterns, population density and settlement patterns, metropolitan development trends, economic patterns as well as the extent of natural energy sources of sun, wind, water, and biomass.[2] All of the components just listed, as well as the relationships among them, comprise the structure of a bioregion, or what might be called its anatomy. These elements are dynamic: Energy, water, and materials flow through them, and this gives life to the system, or what might be called its physiology.

The critical concept to comprehend is that a bioregion functions as an ecosystem, which basically captures solar energy through its vegetation and then transforms this energy through the process of growth, maintenance, storage, species reproduction, and system regeneration. Vegetation in general but forests in particular play a critical role in the hydrological cycle that brings moisture from the oceans and, through the repeated cycle of rainfall and forest evapotranspiration, carries it inland toward the interior of continents. The soils of an ecosystem capture and store water, making it available to plants and releasing it slowly to streams and aquifers. The micro-organisms in soils break down organic materials as well as the minerals in the underlying rock, making these available as plant nutrients. The basic processes by which an ecosystem functions are related to these fundamental flows of energy, waste, and materials through the system.

In general, the more a climate varies, the more surplus energy, water, and materials an ecosystem will store against hard times in stressful periods. Plants and animals in temperate climates, for example, store more energy to survive the winter, or more water to withstand the dry season, than do plants and animals of the humid tropics where the climate is fairly even and, consequently, where energy flows are more continuous throughout the ecosystem.

We harvest these ecological surpluses, and in some cases displace or eliminate other species that might compete with us for these resources. Our near elimination of the bison and antelope habitat in the Great Plains is a case in point. When we harvest more than the surplus produced by an ecosystem and begin to consume the system itself, we are, in effect, mining the resource. This can trap us in a vicious circle in which the system's yield is never enough for us, so we keep using up the system's capacity to produce and the yield keeps diminishing. This is what has happened to most of our nation's ecosystems, especially during the twentieth century.

Part of the challenge of resource management in the American West, where I live and work, comes from the persistence of the boom-bust mentality that has dominated the region since Anglo-European settlement began. To date, we have mined our forests, rangelands, soils, and aquifers as though there is no tomorrow. Only at the turn of the twentieth century, in Theodore Roosevelt's day, did people distinguish between nonrenewable and renewable resources. The establishment of the Soil Erosion Service (later known as the Soil Conservation Service and now the Natural Resources Conservation Service) put this recognition into practice in 1933, but a view of resource areas as something akin to a stockpile of goods dominates attitudes toward resources to this day. When a forest is viewed as a stockpile of timber and not as part of an ecosystem, there is little incentive to reforest. Just clear-cut and move on to the next stockpile, or just clear-cut and replace it with a monoculture plantation. The same principle goes for rangelands, agricultural soils, and aquifers. With ecological awareness, people begin to understand that renewable resources are not just stockpiled in nature, but are produced by living systems; to maintain output, one has to maintain the health of the producing ecosystem.[3]

One of the consequences of deforestation and overgrazing is increasingly unreliable water supplies and destructive periodic flooding. The response is to build more dams, levees, and reservoirs. But this solves only part of the problem, namely, fluctuating water availability. The primary problem remains the destruction of the original water-capturing ecosystems—soil plus vegetative cover in forests and grasslands. The bioregional viewpoint establishes the absolute necessity of the health maintenance of the natural ecosystems from which we obtain our renewable resources and on which, ultimately, our lives and livelihoods universally depend.

This ecologically oriented view, however, does not mean that we ignore human needs or economies. All but a few of us work to make a living. Bioregionalism views human economies as ecosystems within ecosystems, as subsystems of a larger whole. We, too, use energy to transform materials into forms we can use to sustain ourselves. But like other members of the animal kingdom, we depend on the plant kingdom to transform the primary source of energy on earth, which is sunlight, into usable forms of energy—including the fossil fuels on which today's explosive population growth and agricultural, industrial, and technological civilization depend.

Our economies are embedded within larger ecosystems. We depend on these ecosystems to provide us with energy, water, and materials; we, also, depend on them for vital services or "foundational resources" such as water storage, moderation of climatic extremes, generation of oxygen and absorption of carbon dioxide, and the filtering, neutralizing, and recycling of pollutants. And there is that intangible sense of being "at home" when there are rocks, cacti, trees, gardens, and other aspects of life around us that we miss when we become isolated in unfamiliar surroundings.

In economics, the fundamental concept of cost-benefit analysis carries over into the watershed planning instituted by the Soil Conservation Service.[4] In these plans, we find cost-benefit analyses for proposed structures such as dams, sediment basins, or ditches, and for a wide range of soil and water conservation practices applied to the land. In wildlife and range management, the concept of "carrying capacity" is key to evaluating wildlife habitat needs and stocking rates. The carrying capacity of the land, or more properly of the ecosystem, is the number of animals of a given species supported by a given area over the long term. In other words, carrying capacity is a measure of the sustainability of a wildlife species or of sustainable yield for livestock.

Bioregional planning brings together both cost-benefit analyses and carrying capacity or sustainability measures in a way that seeks to balance short-term and long-term costs and benefits. The goal is to help us make a worthwhile living today without compromising the lives and livelihoods of our children and their children or sacrificing the welfare of compatriot lifeforms. Accomplishing this goal requires a recognition of the value of healthy, functioning ecosystems as renewable resource systems. The bioregional approach goes beyond these utilitarian values and states that the quality of human life depends on the health of all life; that we are, in actuality, one immune system. Our health mirrors the health of the ecosystem we live in, and vice versa.

CHALLENGES TO BIOREGIONAL PLANNING

Most elements of modern life impede the implementation of a bioregional approach, in particular those that distort the relationship between our economics and the ecosystem in which we live: Urbanization, energy waste, population growth, and a dominant mechanistic worldview. In addition, the lack of coordination among resource managing agencies and the lack of informed public participation impede progress.

Urbanization cuts off people from nature and undermines our relationship with the ecosystems that support us; and, increasingly, resource management decisions are made in cities far away from the ecosystems affected. A local lumber company in Alabama, for example, with extensive forest holdings in the area, might be acquired by a multinational corporation in, say, Chicago, whose corporate managers might decide to "liquidate their assets" to pay off debts incurred by another division. Since the forest is the asset, liquidation could mean clear-cutting and pulling out. This action fails to account for the long-term production potential of a healthy renewable resource system, in this case a forest, and fails to consider the economic needs of local residents whose jobs rely on the maintenance of the forest ecosystem. The community would likely suffer from heavy runoff and sedimentation, a shortened life of reservoirs and loss of water, and so on. An integrated bioregional approach to renewable resource planning and management can bring back a more sustainable balance between short-term and long-term economic and ecological needs.

The burgeoning of industrial economies is powered by fossil fuels— that vast, yet limited, store of solar energy trapped in coal, oil, and natural gas. Higher levels of material consumption benefit humanity, but the gain in human energy use has simply fed an exploding population rather than raised its standard of living. This trade-off between population increases and a decreasing quality of life is probably the most neglected issue in resource planning and policy making today.[5] We can develop the wisest plans in the world, but the sheer crush of new mouths to feed worldwide is trapping us in a downward spiral of unsatisfied needs and consumed productive capacity. This pressure from a growing population will manifest itself regionally through increasing pressure on a watershed's scarce resources from both internal and external demands. For example, as a result of a surging urban population, the fifth largest tributary to the Rio Grande in New Mexico is the

The Rio Grande, a few miles upstream from Bosque del Apache National Wildlife Refuge near Socorro. The Rio Grande watershed has long been the lifeblood of New Mexico, from late Anasazi to contemporary times. Photograph by George F. Thompson, 1993.

wastewater drainage canal flowing out of Albuquerque. This boom in metropolitan development along the Rio Grande will continue to have a significantly negative impact on the ecosystem of this watershed.

Many challenges face the bioregional planner. The immediate problem is how to devise the means to protect the health and sustainability of local ecosystems against the demands of outside consumers who have no direct stake in the ecosystem's conservation or its renewable resource base. A second challenge is how to encourage informed public debate between growth and the quality of life within the context of sustainable development in a bioregion. This issue will involve every family struggling to make a living and the successful industries that have profited from the lack of coordination, management, and protection of the natural and historic resources in a region. A third challenge is to overcome the compartmentalization—as well as the duplication or conflict in missions—of the agencies responsible for administering

One of the greatest waterfowl and wildlife sanctuaries in the entire nation is Bosque del Apache. The Rio Grande courses through it. During the peak wintertime season, approximately 10,000 sandhill cranes and a few whoopers, 39,000 snow geese, and 50,000 ducks winter here, in addition to herons, hawks, egrets, and eagles. Since 1940 approximately 320 bird species and 400 different mammals, reptiles, and amphibians have been sighted here. Bosque del Apache is, also, part of the largest continuous cottonwood (alamosa) bosque (forest or woods) in the United States. Today, however, alamosa are not generating well because of river channelization, which deprives the trees of a natural water flow. Compounding this problem are aggressive exotics such as salt cedar (Tamarax), which overwhelm the native cottonwood groves. The Fish and Wildlife Service, which administers the refuge, is trying to deal with these problems. Every year, however, Rio Grande water becomes more precious as New Mexico, and especially the Albuquerque area, booms. Photograph by Augustus W. Janeway. From Registered Places of New Mexico: The Land of Enchantment, by Cotton Mather and George E. Thompson (Mesilla: New Mexico Geographical Society, 1995), p. 18.

The Spanish mission church at Isleta Pueblo, thirteen miles south of Albuquerque on the old section of Route 66. A bioregional approach takes account of human handiwork and cultural identity with a place. Photograph by George F. Thompson, 1993.

the resources of ecosystems. Although specialized expertise is needed to deal with different aspects of a problem, specialization has obvious weaknesses: An inability to grasp the whole picture and a susceptibility to influence from vested interests that are equally specialized and unable to comprehend the whole picture. There will always be conflicting claims over scarce resources, but a major function of bioregional planning is to mediate between conflicting agencies and interests in seeking "the greatest good for the greatest number" or an overall "win-win solution" that balances short-term and long-term interests, while maximizing the benefits to society and minimizing harms.[6]

Bioregional planners are interested in improving the quality of our lives and the lives of future generations through an informed citizenry that America's founding fathers knew to be a key to preserving democracy. Consequently, we have a stake in developing and maintaining healthy ecosys-

A vernacular building on the plaza at Isleta Pueblo. Seventeen of the eighteen contemporary pueblos are in New Mexico, and many are situated along or very near the Rio Grande. Photograph by George F. Thompson, 1993.

tems and the productive renewable resource systems on which our lives and livelihoods depend. For example, since the problems of a watershed are held in common, public participation in resource management is needed to resolve problems and to ensure management strategies that work. At the same time, our current education system needs to account for the ecological-economic perspective of learning and to address the bioregional planning process that is the basis for making long-term resource management decisions that ensure sustainable development. Education is the first step toward the long-term sustainability of our communities as well as our soils, forests, watersheds, wildlife corridors, parklands, and historic structures. Geography must, again, become a required course at all educational levels in America in order to achieve a basic source of knowledge and understanding of the interconnectedness between the natural and humanly constructed worlds.

OPPORTUNITIES FOR NEW APPROACHES

The basic assumptions we make about the natural world have profound consequences for the way we interact with that world. Since the discovery of physics by Newton in the seventeenth century, Western society has assumed that nature works like a machine and that the best way to control it is to reduce it to its simplest form, to its components. As we enter the twenty-first century, however, it is now apparent that nature is much more complex than a simple machine; it resembles a living organism.

James Lovelock, in his book *Healing Gaia,* has pioneered the emerging science of geophysiology, which is the study of how an ecosystem functions as a living system.[7] Landscape architects have become proficient at collecting data on the "anatomy" of an ecosystem, for example, by dividing a watershed into components such as soil, precipitation, and vegetation. What is new and revolutionary about the bioregional perspective is that *all* living systems—human, animal, water, plant, soil, and atmospheric—are viewed as one living, dynamic system. Science is finally catching up to what traditional cultures have always known—that the earth is alive.

Through our bioregional inventories, or examinations, we are able to conduct diagnoses of ecosystems that should lead to designs, or prescriptions, for interventions. There are signs that bioregional ecosystem thinking is now moving into the mainstream. For example, in 1992 the Environmental Protection Agency (EPA) initiated a watershed protection approach to solving "nonpoint" or diffuse water quality problems. The EPA finally acknowledged that water pollution does not follow geopolitical boundaries, even though, as we know in the West, water does flow uphill to money.[8] In March of 1993 the EPA sponsored a watershed conference in which groups from all over the United States gathered to share their new efforts in watershed protection. Meanwhile, Bruce Babbitt, secretary of the Department of the Interior in the Clinton administration, launched a biodiversity survey of major ecosystems in order to create baseline data for understanding the current health of our public lands. Solving environmental problems within an ecosystem context makes common sense, and the government is beginning to catch on.

In 1987 Designwrights Collaborative Inc., a nonprofit corporation I established in 1977, brought together all the work in renewable resources, land planning, and water resources to create an integrated, holistic approach to solving pollution problems within a watershed ecosystem context. The upper Rio Grande basin was the crucible for our bioregional project.

The basin is approximately 26,500 square miles, or the equivalent size of Vermont, New Hampshire, Connecticut, Rhode Island, and Long Island combined. Its headwaters are in the San Juan Mountains of southern Colorado, just above Creede, and the river flows through the San Luis Valley into New Mexico, near Taos, and then past Santa Fe, Albuquerque, Socorro, Las Cruces, and the border cities of El Paso, Texas, and Ciudad Juarez, Mexico. Once upon a time the Rio Grande water from Colorado traveled all the way to the Gulf of Mexico. Now the river has been severed due to full appropriation of water in the United States for agriculture, industry, and metropolitan development. As a case in point, below El Paso the river runs out of "American water" at Fort Quitman, Texas: The Rio Grande is fed at this point by unregulated tributary streams from Mexico. And, as we know, Juarez and other Mexican towns and cities tributary to the Rio Grande have no sewage treatment facilities either.

As part of the examination of the watershed's anatomy, Designwrights created a database collected from information from 450 government sources, which resulted in 44 maps and close to 400 pages of text. The inventory of the anatomy, or the collection of baseline data, includes precipitation, surface-water drainage basins, geology, soils, vegetation, and settlement patterns. The inventory maps, for example, indicate our current knowledge about the ancient settlement patterns of the watershed since 15,000–13,000 BC. Projecting this and other maps onto each other is like a carefully choreographed dance. We have maps and data on land grants, metropolitan development trends, landownership, land use, water flow, water rights, water supply, river management, water quality, air quality, forestry and rangeland issues, vegetation, toxics, soil erosion, and much more.

All of these factors are dynamic: Energy, water, and materials flow through them, which gives life to the system; this is what is called the "geophysiology" of the bioregion and how the watershed functions as a living system. Designwrights is currently completing the geophysiology research for the watershed. In particular, we are trying to determine the soil, water, and nutrient retention capabilities of the ecosystem. Because the goal of the bioregional approach is sustainable development, an economic-environmental audit of the industries and municipalities who use the renewable and

One of the many analysis maps prepared by Designwrights Collaborative that reveal the anatomy of the Upper Rio Grande watershed.

UPPER RIO GRANDE BASIN
WATER QUALITY
ISSUES

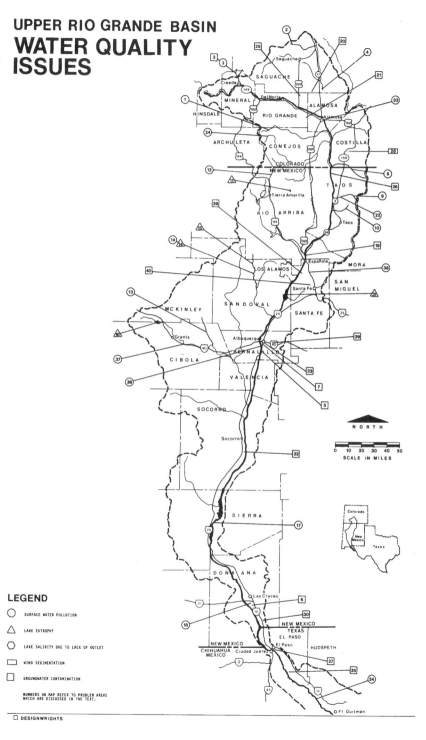

LEGEND

○ SURFACE WATER POLLUTION

△ LAKE EUTROPHY

◯ LAKE SALINITY DUE TO LACK OF OUTLET

▭ WIND SEDIMENTATION

▭ GROUNDWATER CONTAMINATION

NUMBERS ON MAP REFER TO PROBLEM AREAS
WHICH ARE DISCUSSED IN THE TEXT.

▢ DESIGNWRIGHTS

nonrenewable resources in the watershed is being initiated. Designwrights is working with some of the major corporations and resource extraction industries in the Rio Grande watershed to look at their processing systems. Ways to view each industry as an "ecosystem" in itself are being explored, especially in terms of water and waste recycling. We review this major database, which tells us how the ecosystem functions and what are its problems and issues, and then a sustainable development plan emerges.

Of course, sustainable development plans cannot be created or implemented without public involvement. Designwrights has established three task forces: The policy task force, made up of governmental directors for the basin; an interagency task force comprised of scientists in state, federal, and local government agencies; and a stakeholders task force that includes the resource users (farmers, ranchers, the oil and gas industry, Indian pueblos, recreation groups and outfitters, and high-technology industries). In an effort to build consensus to create a framework for ecosystem management in the Rio Grande basin, many issues must be faced and compromises made.

Designwrights has facilitated meetings with the task forces in an effort to foster greater intergovernmental cooperation, an accepted baseline database for the upper Rio Grande basin, and a model for an ecosystem approach that promotes sustainable development. We are halfway through a projected fourteen years on the Rio Grande project.

From all accounts our efforts on the Rio Grande have been very successful. We have established a network database and policy forum that promises to lay the groundwork for a more sustainable and healthier ecosystem in the watershed than would be possible without such partnerships in conservation.[9]

BIOREGIONALISM AND LANDSCAPE ARCHITECTURE

Landscape architects are particularly well qualified to lead bioregional ecosystem planning efforts. Training in ecological concepts, regional planning, and public participation are the basic tools used in the bioregional planning approach. Unfortunately most landscape architects have played a minimal role in this new approach. This is a missed opportunity.

There are many obstacles and challenges to implementing the bioregional approach. It is encouraging, however, that many of our institutions—schools, government, and industry—are beginning to make the shift, albeit slowly. There really is no other practical way to solve our environmental and economic challenges. Our belief systems, ways of doing business, and concepts of how the natural world functions are up for review because the old ways no longer serve us.

One way to respond to the bioregional challenge is for landscape architects to use their knowledge about ecosystems in their small-scale designs. By thinking regionally and acting locally, designers and planners can begin to make a difference.

Clair Reiniger and Associates was commissioned in 1992 by McLeod, Inc. to design a 2,500-square-foot plaza and courtyards for a multifamily housing compound in Santa Fe.

The Epona Garden, a courtyard plaza for a condominium compound in Santa Fe. The design was inspired by the Celtic goddess Epona, and conceived as a river. The flagstone represents the river, the snake pattern is the great horned water spirit, the grass mounds are islands with plantings of river grasses, wildflowers, and aspens. Landscape architect: Clair Reiniger and Associates. Photograph by Benjamin T. Rogers.

School for American Research Presidents Courtyard, Santa Fe, New Mexico. Landscape architect: Clair Reiniger and Associates. Photograph by Benjamin T. Rogers.

This is the approach I take. Whether I am restoring the ecology of a riparian habitat, designing a courtyard, or planning a watershed, I use the same process. As far as the design process is concerned, scale is irrelevant. The parts are reflected in the whole. As the ancient Celtic people knew: as above, so below.

NOTES

1. Kirkpatrick Sale, *Dwellers in the Land: The Bioregional Vision* (San Francisco: Sierra Club Books, 1985), p. 55.

2. Landscape architects and planners from Patrick Geddes and Warren Manning to Ian McHarg and Phil Lewis have advocated this approach for nearly a century.

3. See, for example, Marcy Howe, *Prairie Keepers* (Reading, Mass.: Addison-Wesley, 1994).

4. Watershed planning by the Soil Conservation Service began in the 1930s; the 1954 Watershed Planning and Flood Prevention Act furthered such regional planning. See Frederick R. Steiner, *Soil Conservation in the United States: Policy and Planning* (Baltimore: Johns Hopkins University Press, 1990). Also of interest is David L. Feldman, *Water Resources Management: In Search of an Environmental Ethic* (Baltimore: Johns Hopkins University Press, 1991).

5. See David L. Feldman, ed., *The Energy Crisis: Unresolved Issues and Enduring Legacies* (Baltimore: Johns Hopkins University Press, 1996).

6. See Timothy Beatley, *Ethical Land Use: Principles of Policy and Planning* (Baltimore: Johns Hopkins University Press, 1994).

7. James Lovelock, *Healing Gaia: A New Prescription for the Living Planet* (New York: Crown, 1991).

8. And we also must recognize that about half of all water pollution in the United States is the result of air pollution. See, for example, Richard A. Smith, Richard B. Alexander, and M. Gordon Wolman, "Water-Quality Trends in the Nation's Rivers," *Science* 235 (27 March 1987): 1607–15; also of note is Charles E. Little, *The Dying of the Trees* (New York: Viking, 1995).

9. In 1996, the U.S. Environmental Protection Agency funded the Designwrights–Rio Grande Task Force members in order to create a new official governing organization for ecosystem management. Landscape architects and planners in other regions are engaged in similar efforts. For example, Tom Hunt, a landscape architect and soil scientist with a Ph.D. in environmental studies, has created and implemented a Partners in Conservation program at Wisconsin Power & Light Company in Madison.

8

SIGNATURE-BASED LANDSCAPE DESIGN

JOAN HIRSCHMAN WOODWARD

Look at the landscape around you: You see relationships. As I write, I look from my studio window in Sierra Madre, California, and see an acacia tree in full bloom, a brilliant yellow, explaining my recent bout with allergies and the dominant wind directions. I see lush green plants orbiting a nearby irrigation head, indicating the connection there between plants and water. Remnants of an old orange grove and an enclosing stone wall attest to the former agricultural estate that once stood here, linking me to a previous place in time. Recognizing relationships in landscapes grounds me in place, prods me to alertness, and brings an enthusiasm and zest to everyday life.

The science of ecology informs us about many landscape relationships. It explains, in part, why landscapes look and function the way they do, why they have changed, and how they may change in the future. Designers and planners use this information to understand landscapes because design and planning involve change. The information helps to shape goals and objectives that facilitate beneficial landscape interventions; it drives the models that predict impacts of future change, and eventually it assists the public and the client, as well as the designer and planner, in selecting a course of action. Ecological design recognizes complex relationships between people, the land, and a place, and it shapes decisions that may affect both positive site function and positive human response to that site.

Signature-based design grows out of a fascination with relationships. We can begin to characterize a place by seeing repeated relationships in a particular region. For example, trees that respond to additional moisture in an irrigation channel or along a stream are seen repeatedly throughout semi-arid and arid regions of the High Plains and the American West. Old home-steads and farms in the Middle West still reveal the protective sheath of trees planted to provide shade and protection from wind and soil erosion. Grids of pecan trees in the Deep South and southern New Mexico reflect efficiency and display a resulting beauty in agricultural production. These relationships are both of nature and of culture. They cumulatively characterize an area or region and advance a sense of recognition that potentially can lead to human attachment and vested interest in a place. These characterizations are crafted to a place, become familiar, and are missed when they are gone. They are sig-natures of a place.

The patterns sensed are not isolated objects, but are inextricably linked to the ecological, cultural, and economic processes that shape them. Thus, signature-based design is the act of understanding the signatures of a region or a site in terms of the processes that shape them and then applying these patterns to design and planning. Why? So we can understand what comprises the indicative relationships of a region, so we can determine which relation-ships best meet our current goals, and, finally, so we can artfully and sensi-bly use these to create inspired, conscientious designs and plans.

DETERMINING PATTERNS

According to Diane Ackerman: "Once is an instance. Twice may be an acci-dent. But three or more times makes a pattern."[1] We enjoy identifying pat-terns since they help us to derive order and meaning from chaos. Understanding a region's vegetation patterns is at first a dizzying task, but by reviewing research studies and photographs, and by carefully observing veg-etation, soils, water, and landforms, repeated patterns emerge at varying scales. For example, in the Denver, Colorado, area, the rocky, forested Front Range slopes that rise abruptly from the grassy plains are among the most prevalent patterns in that region. When driving, rock outcrops on the nearby Great Plains grasslands are repeatedly seen, accompanied by islands of trees and shrubs, repeating the same shift as seen from the air. Finally, when walk-ing, seeing perennial flowers bloom in rock crevices where additional mois-ture is available lends a sense of connectedness in scale to observations.

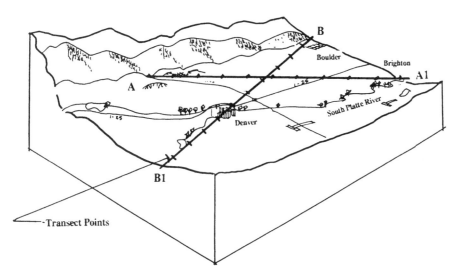

One technique to guide the process of looking for patterns, such as this one for the Denver region, is to draw two transects across the mapped-out region of one's inquiry, so they form an "X" across the region, with stopping points designated at regular intervals. Drive these transects, stop at the designated points, and look carefully for repeated vegetation arrangements at each stop. This will help break apart preconceptions and invite you to see the landscape and its signature patterns with fresh eyes.

In addition to spatial patterns, temporal patterns are evident within a region. Plants are telling markers of disturbance and succession. For example, shifts in forest composition can announce the presence or absence of fire in open space areas. Shifts in plant composition can also indicate disturbance and succession in urban areas. Mae Theilgaard Watts once described the evolution of a house and its garden plants over time: "There has been a definite succession of these plants, and the major ecological force in determining this succession has been *style*."[2]

Planting design eras can be described, based on the predominant ethos, as well as plant and resource availability. In many western communities, which developed after the 1850s, street tree plantings and flower-spotted parks proliferated following the 1893 Columbian Exposition's widespread influence; Victory Gardens emerged in neighborhoods during World War II; a competitive suburban lawn craze followed in the 1950s and 1960s; Xeriscape plants and principles appeared in gardens during the 1980s; and plants interbedded among recycled materials, such as reused concrete sidewalk pieces, designate the 1990s. In unraveling design eras and resultant plant arrangements, designers look for those that meet goals of creating positive site function and human response. In this way, they enlarge their vocabulary of regionally characteristic forms from which to choose when creating site designs.

Determining Regional Processes

Seeing repeated patterns linked in spatial and temporal scale is a satisfying first step in understanding a region's signatures. Simply identifying repeated visual expressions and recreating them in design situations, however, is an inadequate approach to meeting overall goals of positive site function and human response. According to William Marsh: "When we describe the forms and features of a landscape, we are actually observing the artifacts and fingerprints of the formative processes."[3]

Geomorphic, climatic, biotic, and cultural processes are largely responsible for shaping the landscape as we see it. Therefore, understanding these four interacting, formative processes is an essential part of deriving patterns from a place. Geomorphic processes are those activities determining underlying parent material and landforms. Climatic processes include precipitation, wind speeds, radiation, temperatures, lightning strikes and fire frequency, evaporation rates, and overall periods of climatic change. Studying biotic processes yields information about species colonization, adaptations, and succession. Wildlife and insect responses to plant growth also influence plant patterns. Finally, cultural processes include three driving motivators behind creating, shaping, or affecting vegetation patterns: The human need for protection, production, and meaning. Protective processes include efforts to provide protection from sun, wind, cold temperatures, and intruders. Productive strategies involve economics and making a living; thus, efficiency, domestication, technology, and transportation create distinctive forms of settlement, agriculture, and industry. The desire for beauty, pleasure, and meaning results in color concentrations, focal points and framed views, sensory design, repeated forms, a sense of mystery, drama, and symbolism. Political tools involving ordinances and plans institutionalize these cultural processes and ultimately reinforce or change prominent patterns.

By studying these interacting processes we can note the blurred line between human and nonhuman influences, although relative influence is apparent. For example, much of our urban landscape is primarily influenced by cultural processes: The need for protection, production, and meaning.

Geomorphic, climatic, and biotic influences can be overridden with bulldozers, air conditioning, irrigation, and insect spray. Yet the challenge to weave fitted patterns borne of all four processes into an urban setting is tantalizing. Understanding inherent landscape responses to these formative processes can guide us in creating new and retrofitted designs. Specifically, examining landscape responses through the expressive medium of plants is helpful to designers and planners who seek to create distinctive, appropriate designs and plans for a selected region.

Patterns: Vegetation Responses to Formative Processes

These four interacting processes shape distinctive vegetation responses within a region. We can look for these influences and describe how vegetation responds to them. In semiarid landscapes, geomorphic, climatic, and biotic processes interact to shape vegetation responses to aspect; for example, where larger, denser vegetation demarcates north-facing slopes. The repeated manifestations of these influences are then identified as patterns or signatures. It is important to note that patterns are to vegetation responses as weeds are to plants; they are human constructs, where judgment blends with observations. Plants do not grow in patterns unless people see repeated arrangements and declare them to be patterns.

As a demonstration for determining patterns within a region, consider a sampling of influences and resultant patterns for the Front Range region of Denver, Colorado. From the many repeated arrangements of plants found within any study area at a variety of scales, included here are those that reflect "the waterstain." The waterstain is the evidence of water as shouted out by the presence of plants. The cottonwoods tracing sickle-shaped river meanders, the stripes of cornflowers and Queen Anne's lace along the road pavement's edge, and the grasses growing out of concrete weep holes along a channelized stream are evidence of water availability in a dry landscape.

Water is the deciding criterion because of its importance in semiarid and arid regions as both a limiting factor and defining characteristic of the western landscape. Walter Prescott Webb, author of the classic *The Great Plains,* asserted that the primary unity of the West is a shortage of water and that "land in such areas cannot be utilized under the same methods that are employed in the region where precipitation is more than twenty inches."[4] Wallace Stegner's writing prods us to recognize that "aridity, more than anything else, gives the western landscape its character."[5] And Donald Worster describes the West as a "hydraulic society," with water as the defining factor in power and landscape decisions.[6]

The following selected patterns from the Denver area reflect remarkable, complex relationships between interacting processes that evoke a sense of the region's response to the limiting and defining factors of water.

Elevation

Increasing precipitation and evapotranspiration rates, sun and wind exposure, and gradients influence plant responses as elevation increases, creating what John Marr calls "climax regions."[7] Pattern expressions of elevational change include the dramatic stripes and interfingerings of plants seen as one travels from the Great Plains to the foothills of the Rocky Mountains. Elevations are somewhat predictable by knowing what plants are present and vice versa. Ann Zwinger eloquently describes this phenomenon: "The evergreen watermark now begins to stain lower on the slopes as the valley begins to rise."[8] Certain plants survive better at different elevations: Aspen blazing in fall color in montane meadows are most often weakened and stressed in suburban grassland settings, 2,000 feet lower in elevation. Seasonal waves of plants bloom and bear fruit earlier at lower elevations but shed leaves earlier at upper elevations. The upper treeline is determined by harsh climatic conditions above 11,400 feet. Likewise, the lower treeline is determined by droughty, fine-grained soils and competition by grasses. Combined, a distinct band of trees is visible between 6,000 and 11,400 feet.

Aspect

Branson, in his study on north- and south-facing slopes in the Denver area, comments that the "marked contrasts in vegetation types on hillsides with

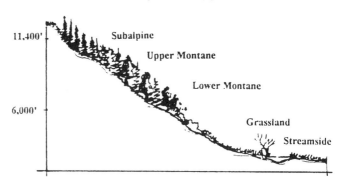

Stripes of vegetation express elevational changes.

North-facing slopes are marked by greater densities of larger plants.

South-facing slopes often exhibit a "patina of dots" pattern.

varying slopes and different exposures are familiar features of most landscapes with moderate to large topographic relief."[9] These stripes of vegetation affiliated with cooler, north-facing microclimates are notably clear at the aerial scale and found not only within the foothills themselves, but also along gentler slopes on the High Plains, where shrubs trace precisely the north-facing slopes. Their order and beauty are remarkable. Likewise, south-facing slopes are notable for dotted patterns of widely spaced plants or significant species changes between northern and southern exposures. Contrasts are notable at smaller scales as well, often wherever there is a vertical surface. Lichens growing on the north side of street trees in urban Denver attest to the manifestation of aspect influences on vegetation.

Water Concentration

Plants respond to varying moisture levels within all the patterns described here, but most notable are those vegetation responses to places of water concentration, such as streams, reservoirs, ditches, wetlands, and at the edges of impermeable surfaces, such as rocks, road edges, and sidewalks. At the largest scale, aerial views of Denver reveal clear meandering traces of water courses, marked by broad-leaved deciduous trees. This has been true since the late 1800s, when the advent of irrigation and perennial streams allowed

Plants form waterstains at the toes of slopes.

Rings of plants around wetlands often mark the availability of water.

Plants in sidewalk cracks respond to water runoff.

water-dependent trees and shrubs to flourish. Prior to this time it is thought that bison trampling and grassland fires prevented the colonization of riparian species.[10] Toes of slope are evident from responding shifts in plant species, densities, and colors. Rings of herbaceous plants indicate, in part, the gradient and relative water availability around a wetland. At the next scale down, shrubs crouching in concave gullies and valley bottoms indicate increased water availability than exists in the surrounding grasslands. At even smaller scales, water and soil collection along road and rock edges, highway embankments, and sidewalk cracks *reliably* results in luxuriant plant growth, often by opportunists from other continents that have found their niche in exotic America.

Soil

Soils greatly affect the availability of moisture for plants, and distinct vegetation changes often indicate underlying contact points between soil types. Within the Plains, for example, ponderosa pine (also called rock pine by early botanists) and shrub islands within grasslands indicate isolated sites of rocky soil conditions, forming reservoirs of water for probing tap roots. In the foothills, stripes of plants respond to changes in soil type, with grasses dominating fine-grained shales and trees and shrubs restricted to the "rocky backbone" of eroding sandstones.[11] Plant responses at a smaller scale provide cultural clues, as compelling today as they were in Watts's time when

Larger plants indicate underlying coarser soils.

she and her colleagues used plants and other clues to decode the age of an abandoned schoolhouse.[12] A former homestead site in the grasslands is evident only through the tracery of shrubs growing where the old foundation broke through the sod and fine-grained soils, increasing water availability for the shrub roots.

Disturbance/Lack of Disturbance

Events causing significant disruption from normal patterns in ecological systems are described as disturbances. It is difficult to generalize about vegetation responses to disturbance in any area, especially in one as complex as the Colorado Front Range.[13] A few of the widespread patterns are disturbance patches from insect and fire outbreaks, although, due to long-term fire suppression, insect-affected forests are more widespread than the fire-affected forests during the past century. Fire patches within the urban/suburban area tend to be small due to rapid suppression. Forest ecologists, however, expect that as urbanization spreads farther into fire-prone forested foothill areas and as fuel loads rise from continued fire suppression, a major conflagration of intense heat and speed could potentially move beyond the control of fire departments, burning forests and houses and setting the successional clock back to a grassland matrix.[14] Grazing, another large-scale disturbance, has resulted in the replacement of native bunchgrasses with exotic broad-leaved herbaceous plants and dotted landscapes of unpalatable remains such as yucca and cacti.[15] Urbanization has occurred over a period of 150 years within the region, but native plants were not completely removed. As habi-

Trees signify rocky reservoirs of available water.

tat decreased, plants migrated into infrequently disturbed remnant areas and have persisted. Thus, traveling through industrial corridors, fugitive native grasses are sometimes glimpsed along railroad right-of-ways, road edges, river corridors, and other unmanicured areas. As Denver's interest in greenway design grew, however, these natives ironically were displaced by turf and trees, victims of what can be termed "vegetation gentrification."

Protection Needs

Human need for comfort and protection from Denver's strong, cold, drying winds and shelter from its summer heat is responsible for a number of plant patterns within the region. Many of these patterns are best seen in areas planted prior to the widespread availability of electricity and air conditioning. Hedgerows lining agricultural fields on the north and west sides of the area form filters, ranging from a line of individual trees to a dense aggregate of conifers and deciduous trees, many imported from similar arid steppe-type environments. Snowfences are used throughout this area to block snow from drifting on highways. Occasionally shrubs and perennial plants can be seen on the windward side of these fences, growing heartily in response to additional moisture concentrating predictably to the north and west of this protective feature. Other microclimate patterns include the square of summershading deciduous trees surrounding farm and ranch homes in the Plains, with an accompanying fence-line square of wind-interrupting conifers surrounding the home and associated farm and ranch buildings. Many homesteads are marked by a single cottonwood tree to the southwest, its leafy

Fugitive plants populate seldom-disturbed corridors such as railroad right-of-ways, streams, and roads.

Homestead trees provide summer shade but permit winter light.

shade reducing glare and providing comfort. These plant patterns frequently can be seen long after the houses have been removed and land uses have changed. In urban settings, the need for climate control and visual order was derived from dense street tree plantings and cooling urban parks and parkways, originally envisioned in 1858 and eventually threading throughout the Denver urban core.[16] More recent protection patterns are visible in the region; more than one suburban resident has strategically placed cacti beneath windows to dissuade potential intruders.

Production Needs

Productive vegetation patterns are those in which plants are managed for production of food, either crops or grasses intended for grazing. Aerial views of the Denver area reveal quilts of various themes: Squares aligned with the American Survey, 133-acre pivot-irrigated circles, grids of orchards and fields, and fence-line and canal-line plants. Sunflowers often are seen lining the edges of plowed fields, forming a bright yellow frame around verdant crops. At smaller scales, one can enjoy the predictable association between fruiting shrubs and their inevitable location at the base of a bird-perch fencepost. Kenneth Helphand in his book on Colorado identifies signs of rural prosperity: "Substantial farmhouses, well-fenced and well-farmed fields, and a 'vast congregation of grain and hay stacks'." Lawns appearing in Denver's suburbs are an "atavistic attachment to the land and a reminder of a rural past,"[17] but unlike the small garden patches prevalent throughout urban and suburban backyards, they do not serve direct productive needs. Edible garden patches

Urban reprieves provide shelter from harsh climatic conditions.

rise and fall in number throughout Denver's history, peaking in 1944, when forty-two thousand Victory Gardens were planted to support the war effort.[18]

Order Needs

Vegetation responses to human needs for order and pleasure are most distinctly seen during times when water availability is scarce: Priorities become very clear when seedlings must be watered with buckets from a stream or well. As early as 1864, cottonwood branches were trimmed and placed along Denver's streets to provide eventual shade and a sense of aesthetic order. Tree plantings were later supported and proliferated by the Denver irrigation ditch network. As homes were built, plants also defined property boundaries, with trimmed hedges planted along otherwise invisible lines separating adjacent properties. Parks were developed to provide a sense of urban oasis and, also, to serve as "passive beauty spots" in the hard urban environment.[19] Introductions to the city parks and civic buildings featured blazing

Birds sow plants by fenceposts.

Attractive plants mark entrances as urban "beauty spots."

"Polite introduction" plants appear at suburban town entrances.

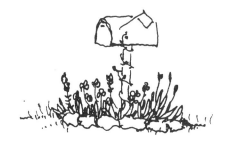

"Polite introduction" plants occur at the residential scale near mailboxes.

announcements by annual flower beds. These are now repeated at larger scales at freeway entrances to cities within the region, as well as at smaller scales in commercial and residential development entries. At the smallest scale, mailboxes and connections between driveways and front doors receive special attention in introducing one's sense of order and beauty. Overall, vegetation patterns are driven by the need for polite introductions, property definitions, marking movement corridors, and making homes visible or invisible. These vegetation responses to the four formative forces are clearly influenced by both nature and culture.

APPLYING PATTERNS

Objectives and Guidelines

This method of understanding processes and resultant patterns supplies us with a wellspring of regionally derived, familiar forms from which to draw design inspiration, but two inadvisable design temptations inevitably emerge. The first is to sieve through the patterns, selecting those that appeal visually to us, and then recreate them randomly at a new location. Many attractive garden design books are filled with beautifully photographed patterns inspiring designers and homeowners to do just that: To disembody patterns from their processes and piece them into purely aesthetic designs. A thorough site analysis should precede pattern application to relate site processes with those shaping regional patterns. For example, the north side of a building provides a cooler microclimate in the northern hemisphere that is more appropriate for applying plant groupings that are more shade tolerant or are from higher elevations. Climate and landforms should be considered before applying patterns randomly to a site.

The second temptation is to consider all patterns equally useful in design simply because they are characteristic of a region. Many exceedingly common patterns within a region are inappropriate for future applications. In the Denver area, for example, juniper shrub belts cinch tightly around suburban home foundations, surrounded by a larger ring of turf. Turf and shrubs clad both northern and southern exposures of a property, obscuring the inherent regional clarity of aspect patterns and requiring irrigation to supplement higher evapotranspiration rates along the southern exposure. These patterns do not meet overall planting design goals of creating positive site function and human response. Therefore, carefully crafted regional objectives are needed to set the stage for appropriate regional design applications. Patterns that fail to meet these objectives should not be considered as future design models.

The following regionally based objectives are shaped for the Denver area, but also apply to most design schemes in any region:

Acknowledge and design for flows:

- Decrease off-site water importation and flow.
- Decrease heating and cooling requirements.
- Provide for movement and habitat needs.
- Maintain nutrients on a site to the extent possible.

Respect cultural, physical, psychological, social, and budgetary needs:

- Allow for individual site interpretation.
- Acknowledge historical, geographical, and cultural affiliations.
- Provide comfort, visual and sensual pleasure, safety, and movement.
- Provide settings for interaction and privacy.
- Create designs that are affordable to maintain over time.

Guidelines based on regional objectives and patterns present research findings in a palatable form for landscape decision makers' use. These guidelines are intended not to restrict designers' creativity; rather, they should open up possibilities and options based on using patterns to create positive site function, human response, and regional distinctiveness. Thus, forms generated can be geometric or nonlinear. The species one selects can be native, naturalized, or imported, but one should avoid detrimentally contagious species such as Russian olive trees, salt cedar, purple loose strife, and other habitat conquerors. Design concepts can be derived from a favorite artist or a client's quirks. The method is inclusive of all these choices. Guidelines are simply intended to help determine where to place plants in accordance with larger geomorphic, climatic, biotic, and cultural processes as expressed through plant patterns in the selected region. A sampling of guidelines, applicable at the full variety of scales, follows:

- Where grades change, celebrate the differences between northern and southern exposures at similar elevations by placing larger plants at greater densities on north faces, or selecting more mesic species.
- Announce the presence of a water concentration at slope breaks or concavities by using larger plants than on slopes.

- Plan for and incorporate into designs plants that respond to breaks in impermeable surfaces.
- Where water concentrates, mark the gradient changes with plants of different moisture requirements.
- Plan for and incorporate plants dispersed by wildlife at edges such as fenceposts, telephone poles, and other vertical surfaces.
- Reflect soil shifts from fine-to-coarse-grained materials with smaller-to-larger plants.
- Utilize trees associated with homesteads on southwest building corners to recall earlier planting patterns and to provide microclimate comfort for homes.
- Utilize notable plants in key locations to provide "polite introductions" or "beauty spots."

In applying patterns and guidelines to design, designers can use their preferred design process of interviewing clients, analyzing site and regional contexts, and deriving appropriate concepts. An additional step is to scrutinize the design site and vicinity for repeated vegetation patterns that meet regional and site objectives. Guidelines can be streamlined to suggest the use of these patterns. Following the application of patterns to the design site, spatial and temporal scales must be considered. Examples of applying this process are illustrated through the following residential design project in Boulder, Colorado.

Site-Scale Design

The site is typical of upper-middle-class homes within Boulder's southernmost suburban development, constructed during the early 1980s. The home is located on the open space–suburban interface and has 180-degree views of the shift between the Rocky Mountains and the Great Plains. Soils are well drained and rocky, with scattered clay lens. The surrounding open-space vegetation is composed of ponderosa pines invading a remnant tallgrass prairie. The pines, having previously been outcompeted by fire-adapted grasses, are taking advantage of adjacent suburban fire suppression policies and are increasing in density.

Following client interviews to shape site-specific objectives, site patterns prevalent on-site and within the vicinity are described and dia-

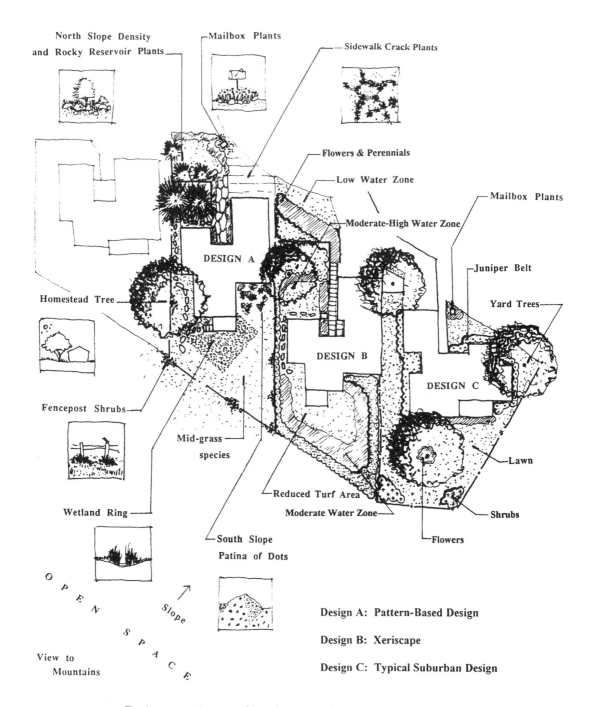

North Slope Density and Rocky Reservoir Plants

Mailbox Plants

Sidewalk Crack Plants

Flowers & Perennials

Low Water Zone

Mailbox Plants

Moderate-High Water Zone

Juniper Belt

DESIGN A

Homestead Tree

Yard Trees

DESIGN B

DESIGN C

Fencepost Shrubs

Mid-grass species

Lawn

Wetland Ring

Reduced Turf Area

Moderate Water Zone

Shrubs

South Slope Patina of Dots

Flowers

OPEN SPACE

Slope

View to Mountains

Design A: Pattern-Based Design

Design B: Xeriscape

Design C: Typical Suburban Design

This plan compares three types of design: Pattern-based (or signature-based), Xeriscape, and typical (or traditional) suburban.

grammed. These are integrated into the design, using applicable guidelines. Three popular design approaches are illustrated for comparison. Xeriscape design (Design B, page 216), or water-conserving landscape design, involves zoning plants for microclimate control, reducing turf areas, and reducing evapotranspiration through the use of mulches and efficient irrigation. Xeriscape design promotes the "greening" of semiarid garden landscapes while encouraging water conservation. This is its principal goal; designing for regional distinctiveness is not a stated Xeriscape goal.[20] A more typical suburban response to residential landscape design is also presented (Design C).

The signature-based design incorporates overlapping patterns that are reflective of a site and sympathetic to regional processes (Design A). For example, the north side of the building behaves as a large rock outcrop would: It creates a cooler microclimate and water evaporates less quickly here. Drawing from north-slope patterns results in a concentration of larger, denser plants; in this case, pines. These must be carefully placed, however, to avoid branches that make contact with the roof and increase wind damage or fire hazard. The north-slope pattern overlaps a water concentration pattern and is acknowledged by the location of larger plants at the hinge between slope and toe of slope. Also, the contact between permeable and impermeable surfaces invites larger plant growth and reinforces the presence of pines. Likewise, fencepost shrubs, taking advantage of increased nutrients and water, provide reinforced property boundaries, a protective need. One post is left unplanted, allowing the clients to await patiently its inevitable sowing. The homestead tree, a pattern from the mid-1800s, is placed according to microclimate needs, historical precedence, and water concentration, since gutter water supplements runoff at this location. The wetland ring pattern guides planting of more mesic species at the site's low point, surrounded by slightly less mesic species, and then ringed by xeric midgrass species. Urban order patterns guide the use of flat, rectangular paving stones in the front walkway, and water concentration patterns guide the use of scented herbs between pavers and along the stone edges. Order also determines larger plants next to the roadway, but so do water concentration patterns. "Polite introduction" patterns beckon when placing plants beneath the mailbox, but small-scale aspect patterns guide the denser placement of flowers on the north side of the post. Overlapping patterns are desired; the more the better, so that the resulting design begins to tell a story about climate, soil, landform, birds, plants, and the landowner.

A bird's-eye view of signature-based residential design.

The overall composition is guided by a designer's or homeowner's taste for formality or naturalness, spatial needs, individual program desires, and plant selection desires. For example, plants shown here are arranged on a grid, responding to the building's lines, but shifted when responding to mountain views and fence orientation. Many homeowners, however, prefer curvilinear lines. The design shown above is additive in that it assumes a clean grassland slate with a house and neighbors and responds to resulting processes with plant additions. A subtractive approach could also be taken, removing trees and shrubs and exposing grassland areas. These decisions are left to the discretion and creativity of the designer, the client, or both.

The pattern-based approach offers information about how plants respond to formative processes. As long as principles are recognized, designers freely interpret the application. The approach does not restrict using plants with higher water requirements, and a lawn or turf substitute can replace the wetland ring area, for example, if children's play or pet use are issues. It should be located in the most waterstained, level area, appropriate for turfgrass. Planting mesic lawn species uniformly on south- and north-facing slopes, however, would not follow objectives, guidelines, or patterns and is not recommended.

Larger Temporal and Spatial Scale Considerations

It is useful to project forward to consider how an individual design will change over time. If we were to complete all drawings of a single residence along the *y*-axis (time), we would see the maturation of the planting design

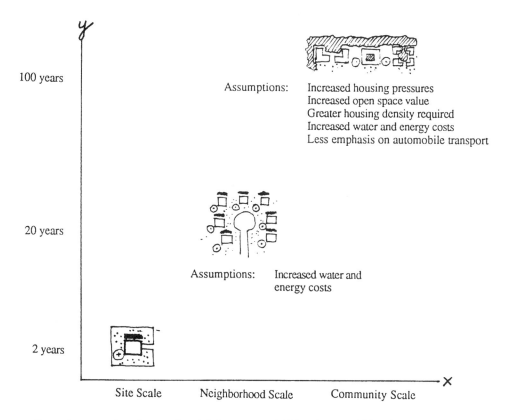

Comparing a sampling of pattern-based designs over spatial (x) and temporal (y) scales.

over a one-hundred-year period. Homestead trees will mature, north-face plant concentrations will continue to take advantage of cooler microclimates, and xeric grasses on southern exposures will self-perpetuate to form sod. As forecasted, this will reduce heating, cooling, and maintenance requirements, as well as meet other stated objectives over time.

In projecting beyond a single residential design, how might existing neighborhoods and new communities appear if signature-based design was employed at increasingly larger scales, as represented by the x-axis. First, we need to know what assumptions we are making about conditions surrounding our site in the future, such as that land, water, energy, and open space value will increase. Based upon these assumptions, signature-based designs adopted by the original single-family residence likely would spread to other homes in the neighborhood, due to the benefits offered, and to a neighborhood "contagion" effect: This is a familiar pattern in neighborhoods, where one person's innovation is "borrowed" and incorporated in adjacent properties. Over a one-hundred-year period, assumptions are made that land and energy value increases may spark redesign of single-family residences to higher-density housing with reduced automobile access. Signature-based design can also be applied at this larger-scale, higher-density design scenario. This type of projection forward is a necessary step to envision the results of design over time and space.

Evaluating Designs

We need to evaluate our design work and compare pattern-based design to the two neighboring designs described earlier: Traditional and Xeriscape-based design. The Xeriscape design (Design B, page 216) acceptably meets objectives. The design is based on popular perennial border design forms. It is a useful approach that conserves water and is pleasing to many clients. It is a base from which to build more distinctive design forms. The traditional design (Design C) of lawn, foundation shrubs, and yard trees is based on the juniper belt and lawn design forms prevalent throughout the study area; the resulting typical suburban design fails to meet most objectives.

Like Xeriscape, pattern-based planting design (Design A) will help to conserve resources and reduce landscape expenditures by placing plants where they will survive better with less maintenance. This appeals to developers, homeowners, and municipalities alike. Pattern-based design approach

Three Design Approaches Evaluated in Terms of Regional Objectives.

Evaluation Criteria	Signature-Based Design A	Xeriscape Design B	Traditional Design C
• *Acknowledge and design for flows:*			
Decrease off-site water importation and flow	+	+	−
Decrease cooling and heating requirements	+	√	−
Provide for species movement and habitat needs	+	√	√
Maintain nutrients on-site as much as possible	+	√	−
• *Respect human psychological, cultural, physical, social, and economic needs:*			
Allow for individual site interpretation	+	√	−
Acknowledge history and cultural affiliations	+	√	√
Provide comfort, visual and sensual pleasure, safety	+	√	−
Provide settings for interactions and privacy	+	+	−
Create designs that are affordable over time	+	+	−

+   Design meets objectives well
√   Design moderately meets objectives
−   Design does not meet objectives

differs from Xeriscape, however, by providing processes and patterns to inspire form-generation and to provide more choices than those forms commonly distilled from temperate climate designs. Drawing on these expanded choices can help to counteract today's prevalent homogeneity in planting design and move toward more appropriate regional designs.

Questions arise, however: If the signature-based, or pattern-based, design becomes incorporated into municipal codes, do we run the risk of creating new landscape homogeneity? Designers' creative explorations and homeowners' imaginative interpretations of place should mitigate this potential risk, and this approach encourages such exploration and imagination within the parameters of regional processes.

Does this method advocate purging or redesigning Denver's notable City Beautiful parks, lawns, and median strips because they do not show discretionary use of water? In a regional sense, these historical "beauty spots" *do* meet the criteria for using water where it is most valued. Denver's legacy of parks and parkways is integral to its distinctiveness. These must not be redesigned with waterstain patterns unless they are part of the original design. City Beautiful designs must be respected and preserved as a reminder of the past attitude toward civic design and the relationship between landscape design and cultural and political institutions. New design, however, should reflect regional processes and the necessity of resource conservation. We must create a new aesthetic based on responsible application of our resource awareness.

Finally, do the patterns distinguish Denver from other semiarid cities such as Cheyenne, Salt Lake City, or Santa Fe? Yes. Many of the patterns described are common to most semiarid cities, but many also isolate trends and habits of a particular region. Helphand indicates a pattern frequently seen in Denver, based on context: "There is a Colorado landscape aesthetic . . . it includes mountain silhouettes and distant vistas, piñon pines on red slopes, golden aspen in wavy bands, wildflowers in meadows and rock crevices, the soft band of trees along a stream, and rocks. In popular and personal form, these elements are miniaturized and condensed in residential landscapes."[21] Many of the landscape features will be similar but not identical between semiarid regions. Cultural expressions based on history, geography, and contemporary influences are expected to provide distinctive patterns. Part of the challenge is rooting out patterns that do not travel well.[22]

MOVING FORWARD

Prospect is defined as an outlook, a possibility. Early authors of ecological design and planning approaches were ignited by the prospect of applying ecological principles to select suitable land-use locations and to accommodate necessary natural processes. The word *ecological* was needed at the time to distinguish this type of design from *aesthetic* design, which did not recognize complex ecological relationships on a systematic basis. Numerous successful applications of ecological designs show the metamorphosis from possibility to reality. Yet many ecological designs have also been critiqued for not accommodating fully people's need for order, meaning, and beauty. Now we can anticipate the next prospect: Where understanding ecological relationships and human desires are so ingrained in all design and planning processes that no "ecological" or "aesthetic" modifiers will be necessary. Understanding ecological relationships and human needs must become the norm if design and planning disciplines are to move forward responsibly and creatively.

Signature-based design reflects this new prospect. This design approach fulfills both goals of design: Using the medium of plants to create positive site function and positive human response. From a functional standpoint, it makes sense to design in accordance with dominant processes to save energy and resources and to increase the likelihood of a design's integrity and maintenance over time. As more people are drawn to live in cities such as Denver and Albuquerque, the cumulative savings from such modest individual measures will become increasingly important.

The goal of creating positive human response is also fulfilled through signature-based design. Instead of settling for developers' mass-marketed preconceptions of landscape beauty, we can implement patterns to tell a story, filled with information and fondness for the places where we live and work. Our mailbox and entryway treatments, homestead trees, and striking north-facing slope densities become intelligible "words" that combine to form "sentences" describing responses to order, protection, and aspect. These sentences then build to describe the (con)text of the region: The geomorphic, climatic, biotic, and cultural processes ultimately responsible for the entire design language.

Legible designs can be built from the seamless consideration of what are, unfortunately, still considered opposites: Nature and culture, past and present, small scale and large scale. It is my hope that evidence of this work over time will signify that what we ultimately scribe with signature-based design is the word *respect*.

NOTES

Illustrations by Kiku Kurahashi and the author.

The author gratefully acknowledges the support and assistance of an invaluable advisory group: Carolyn Etter, Kenneth Helphand, John Lyle, and Frederick Steiner. Grants from the Landscape Architecture Foundation and California State Polytechnic University, Pomona, have provided important financial support, and Kiku Kurahashi's illustration skills have greatly enhanced this work.

1. Murphy, Neill, and Ackerman 1993, p. 11.
2. Watts 1982, p. 320.
3. Marsh 1991, p. 43.
4. Webb 1931, p. 8.
5. Stegner 1992, p. 46.

6. Worster 1985, p. 7.

7. Marr 1961; Marr and Boyd 1979.

8. Zwinger 1988, p. 6. See, also, Mather, Karan, and Thompson, 1992, pp. 26–27.

9. Branson 1989, p. 1.

10. Knopf 1986.

11. Marr 1961, p. 21.

12. Watts 1982, pp. 137–47.

13. See Marr 1961; Peet 1981; and Veblen and Lorenz 1991.

14. Edminster, U.S.D.A. Forest Service Ecologist, personal communication, 22 July 1994. See, also, Little 1995, pp. 81–92 and 131.

15. Clark et al. 1980.

16. See Wilson 1989, especially chaps. 8 and 11.

17. Helphand and Manchester 1991, p. 147 and p. 171.

18. U.S.D.A. and State Agricultural Colleges Cooperating Extension Service Annual Report 1944.

19. Etter 1986.

20. Burand 1992, p. 2.

21. Helphand and Manchester 1991, p. 171.

22. Ryden 1993.

REFERENCES

Branson, F. A. 1989. "Contrasts of Vegetation, Soils, Microclimates, and Geomorphic Processes between North- and South-facing Slopes on Green Mountain near Denver, CO." Denver: U.S. Geological Survey Water Resources Investigations Report. 89–4094.

Burand, S. 1992. "Xeriscape: Yesterday and Tomorrow." *Xeriscape Colorado! Newsletter* (Denver).

Clark, S. V., P. J. Webber, V. Komárková, and W. A. Weber. 1980. "Map of Mixed Prairie Grassland Vegetation, Rocky Flats, Colorado." Boulder: Institute of Arctic and Alpine Research Occasional Paper No. 35.

Etter, D. 1986. "A Legacy of Green." *Colorado Heritage* 3: 9–16.

Helphand, K. I., and E. Manchester. 1991. *Colorado: Visions of an American Landscape.* Niwot, Colo.: Roberts Rinehart.

Knopf, F. L. 1986. "Changing Landscapes and the Cosmopolitanism of the Eastern Colorado Avifauna." *Wildlife Society Bull.* 14(2): 132–42.

Little, C. E. 1995. *The Dying of the Trees: The Pandemic in America's Forests.* New York: Viking.

Marr, J. W. 1961. *Ecosystems of the East Slope of the Front Range in Colorado.* Boulder: University of Colorado Press.

Marr, J. W., and W. S. Boyd. 1979. "Vegetation in the Greater Denver Area, Front Range Urban Corridor, Colorado," U.S. Geol. Survey Misc. Investigations Series Map I–856–I.

Marsh, W. M. 1991. *Landscape Planning: Environmental Applications.* New York: John Wiley & Sons.

Mather, C., P. P. Karan, and G. F. Thompson. 1992. *Beyond the Great Divide: Denver to the Grand Canyon.* New Brunswick: Rutgers University Press.

Murphy, P., W. Neill, and D. Ackerman. 1993. *By Nature's Design.* San Francisco: Chronicle Books.

Peet, R. K. 1981. "Forest Vegetation of the Colorado Front Range: Composition and Dynamics. *Vegetatio* 45: 3–75.

Ryden, K. C. 1993. *Mapping the Invisible Landscape: Folklore, Writing, and the Sense of Place.* Iowa City: University of Iowa Press.

Stegner, W. 1992. *Where the Bluebird Sings to the Lemonade Springs: Living and Writing in the West.* New York: Penguin Books.

United States Department of Agriculture and State Agricultural Colleges Cooperating Extension Service. 1944. *Combined Annual Report of County Extension Workers* (Denver).

Veblen, T. T., and D. C. Lorenz. 1991. *The Colorado Front Range: A Century of Ecological Change.* Salt Lake City: University of Utah Press.

Watts, M. T. 1982. *Reading the Landscape of America.* New York: Collier Books.

Webb, W. P. 1931. *The Great Plains.* New York: Grosset and Dunlap.

Wilson, W. H. 1989. *The City Beautiful Movement.* Baltimore: Johns Hopkins University Press.

Worster, D. 1985. *Rivers of Empire: Water, Aridity, and the Growth of the American West.* New York: Pantheon Books.

Zwinger, A. 1988. *Beyond the Aspen Grove.* Tucson: University of Arizona Press.

GALLERY II

PHOTOGRAPHS BY STEVE MARTINO

Suburban front yard, Phoenix

Before (1976): A fairly typical suburban situation of a new characterless house being plopped down on a subdivision lot where all traces of the natural landscape have been erased.

226

"BEFORE" AND "AFTER" PICTURES OF MARTINO PROJECTS

After (1983): The project captures space from the required but useless front yard and creates an entry court that also mitigates the interior house views to the street. This was an early attempt by me to create a "desert landscape." Desert plants from Arizona, Australia, Mexico, South America, and Africa were used to supplement the native species that were commercially available.

The Arizona Cardinals training facility

Before (1990): A facility, jointly owned by a municipality and an NFL football team and situated on an alfalfa field. The owner requested a desert character for the landscape.

After (1995): By now I was well experienced in desert building and restoration, and so I developed a landscape process that brought the landscape well beyond the project's modest budget. This project says that eighty years of farming activity can be looked at as a temporary land use.

Arid zone trees

Before (1988): An Arizona cotton farmer anticipating future water cost wanted to change his crops from cotton and grapes to desert trees.

After (1992): *The farmer wanted an entry garden to showcase his trees. The entry wall's elements develop and define the nursery entry. A secondary goal was to experiment with methods of returning the farmland back to desert once it is taken out of production.*

Ullman Terrace

Before (1989): A parking lot and storage area behind a notable historic building at the Desert Botanical Garden in Phoenix.

After (1992): I approached the garden and volunteered to create a prototype public space that would expose the public to the special character of the Sonoran Desert. This highly popular "garden" is rented out for private functions and booked months in advance. It has become a model for other projects as well as public space in general.

Hawkinson residence, Phoenix

Before (1992): This modest subdivision house was built on a postage-stamp-size lot next to a collector street. The owner wanted a refuge from life beyond the wall.

After (1994): New walls screen the fussy window slots in the existing subdivision perimeter wall. The walls relate the space back to the house, create secret rooms, and amplify and direct the fountain's sound back to the house. The space has been transformed from a very small yard to the biggest room in the house.

PART III

RESPECT

9

BEYOND STEWARDSHIP TOWARD PARTNERSHIP

SALLY SCHAUMAN

Stewardship is a sacred word in landscape architecture. Environmentalists intone it endlessly in mission statements as a ritualistic blessing on the worthiness of those who set goals. To say that we will be stewards of the landscape implies we will do what is right. As landscape architects, most of us try to do our best; we use the word a lot. We chant "stewardship" while the world's environment degrades increasingly toward a wasteland. The destruction of our human habitat has become so complete that eminent biologists, such as Edward O. Wilson, are now asking the question, "Is humanity suicidal?"[1] The magnitude of our self-destruction compels us to question the relevancy of stewardship, to question our ability to do what is right in the landscape. Now is the time to examine our failures and to rechart a future. Now is the moment to come out from under the comforting mantle of stewardship and to redefine radically our relationship with the landscape.

It is clear why stewardship is so popular: It is a hopeful word, it appeals to our sense of worth, it even sounds righteous. Stewardship of the landscape is a notion that fits with the conventional wisdom that human beings have a God-given dominion over the earth. As Keith Thomas asserts in *Man and the Natural World,* the ascendancy of man (his word) over the natural world became complete in the minds of men during the medieval era when theology "elevated him to a wholly different status, halfway between the beasts and the angels."[2] While evoking stewardship as a call to do what is right, man recognizes the continuing degradation of the earth.

Man's guilt for the degradation requires explanation. In Western literature, two themes are common. First, there is the direct "not guilty" plea (i.e., "he did it, not me!"). Simply put, I am a steward, but my brother is not. This version is heard often when one group accuses another of abusing a landscape. A familiar example is when landscape architects and planners blame developers for landscape degradation. Another theme is the guilty-by-reason-of-ignorance plea or the "they misread *Genesis*" notion. In this version, degradation is blamed on a Judeo-Christian tradition that overemphasizes the dominion command of God in the Bible and neglects God's admonition to care for our earthly gifts. In other words, some American environmental writers surveying the damage declare that religion is the culprit, not individual decision makers.[3] In both pleas, and in other variations, the basic premises do not change. Man controls completely from a superior position; he is either an intelligent sinner or an ignorant reader of Western religious tradition. Some writers blame more than religion and point to Western culture as the culprit. They describe white man as more egocentric than the yellow, brown, or red man; thus, white man is a global culprit. The fact is that all of the earth, everywhere, is damaged. Try to imagine a square mile on earth that is not stressed in some way by the actions of human beings. Even remote beaches give evidence of oil-soaked wildlife, trees are dying all over the globe, and the most tended agricultural landscapes erode. No one religion, no single race or gender, and no specific culture can be blamed for the advanced state of the earth's environmental degradation.

Perhaps because the ecological situation is so desperate, people seek a quasi-spiritual word such as *stewardship* for solace, to give us and the land some hope. If all of us can be stewards, if all of us will just do what is right, then surely the world's environmental condition will take a turn for the better. Certainly, the word *stewardship* is a convenient sound bite for politicians and an effective buzzword around which to organize citizen groups. Perhaps for the general public and for the neophyte environmentalist the concept of stewardship has efficacy and merit. But for an increasing number of environmental professionals, and especially for environmental designers and landscape architects, stewardship today rings more like a shallow commitment. However benevolent it seems, it is not benign.

Stewardship's roots are embedded firmly in the assumption that people *control* the earth. Some still hold out the promise of better stewardship as a redeeming factor, but most of us should acknowledge that our attempt at stewardship has largely failed. For landscape architecture, the evocation of stewardship means we naively believe that we are still working with a healthy landscape into which we can gently fit sensitive designs; we still see the landscape through the gaze of benevolent protection. We should know better. Few designs endure as healthy ecosystems for either people or other species, and few developed landscapes have grown healthier because of our designs. Certainly landscape architects have made parts of our earth more livable and socially valuable. Likewise, the work of landscape architects have made some landscapes a bit healthier, but these are so scarce among the massively abused landscapes that they too often make little difference. For environmental designers, stewardship has turned out to be an arrogant ethic that has produced sorry results while allowing us to forego our penance for destroying the earth.

When environmental designers evoke stewardship as an ethic, they rarely refer to religion as Ian McHarg and Nancy Denig did, and they usually point to Aldo Leopold as the spiritual leader for their fervor. Since Leopold, environmental design orthodoxy has held that active stewardship would conserve our planet's health. Yet Leopold neither chose stewardship as *the* operative word of his proposed land ethic nor as the main way to describe man's ethical relationship to the landscape:

> Health is the capacity of the land for self-renewal.
> Conservation is our effort to understand and
> preserve this capacity.[4]

Leopold wrote about man as a member of a biological community. He was hopeful that we would recognize our human needs as a part of the biological community and that we would not trade off these needs solely for economic benefits. Leopold was accurate about our biological community needs, but he was overly optimistic about man's motives and, unfortunately, he was not a prophet of human actions. We now know more about the relationship of human health to the natural world. For example, people are healthier when they can see and interact with nature even if only in small portions or even if it is only nearby. We have defined biological and psychological needs for the landscape. But this new knowledge of our need for nature nearby has not changed our actions; we still assault the landscape at a rate far greater than our ability to conserve, much less to preserve it. Sadly, in the sixty-three years since Leopold first discussed the need for a land ethic in print, we have "managed" our planet to the brink of its limits to self-renew. The health of our habitat, and especially the urban environment, is totally and perhaps terminally afflicted.

The time for Leopold's notion of conservation for the land's self-renewal is almost gone forever. We must act now to heal what we have almost destroyed. Landscape architects can act in three basic ways: They can advocate forcefully for the full range of biological and social values of the landscape; they can radically redefine an ethical relationship to the landscape; and they can lovingly begin to restore the damaged landscape bit by bit.

Landscape architects must be aggressive and steadfast advocates for the full range of landscape—urban, rural, and wild. The landscape has intrinsic biological and spiritual (or emotional) value for all people who inhabit it. Basically, people feel better and are healthier when they can see, touch, and connect physically or mentally with the land. The landscape can improve water quality and reduce flood damage; it may even enhance air quality. We know these things to be true in our hearts and in our heads, yet we still act as though the landscape's only value is the one given it by the tax assessor or real estate agent. The main causes of landscape degradation are the myths that the supply of land is unlimited and that its biological and social values defy accountability. Landscape architects and scholars engaged in landscape research know differently. The landscape's range of values must be recognized and taken into account; they cannot be trivialized or marginalized. The landscape is not merely a setting for architectural or engineering designs. We should demand that landscape accountability start now.

Recently, two landscape architects, each following different professional directions, discussed this basic need to account for landscape value. Martha Schwartz describes how the persistent undervaluation of the landscape leads to our current urban blight: "our cities . . . are not only environmentally degraded, they are also visually and spiritually degraded . . . these neglected landscapes add up, piece by piece, to the ubiquitous ugly environment so identifiably American."[5] Anne Spirn echoes the same conclusion. She points out that, amid a renewed interest in special landscapes such as "private gardens, public places as landscape art, wilderness preservation and global landscape change . . . most of the everyday landscape of city, suburb, and region within which we all live receives little or no attention." She further characterizes the landscape as "communal, long-term intellectual, spiritual, and complex," thus not valued by our society, which "promotes the individual, the immediate, the material, and the straightforward."[6]

How do we promote the value of the everyday, common landscape? Should it be an index of its naturalism, its nearness to human life and culture, or its site-specific ability to improve air, water, wildlife habitat, or soil quality? Should it be its ability to be memorable, to sweeten our dreams, and to lift our spirits? My answer is—yes, all of these and more. Every square foot of a landscape not occupied by structures has an ecological value, a psychological value, or both to the human species. All are important, regardless of their present natural conditions, and none should be overlooked or trivialized. We should consider carefully how we envision change in any landscape, how we might diminish or enhance its values, and how it may be more important than any structure we can place in it.

First, do no harm to the landscape. Design? Yes. Change the landscape? Yes, but, *first,* do no harm. Basically, take the landscape seriously. Landscape architects must admonish their clients and their colleagues that the landscape is not an endless ingredient to be wasted with impunity. Landscape architects can advocate ethically on the landscape's behalf because a healthy landscape that is esteemed for its special values is a gift, intrinsically tied to our individual and public health. Landscape architects are in a unique position to be advocates for the values of place, as revealed in landscape.

Advocacy for the landscape is similar to, but not the same as, a biologist advocating for the welfare of fish or bird species. Leopold recognized that specialization among conservationists means that each analyzes a natural process or component from a different perspective and, thus, arrives at different and often conflicting conservation goals. Simply put, "conservationists are notorious for their dissensions."[7] The roots of many contemporary dilemmas in conservation are grounded in these basic, differing mind-sets. For example, some foresters see old-growth timber as a crop, albeit with a very long harvest cycle, whereas most biologists see old-growth timber as a habitat, a home. Leopold believed that valuing land for a single purpose or only through the lens of specialized resource conservation professions such as forestry, agronomy, or soil science leads eventually toward neglectful or even malevolent actions on the land. His thoughts and writings remain timely and imperative. If we allow the evaluation of the landscape to depend on the values derived from the viewpoint of a single scientific discipline, then we will never conserve any landscape, for narrow economic values will always stand out as more compelling commercial opportunities for private gain.

Landscape architecture is uniquely qualified to answer questions about landscape values: How much is this site, even this tiny spot of touchable nature, worth to an urban person? To the people who drive by each day? To the executive who sees it through an office window and gains mental respite? To the child who walks through it every day and dreams a future? To the taxpayer who pays increasingly higher water assessments because natural storage and cleansing of stormwater no longer occurs? And to the songbirds and ants and other creatures and plants who call it home? The scholars and students of landscape architecture should be able to answer these questions. Putting these and other answers together to accrue a "natural" value for an urban site is within the intellectual reach of landscape architectural researchers and practitioners.

Synthesizing an understanding of landscape, integrating compartmentalized knowledge into a holistic concept, has always been a major expertise of landscape architects. This synthesizing intellect is a fundamental mind-set for landscape architects. They know how to put together landscape facts such as wind direction, slope, and soil conditions; now they must do a better job synthesizing all values for a landscape and, in particular, be more clear as to why and how the living landscape's value to all life-forms is greater than the sum of the values of its parts. Landscape architects already know this, but few have acted upon such knowledge. Why? Basically, they are shy and uncomfortable taking action that will bring them into conflict with other professionals and disciplines.[8] Heretofore, they have chosen the safe route, to hide under their banner of stewardship, pretending that all design actions are benevolent rather than adamantly advocating a complete set of values for a landscape and, thus, to risk being critical of designs done by other landscape architects and architects. Our abused habitat can no longer afford shyness or politeness.

If we treat the landscape in ways that reflect its multiple biological, spiritual (emotional), and psychological values for people, will the landscape become healthier? Yes, but perhaps not in time to save all urban landscapes. We can slow landscape abuse, but to imagine that we can restore everything we have damaged is arrogant. Remember, Leopold's description of a healthy landscape meant *its* capacity to renew itself and *our* capacity to help it do so. His land ethic promotes the consideration of biological and aesthetic landscape values. Yet, as Charles E. Little so brilliantly states in *Hope for the Land*, Leopold's intelligent reasoning has not led to a change in attitudes toward the landscape.[9] Does a shift in the value basis for land mean that a shift in human attitudes will occur? No, quite the contrary. A shift in attitudes is required before, or at least concurrently with, a shift toward accruing natural landscape values. Before we can look more broadly at valuing a landscape, we must, first, drastically change our thinking about land and the landscapes we create.

We need more relevant ways to conceptualize the landscape, to give it renewed meaning, to ensure that we do not force future generations to be alienated from it. We must redefine our relationship to the landscape, especially in light of our failure to steward it. Stewardship is no longer an ethical option; it does not work. What will? Again, Leopold has a clear answer:

> It is inconceivable to me that an ethical relationship to land
> can exist without love, respect, and admiration for land,
> and a high regard for its value.[10]

Clearly, Leopold had more in mind than simply a broadening of landscape values. Love, respect, admiration—these are words we reserve for human relationships, to describe the best of our feelings and attitudes toward not a mere equal, but a special one among equals. Perhaps the closest contemporary notion to this relationship is to think of a spouse or partner. Unlike a steward who controls, however benevolently, partnership means sharing. Partnership implies an equal status of independent entities.

Currently, the concept of a partner is widening in personal and business relationships. For example, "partnering" has become a desirable approach in the construction industry, where designers and builders "partner" the construction of a project. And since people are already connected biologically to the land and the built landscape, it seems reasonable to acknowledge this connection and to celebrate the link as a partnership. Yet, although people are biologically equal in most respects with the living landscape, we are often blind to this equality. Because we have extraordinary power and clever mechanisms to alter a landscape drastically in a short time to fit our often selfish needs, most of us mistakenly think of ourselves as superior. Because people dream, remember, and solve problems, most of us think of and treat other living entities, who we do not believe do those things, as inferior. Thus, as a species, we fail to see the power and ultimate effects a living landscape has on our lives. The landscape has no dreams or memory, but it manifests cease-less natural processes, often more subtle than we can perceive, always more long-term than our patience can measure, but, ultimately, natural processes that are perpetual, powerful, and equalizing. Occasionally, nature provides us sudden gifts of floods or prolonged presents of drought to remind all crea-tures of the power of the seemingly silent, "inferior" living landscape.

Partnering the landscape. Partnership with the landscape. What does this concept mean for ordinary landscapes, the ones we see and touch every-day? To garden? To design memorable places? To create art and culture? To preserve history? Yes, all of the above, but most importantly with a change in our collective attitude. And none of these can be done ethically, as Leopold reminds us, "without love, respect, and admiration for land." That means to design and plant and build with the health of the landscape, our partner, in mind. To design, plant, and build so as to prolong and enrich the landscape's natural ability to be a healthy habitat for all creatures. This means abandon-ing the notions affiliated with stewardship that man knows best, or that syn-thetic products are appropriate substitutes for the natural processes of soil building and fertility. This mainly means to plant and harvest with the well-ness of the garden Earth itself, not the size of our harvest, as a first priority.

For designers and planners, partnering the landscape means, first, to do no harm: To design and create so as to leave intact or enhance the landscape's natural abilities to absorb runoff, to cleanse water, and to provide habitat. This does not mean that designs or plans should necessarily imitate Nature's forms and patterns or mimic natural landscapes. It means that designers and planners are set free to explore all creative possibilities as long as the overall natural values of the site are enhanced or remain intact. One can design habi-tat with the wellness of the natural habitat in mind via patterns that fit human designs. For example, if we assume that landforms, climate, and soil "patterns" the resultant vegetation and that biological integrity is a holistic measure for water quality, then this knowledge of patterns can be used to guide designs to improve water quality at all scales from a single site to a regional watershed. Most of us have, with great arrogance and a smug sense of ourselves as stewards, assumed that we need only construct *our* own habi-tat and that we only have a consumer relationship to other species. Now we have an opportunity, perhaps as a penance, to design our community as an urban habitat with the wellness of the earth in mind. The goal is not to pass an environmental problem created by a design on to another site. The goal is not to assume that another site or design in a watershed or region can compensate for the loss of cumulative natural values attributable to biological, physical, and psychological factors resulting from a site design. The goal is not to be the designer who does the least harm to a site. To repeat, the first goal is to do no harm to our partner, the landscape.

Advocating for the cumulated natural values of our partner, the landscape can inspire us to be better designers, but these actions can also help us to restore the abused ordinary landscapes that surround us. If we can view the common landscape as a partner with potential cumulative natural values, we may be able to reverse in small but significant ways the damage past design and planning ignorance has caused. This means our second goal is to restore and recycle built landscapes. Restoration and recycling means to redesign urban areas at any scale so they have a chance to self-renew some of their lost natural functions, so they have an opportunity to regain their natural values as healthy spaces within the biological community.

Restoration and recycling are not new concepts. Designs such as Gas Works Park in Seattle are evidence that derelict landscapes can be recycled to better health. But landscape architects and planners have limited their thinking mainly to large, derelict areas and to parks and other spaces for human use. Two notions thwart our ability to include other urban landscapes in restoration and recycling: First, the mistaken belief that, once land is modified or built upon, it can never revert to nature; and, second, the persistence in "ecological thinking" that the only goal in restoration is the creation of natural landscapes. Thankfully, a few historic examples can guide our thinking about design. More importantly, perhaps, a national grassroots movement is now underway to restore urban remnants, and this civic energy is an ideal outlet for the expertise provided by landscape architecture.[11] Let us consider one historical example of urban restoration, several examples of grassroots efforts in restoration, and the work of one landscape architect, Peggy Gaynor, who is committed to a partnership with the landscape.

Portland, Oregon, rightfully enjoys a national reputation as not only an environmentally conscious urban area, but also a vibrant economic community. The city is consistently selected as one of the best places to live, work, and visit in the United States. Much of the central business district has been changed during the past two decades as Portland installed bus malls, light rail for mass transit, civic architecture, urban parks, and innovative landscape architectural designs. Portland deserves this fine reputation because the city considers a wide range of landscape values, including social ones, whenever it plans for changes and because it recycles older, dysfunctional parts of the city without diminishing their historical value. More importantly, the city has been bold enough to recycle still-functioning sites when these functions have prevented the landscape's multiple values from being realized. The most impressive example of this recycling is the conversion of a four-lane, limited-access highway to a riverfront park named for a former governor.

Until 1968, Harbor Drive was the main north-south route for vehicular movement through Portland. Without traffic lights and with ramped side traffic, the arterial was an engineer's delight but a pedestrian's route to suicide. When an interstate highway loop provided an alternative north-south route, the Portland Development Commission and the Portland Planning Bureau seized the opportunity to vacate Harbor Drive, tear it up, raze a few adjacent buildings, and design Tom McCall Park, a greenway along the entire length of the Williamette River as it flows parallel to the downtown area.[12] While the interstate highway construction gave Portland the opportunity to make this change, it is important to note that, in 1970, many other U.S. cities would not have taken such creative advantage of opportunities. If Portland were designing this park today, it would be possible to take advantage of the

Willamette River Harbor Drive as it existed in January of 1958. Courtesy of Oregon Historical Society.

Tom McCall Park as it appeared in 1993. Photograph by Sally Schauman.

green spaces to store and biofilter storm runoff and to provide better linkages to other green spaces and wildlife habitats. Nevertheless, Portland's Tom McCall Park is a creative urban retrofit/recycle design that many other cities—large and small—have yet to consider. The decision to recycle the riverfront has been so popular that Portland is considering ways to relocate Interstate 5 away from the opposite riverbank to create even more green spaces downtown.

If we define urban retrofit as the redesign of an existing area to reestablish partial natural functions for that site, then the opportunities are almost unlimited. If designer and planners throw out their self-imposed limits—and the belief that, once a site is built upon, it cannot be reworked to regain a more natural state—then opportunities for retrofitting small sites exist literally everywhere. Individually, retrofitting a small site may not seem worth the effort, but the aggregate values of individual designs will change the character and health of a property and an urban area or community over time.

Countless possibilities arise when we appreciate that any underused urban landscape is an opportunity to follow Leopold's admonition for us to allow the landscape to self-renew its natural functions. For example, urban planners once required high ratios between the number of parked cars to a building area. Air pollution abatement regulations now in effect in major U.S. urban areas encourage car pools and mass transit. As a result, fewer single-occupancy vehicles are driven to work and, thus, fewer paved parking areas are needed in many built areas. A windshield survey in a large industrial area in Seattle reveals innumerable paved parking areas that clearly are not being used. Parts of these underused paved areas can be peeled back, allowing for water infiltration, thus reducing stormwater problems.

Similarly, underused paved or riprapped areas along waterways can be uncovered to allow for vegetation and to improve habitat. Countless piped stormwater systems can be unpiped or uncovered, a process commonly known as "daylighted." Currently, many urban areas are separating combined sewer systems, installed decades ago, because in these systems both stormwater and wastewater must pass through sewage treatment facilities, which in turn raises treatment costs. In addition, during heavy storms, these combined systems fail, overflow, and cause dangerous and costly water pollution problems. Rather than putting both wastewater and stormwater back into separate pipes, one solution is not to pipe stormwater but to allow it to follow on the surface in designed urban stream corridors with areas interspersed for small, constructed wetlands to store floodwaters and to filter out pollutants. More than a decade ago, Bellevue, Washington, a city within metropolitan Seattle, chose not to pipe any stormwater because a thorough study concluded that a piped system would be more costly in the long run. Now Bellevue enjoys its many stream corridors as green space conduits for both stormwater and wildlife.

Opportunities for the landscape to self-renew its natural hydrological processes are only one part of the potential for total urban restoration. Another involves reforestation with diverse vegetation on underused urban sites. For example, many steep slopes and remnant urban lands either have no plants or are covered by a few invasive species. In both situations, more diverse plant material can be introduced to improve wildlife habitat and, in some cases, to better soil building and erosion control.

Seattle is a typical urban area with many retrofit and restoration possibilities. The city's nickname, Emerald City, does not come from its appearance as a green urban area—which it is not. The name was chosen because of the lush growth of evergreen trees on surrounding hillsides that had not yet been developed. Seattle is a beautiful, exciting city that is surrounded by an emerald landscape. Within the city natural landscapes are not abundant, but the opportunities to retrofit are easy to find. For example, students in the Department of Landscape Architecture at the University of Washington studied an industrial area and shopping center south of the city. They found numerous potential retrofit pockets of underused landscapes within the street right-of-ways, unbuilt fragments of property, and paved areas. Their study illustrates where and how small constructed wetlands and biofiltration ditches can be located to store stormwater during local flooding and to improve the water quality before the water drains into the adjacent Green River. Some of these sites, also, can be used as vest-pocket parks where employees can rest or lunch during their work day. Since both the quality and quantity of water are problems in Seattle, the potential of each of these small retrofit sites adds up to a major environmental benefit for the community at a low cost.

Technology already exists to design constructed wetlands to store floodwater, and to enhance the quality of both stormwater and wastewater.[13]

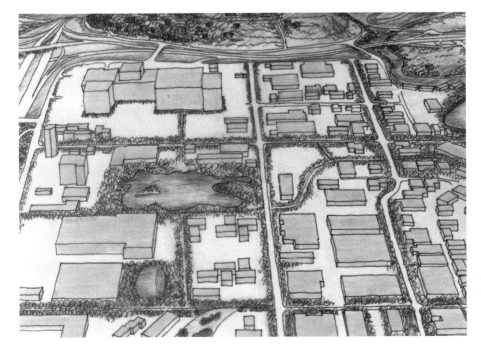

Bird's-eye view of a shopping and commercial area in the Seattle suburb Tukwila showing the potential retrofit sites.

Constructed wetlands will become more common sights in every region of the country. Now we have the opportunity to use these newer techniques as the basis for restoring our abused urban environment. We have the opportunity to peel back unused pavement in older urban areas, to construct small wetlands and filter strips that not only improve water quality, but also increase wildlife habitat and provide nature nearby for people. Small constructed wetlands can be located in strategic places along stormwater drainage systems in underused sites within newer commercial and residential areas. With good ecological planning and design, these places can become valued green spaces for the community.

Retrofitting the built landscapes or partnering the landscape is not an activity or plan to make Main Street a muddy road again, but an opportunity to find self-renewal in all underused urban remnants so landscapes can revive their multiple natural functions. The means and the opportunities to retrofit exist, so what about motives? Does the public care about retrofitting abused urban landscapes? Does anyone value these small, seemingly insignificant recycling and healing opportunities? A resounding yes. The public seems to recognize the retrofit opportunities and, at present, seems to care more about acting than do most government officials and planners, professional architects, and landscape architects. In the United States, grassroots groups are retrofitting and restoring urban remnants everywhere. Americans seem to understand intuitively that small neighborhood efforts to "partner" the landscape toward self-renewal make a difference, in the health of the earth and the community as well.

Examples of grassroots involvement exist in hundreds of American communities nationwide. Creek People, a coalition of approximately twenty neighborhood groups in the Seattle area, is typical. Each organization in the coalition is working toward a riparian restoration project—uncovering (daylighting) a piped stormwater system, restoring a creek's hydrologic function or habitat value, pressuring government not to pipe an existing open-water drainage, and so on. A typical Creek People group is the Ravenna Creek Alliance. Neighbors formed the Alliance to force the Municipality of Metropolitan Seattle (METRO) to rethink its plan to pipe stormwater that drains from Ravenna Creek. (The creek runs at the surface through a popular urban greenway and then disappears underground into a combined wastewater and stormwater sewer system.) METRO had planned to separate stormwater from wastewater at the point where the creek goes underground,

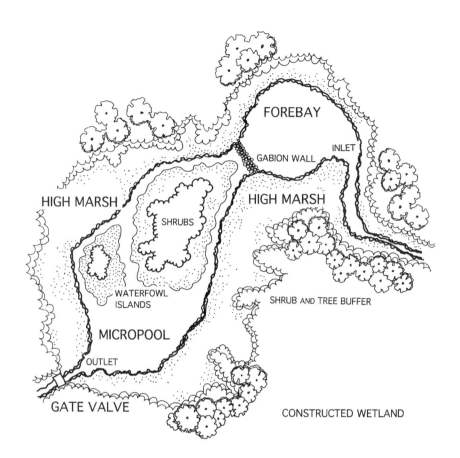

FOREBAY

INLET

GABION WALL

HIGH MARSH

HIGH MARSH

SHRUBS

WATERFOWL
ISLANDS

SHRUB AND TREE BUFFER

MICROPOOL

OUTLET

GATE VALVE

CONSTRUCTED WETLAND

*A plan view of a
constructed wetland
(after Schueler 1987)
designed to purify
stormwater draining
from a multifamily
residential site.*

to pipe the wastewater to sewage treatment, and to pipe the stormwater to Lake Washington. Pipe, pipe, pipe. (Tax dollars, tax dollars, tax dollars.) The proposed stormwater pipe system, more than 4,000 feet long, would have been buried under several streets and residential areas, a shopping center, and the attractive University of Washington campus. METRO provided a community action grant so that the Alliance could make the public aware of the daylighting opportunities and also pledged $800,000, the estimated amount it would cost to pipe this water, toward daylighting. The City of Seattle acquired funds for the acquisition of open space along the route and negotiations are underway with major property owners. Although the proposed "daylighted" Ravenna Creek will flow in a narrow corridor in places and will be routed through the shopping center's parking lot, the citizens and the merchants believed the increased green space (and its associated values) created by daylighting to be well worth the effort.

A retrofitted water edge site along the Duwamish River in Seattle that was stripped of riprap and paving, and is now healing and becoming a natural mudflat with significant ecological value for juvenile salmon. Photograph by Curtis D. Tanner, U.S.F.W.S.

In the most industrialized part of Seattle a multimillion dollar restoration project has begun along the Duwamish Estuary. As Seattle grew, the estuary became a major industrial and commercial area and, as a consequence, was filled in. But now, along the Duwamish River, which runs through many Port of Seattle facilities, small sites are being uncovered and regraded so that the landscape can begin to self-renew into its original form as an estuary. This area, south of the familiar Seattle Kingdome, was once a major Puget Sound estuary, a special place for marine life to begin and for young salmon to gain strength before venturing into the Pacific Ocean. All of the restoration sites are relatively small, less than ten acres, and only one or two have plans for associated recreation. The most common restoration techniques are simply to peel back the hard surfaces and to regrade the water's edge so that the uncovered landscape can heal itself as the mudflat edge of a marine estuary it has always wanted to be.

In another community project, a neglected hillside in Seattle became a wonderful green space. Highly visible, yet unnoticed by most motorists who speed by, the site is a steep hillside that overlooks the intersection of Interstates 90 and 5. It is covered with grasses and Himalayan blackberry vines. The property was within the jurisdiction of the Seattle Parks Department, but was never developed for recreation because of its steepness. Citizens recognized that this landscape had potential as a filter for the airborne toxicants spewing forth from the quarter million cars that pass by the site every day, and as a view of nature for hundreds of workers in nearby downtown offices and patients and others in the nearby hospitals. The Mountain to Sound Greenway, a grassroots group dedicated to creating a greenbelt along Interstate 90 from Puget Sound to the Cascade Mountains, chose this site for its first project area. The group decided that planting this neglected but highly visible hillside was an appropriate demonstration of its vision for a regional greenway. A work group organized from several civic clubs and neighborhood volunteers planned this reforestation project. More than 560 trees were planted in one day; the group dedicated its efforts and the landscape to the memory of Dr. Jose Rizal, a Philippine national hero who envisioned the creation of the Philippine nation and was executed for his views in 1896. Thus, the restored hillside not only inaugurates an extensive greenway, but also honors a hero of the nearby Filipino-American neighborhood. To ensure survival of these trees, a maintenance program was planned by the City of Seattle Summer Youth Employment Program, the Rizal Park Preservation Society, the Pacific Medical Center and Clinic, and the neighborhood group.

In these case studies—Ravenna Creek, the Duwamish Estuary, and Dr. Jose Rizal Park—the restoration, retrofitting, and recycling of a built or neglected landscape came about because citizens cared about their community landscapes. This type of neighborhood partnering of landscapes nearby is neither rare nor indigenous to the Pacific Northwest. Similar energy and efforts exist elsewhere—from the efforts of Bob Bersson and numerous volunteers to restore the Blacks Run Creek in downtown Harrisonburg, Virginia, to the efforts of Judy Guttierez and citizens in Las Cruces, New Mexico, to heal traffic corridors with attractive islands of green. It is clear that people value unspectacular landscapes and do not want to be alienated from any opportunity to experience nature in their immediate surroundings. These civic efforts are evidence that people value common natural elements and do not demand picturesque or ornamental landscape designs reminiscent of eighteenth-century England, that people expect natural elements to be easy to see and touch; that is, they value landscapes that are close at hand, in their own neighborhood, and not merely available in remote parks or wilderness areas. People understand that, by nurturing the landscape's potential to self-renew, human beings are once again connecting with an essential and eternal process. This citizen-based partnering of our abused built landscapes goes beyond stewardship because it does not depend on human control, on people improving by imposing on nature. Rather it recognizes that natural processes are powerful and more desirable ecologically, it demonstrates a sharing of the earth, and it recognizes that small gains in the landscape's wellness are tied to our own human health.

Current citizen activity is ongoing largely without massive funding from environmental lobbies, without government planners, without professional designers, and with little landscape architectural involvement. Perhaps soon the status quo will wake up and take notice. A few landscape architects, however, are gaining national reputations for landscape restoration and ecological designs, but few work primarily with citizens' groups in restoration.[14] One of the best is the Seattle landscape architect Peggy Gaynor. Gaynor's office works on a wide range of project types, but much of her work can be characterized as "partnering" the landscape. Her forte is to organize

Constructed wetlands in the parking area of Atlantic City Boat Ramp, Seattle. Designed by Peggy Gaynor, A.S.L.A.

and direct the energies of citizens who want to improve a small bit of an abused landscape.

In one example, the 24th Street Landing, Gaynor orchestrated the public effort to clean up the terminus of a street ending at an urban waterway in an industrial neighborhood. The tiny site was "parked" with cars and covered with oil, bits of pavement, debris, and invasive blackberry vines. Gaynor's group tilled up oil-soaked compacted soils, regraded the land for better drainage, improved water quality, replanted a variety of native trees and shrubs into a natural beach, and rebuilt a pier for public access. This work was done mainly with donated time and materials. In another instance, the city planned to pave a gravel parking lot adjacent to the Atlantic City Beach boat ramp along Lake Washington because of general wear and tear on the site. As a trade-off for the covering of this water-absorbing landscape, Gaynor convinced the city and the engineering consultant to construct mini-wetlands within large parking lot islands dividing the rows. In this way the landscape gained more natural functions as a place to detain stormwater, improve stormwater quality, and provide a natural wetland aesthetic before it drained into the receiving public waters of Lake Washington.

Not all of the restoration projects done by Gaynor Landscape Architects result in actual self-renewal of natural landscape processes; some are only symbolic of the processes. While these may seem less crucial, they are important for teaching purposes. The educational value of these designed symbols of nature is especially important to children. For example, Gaynor was asked to provide a master plan for an old school site in the Richmond Beach area of Seattle, which included a drainage problem caused by a high wall (built during the Works Projects Administration era in the 1930s) that cut through a natural flow of underground water. The typical engineering solution was to pipe the "problematic" groundwater to a storm drain. (Pipe, pipe, pipe—will engineers and city managers ever learn ecology and aesthetics?) Instead Gaynor captured and revealed the leaking water into a mini-wetland, with rocks and various vegetation along the base of the wall, before the water flows into a french drain and then away to Puget Sound. Her creation was an inexpensive solution to the problem of errant water, and it created a safe, wonderful place for children to explore. No great wetland values were created, no measurable improvement in landscape health resulted, but kids dearly love it.

Children playing in the "symbolic" wetland designed by Peggy Gaynor, A.S.L.A..

Much of Gaynor's landscape partnering occurs in urban riparian corridors. Often these linear landscapes become gouged by erosion, denuded of plants, susceptible to pollution from home yards, parking lots, and play fields that drain into them and make them devoid of any fish-spawning areas. Such was the case in Bellevue, Washington, along 140th Avenue, N.E. This degraded landscape within a city park came to the Gaynor's attention when an adjacent road was planned for widening. Here Gaynor rerouted the creekbed and added rocks, plants, stumps, and logs to enable this riparian landscape to heal itself. She then created a series of biofiltration swales and ponds to intercept and purify the runoff from the adjacent ball fields before the water drained into the creek. Next, she designed a boardwalk system around and through the site instead of the typical sidewalk, thus allowing

Plan view of the design by Peggy Gaynor, A.S.L.A., for the riparian corridor along 140th Avenue, N.E., Bellevue, Washington.

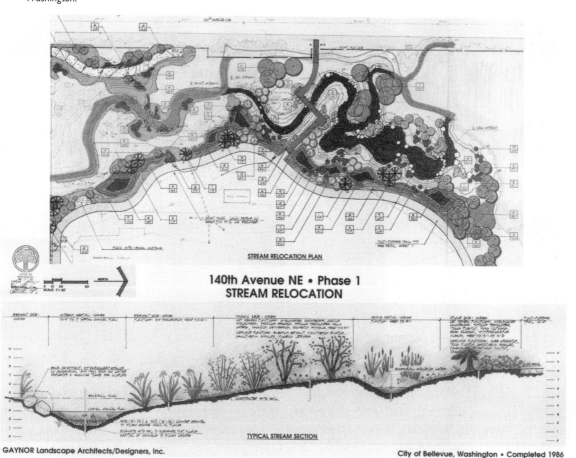

140th Avenue NE • Phase 1
STREAM RELOCATION

GAYNOR Landscape Architects/Designers, Inc.

City of Bellevue, Washington • Completed 1986

The completed boardwalk, part of Peggy Gaynor's project for 140th Avenue, N.E., Bellevue, Washington.

more room for the creek to meander and for people to enjoy the landscape from areas higher up. Finally, she designed a set of interpretive signs. As a result, the small site became a natural oasis for wildlife and people, surrounded by, but oblivious of, nearby vehicular traffic.

Gaynor's design philosophy is an appropriate guide for partnering the landscape. It is to create opportunities for self-renewal wherever and whenever possible, to create symbols if site constraints will not allow self-renewal to occur, to create art where art or the landscape has the potential to stimulate, and to design for the health of the landscape in every instance. Her designs nurture the landscape in a way that goes beyond traditional ideas of land management. Her work involves the basic notion of being responsible for giving the natural landscape a chance to heal itself. Her working concepts for self-renewal are to uncover the landscape, to "unpipe" surface water, to treat and store water on a site, and to seed and plant whenever possible. Gaynor's projects reflect the ethical relationship to the landscape as described by Leopold, a concern for ecological integrity and beauty, and, importantly, a relationship of respect for a partner.

Tom McCall Park in Portland and Gaynor's retrofit designs give us a clear message that the built landscape can be given a chance for self-renewal. Now we must seek as many opportunities to heal the land as we can. We must not be thwarted by the blight and ugliness of our built landscapes, but rather we must analyze them for retrofit potential. The overlay suitability analysis system developed by McHarg helped us to see the value of the natural systems as they layered upon each other and interconnected with one another. Now we need to consider how the layers of human impact have disconnected people from natural elements in their communities and smothered the natural functions of the landscape. We can use the overlay analysis method to consider human impacts in relationship to the underlying natural systems to find restoration potentials. A major design challenge that landscape architects will face in the twenty-first century is how to develop methods and processes to peel back the layers of human impact and intervene in a therapeutic way so that the built landscape naturally heals from past abuse.

The success of grassroots efforts across America to restore landscapes should convince government officials, city managers, planners, and landscape architects that, when a self-renewal potential in a landscape is found, the public will support and contribute to restoration efforts. Indeed, restoration, recycling, and retrofitting the landscape are ongoing throughout the world. We only have to turn to the Dutch, who are letting the North Sea back into areas they have previously struggled to control.[15] For the most part, restoration has been thought of as a solution to a large-scale system, such as the Kissimmee River in Florida, or to small, mainly natural, sites. But the built landscape is our own habitat, our own backyard, our own community. Citizens recognize the benefits of having nature nearby. Landscape architects need to build on this public recognition. Landscape architects can make a difference in the restoration of built landscapes, but they need to move beyond the idea of stewardship as a gift that people bestow upon the earth, and toward the idea of a partnership with the landscape treated as an equal.

NOTES

1. Wilson 1993, p. 24.

2. Thomas 1983, p. 31.

3. Landscape architect Nancy Denig discusses this genre of writing in her rebuke of Ian McHarg for "sadly misleading" in *Design with Nature*. McHarg (1969) writes of his belief that the Judeo-Christian tradition fosters Western man's conviction that he has dominion; hence utter control over nature; thus, an excuse to degrade the planet. Yet Denig states that "Judeo-Christian man is called, instead, into a relationship with nature founded on dominion, stewardship, and co-existence" (Denig 1985, p. 103).

4. Leopold 1949, p. 258

5. Schwartz 1991, p. 95.

6. Spirn 1991, pp. 92–93.

7. Leopold 1949, p. 258.

8. Gary Mason, a landscape architect based in California, believes his experience with professional conflict is typical. Mason tells how the project designer, another landscape architect, berated him severely after Mason testified in a public hearing against the leveling of 2,800 mature oak trees in a Walnut Creek, California, project (Leccese 1992). The project site is a savanna landscape, a woodland of large, spreading deciduous trees with a ground cover of grass and low herbaceous plants. Savanna woodlands are among the most desirable throughout the world as housing sites because of their attractive appearance (open yet shaded by large, beautiful trees), generally gently undulating slopes, and well-drained soils. Because these sites are so popular as home sites they have almost disappeared in California.

9. Little 1992, pp. 7–14.

10. Leopold 1949, p. 258.

11. Much of the citizen efforts have focused on identifying, conserving, and expanding greenways within urban areas and surrounding communities. Charles E. Little (1990) has written the definitive history of this movement.

12. Ashbaugh (1987) discusses the remarkable conversion of this landscape in more detail.

13. The term *created wetlands* generally refers to those areas created for multiple functions where no wetland had previously existed; *restored wetlands* means that the function(s) of an existing wetland are increased (Soil Conservation Service 1992). At present the term *constructed wetlands* generally refers to those areas that have been constructed for a single purpose, specifically wastewater treatment (U.S. Environmental Protection Agency 1987 and Marble 1992). Increasingly, however, constructed wetlands can be used to treat stormwater to improve its quality (Schueler 1987). The detention of stormwater in constructed basins is a common practice in many parts of the United States The next step in ecological design and planning is to construct facilities within a drainage system that treat the stormwater to improve water quality. Ultimately, the planning and design goal is to store floodwater and treat all water on a developed site before releasing it into a stormwater system.

14. Steiner and Johnson (1990) discuss three landscape architectural firms in Philadelphia that focus on ecological design almost exclusively; and Lyle (1985) describes ecological

designs that he and his students have done in Southern California. Also, Tom Hunt, known to many as the Land Doctor, is working miracles in restoration work on lands owned by Wisconsin Power & Light Company, especially the Lake Wisconsin Watershed Restoration Project near Merrimac. Hunt, also, founded and still directs the Partners in Conservation Program as part of his work for Wisconsin Power & Light Company in Madison.

15. See Meto J. Vroom's essay in this book.

REFERENCES

Ashbaugh, James G. 1987. "Portland's Changing Riverscape." Pp. 38–54 in *Portland's Changing Landscape,* ed. Larry W. Price. Portland, Ore.: Portland State University and the Association of American Geographers. (Occasional Paper 4).

Denig, Nancy Watkins. 1985. "On Values Revisited: A Judeo-Christian Theology of Man and Nature." *Landscape Journal* 4(2): 96–105.

Leccese, Michael. 1992. "I Profess." *Landscape Architecture* 82 (January): 54–57.

Leopold, Aldo. 1949. *A Sand County Almanac.* New York: Oxford University Press.

Little, Charles E. 1990. *Greenways for America.* Baltimore: Johns Hopkins University Press.

———. 1992. *Hope for the Land.* New Brunswick, N.J.: Rutgers University Press.

Lyle, John T. 1985. *Design for Human Ecosystems: Landscape, Land Use, and Natural Resources.* New York: Van Nostrand Reinhold.

Marble, Anne D. 1992. *A Guide to Wetland Functional Design.* Boca Raton, Fla.: Lewis.

McHarg, Ian. 1969. *Design with Nature.* Garden City, N.Y.: Doubleday/Natural History Press. 1992. Reprint, New York: John Wiley & Sons.

Schueler, Thomas R. 1987. *Controlling Urban Runoff: A Practical Guide for Planning and Designing Urban BMP's.* Washington: Washington Metropolitan Water Resources Planning Board.

Schwartz, Martha. 1991. "The Landscapes of Neglect." *Progressive Architecture* (August).

Soil Conservation Service. 1992. Chap. 13 in *Wetland Restoration, Enhancement, or Creation.* Engineering Field Manual. Washington: U.S. Department of Agriculture.

Spirn, Anne Whiston. 1991. "Seeing and Making the Landscape Whole." *Progressive Architecture* (August).

Steiner, Frederick, and Todd Johnson. 1990. "Fitness, Adaptability, Delight." *Landscape Architecture* 80 (March): 96–101.

Thomas, Keith. 1983. *Man and the Natural World.* New York: Pantheon Books.

U.S. Environmental Protection Agency. 1987. "Report on the Use of Wetlands for Municipal Wastewater Treatment and Disposal." Washington: Office of Water.

Wilson, Edward O. 1993. "Is Humanity Suicidal?" *New York Times Magazine,* 30 May.

10

FOSTERING LIVING LANDSCAPES

CAROL FRANKLIN

*A land ethic, then, reflects the existence of an ecological conscience,
and this in turn reflects a conviction of individual responsibility for the
health of the land. Health is the capacity of the land for self-renewal.
Conservation is our effort to understand and preserve this capacity.*

ALDO LEOPOLD[1]

SUSTAINABLE LANDSCAPE DESIGN—A DEFINITION

Everywhere the landscape is deteriorating—a direct result of the attitude
that land is a commodity and that natural and cultural values are expendable. As awareness of global environmental problems increases, however,
we are witnessing a revolution in attitudes toward the natural landscape at
every level and a desire to design and plan in an environmentally responsible way.

The basic premise of sustainable landscape design is to allow the ongoing processes that sustain all life to remain intact and to continue to function
along with development. While the first tenet of sustainable landscape
design, and one that is actually often overlooked, is "don't destroy the site,"
in reality we have already destroyed too much and we can no longer measure
the sustainability of a design by its minimal impact on the natural systems of
a site. Today, almost every site on which landscape architects work has been
abused. Sustainable design must go beyond the modest goal of minimizing
site destruction to one of facilitating site recovery by reestablishing the

processes necessary to sustain natural systems. This approach is not "naturalistic landscaping" or "preserving endangered species" but the preservation, restoration, and creation of self-sustaining, living environments.

Sustainable design is not a unified philosophy for which there is one accepted, rigorous method. Perhaps most important, it is a process of raising consciousness and changing basic attitudes—attitudes so ingrained we are often unaware that they shape our design and management of the land.

These changes require that we actually see the present deterioration of the landscape, that we recognize the impacts of our interventions, and that we understand each site and each piece of a site as parts of larger systems.

BASIC ATTITUDES AND PREMISES
OF THE SUSTAINABLE DESIGN PROCESS

Sustainable design is not a reworking of conventional design approaches and technologies, but a fundamental revision of thinking and operation—you cannot put spots on an elephant and call it a cheetah. With sustainable design the presumptions of how a site is dealt with are different. The kind of data gathered and the way we interpret these data are also different; even the methods by which we design are different. It is the sum of these changes that results in a different design.

The key to sustainable design is the systems approach—sometimes called a holistic view. Most of us are aware that nothing exists in isolation and that everything is interconnected. Many of the skills of the design professions (which include engineering), however, are geared to solving arbitrarily defined problems and providing solutions that may appear reasonable from the point of view of a single professional discipline or single client but cannot resolve the multidimensional problems of the land. With sustainable design, we are not looking at single-focus solutions to single-focus problems, such as drainage, sewage disposal, or erosion control, but rather at the management of a whole set of resources.

A second premise on which sustainable design is based is that product and process are one. Therefore, the process by which an end is achieved is often given as much, or nearly as much, weight as the product, because it is recognized that only by changing the design process is it possible to change the design result. These changes in the design process affect who participates, how they participate, and ultimately how the project is defined or redefined.

Who participates and how do they participate? The sustainable design process is inclusive and basically democratic; it is a relationship of consenting equals that builds consensus as a project proceeds. In traditional design relationships, we successfully divorce many of the obvious partners from the design process. Redefining the players and their roles, breaking down old boundaries, and empowering new parties in new partnerships are critical to a sustainable design process—which is inherently representative, interactive, and consensual. The traditional design process, even with modifications, is too exclusive, linear, and compartmentalized, with little real communication or coordination among team members and many potential team members unrepresented or participating only in subordinate roles. The sustainable design process requires inclusive partnerships that are new and unexpected, in which all concerned parties are empowered to advocate their needs and desires.

With a sustainable design process, team members interact as equally empowered partners. The client becomes a "partner" in the design and its realization—rather than patronized as a necessary inconvenience to be told what to do by the experts or "master builders." The design professional is also an equal participant—not a "hired gun" subservient to the client. Most importantly, the land, the people living and working on it, and those who will be using the project are full participants. And to ensure sustainability, "the unseen users, who are the other players at the table, are the future generations."[2] With this inclusive participation in the design process, there is a recognition that all site values are important and must be respected, understood, and represented. While often there is considerable fear, on the part of both designer and client, that the inclusion of so many people will be unwieldy and delay a tight schedule, structured participation of the stakeholders allows this process to proceed smoothly. If there is an appropriate level of involvement, there will be real consensus, as unrealized connections and unexpected allies are brought to light.

For participation to be more than window dressing, continuity is a critical factor. To ensure the truth of the vision to the end, sustainable design requires stakeholder participation from soup to nuts—from the development of the program, through the design of the building and site facilities, to construction review and beyond to a program of assessment and repair that is built into a completed project.

In addition to the type of participation, the structure of the work process is different. In contrast to traditional design methods, the sustainable design process is rarely linear. Instead, the work is characterized by a focus on the whole project and by feedback loops that create changes in the structure of the work process throughout the lifetime of a project. For example, the methods of installation and the resources of the contractor or volunteer work force may be explored at the very beginning of the design process and this knowledge used in crafting the design.

Lastly, the sustainable design process affects how the project is defined or redefined. There are few sites that are self-contained packages where planning and design simply entail designing the required building and landscape for the proposed client. Site programs and clients come and go, but the land remains. Providing long-term solutions to site problems can require looking outward to the larger context and confronting impacts to the site that occur beyond site boundaries. Solutions may include the redefinition of the project scope, a change in the physical boundaries of a site, or the recognition of larger jurisdictional boundaries and the involvement of wider groups of people, such as owners of adjacent properties or multiple agencies.

DEFINING SITE VALUES AND FRAMING APPROPRIATE SITE GOALS

To frame appropriate site goals, the designer must ask, "What values are critical to the site, and how should they be protected and even enhanced by site development?" Because we are seeing today, on almost every site, accelerating and destructive environmental trends such as erosion, compaction, excess stormwater runoff, and takeover by invasive exotic plants and animals, every project design should be considered as a part of a larger strategy to resolve these critical issues. The goal of every project should be to leave the site in a better condition than it was found.

Another critical impact of conventional development is the increasing fragmentation of natural systems. Today the natural landscape remains only as small islands surrounded by a fabric of development. These islands gradually lose their ability to support a variety of plant communities and habitats, and they are extremely vulnerable to invasions by exotic plants and animals. Sustainable design must involve serious efforts to reverse this scenario by (1) creating strategies to reconnect fragmented landscapes and establish contiguous networks with other natural systems, both within a site and beyond the site boundaries, and (2) reestablishing the widest possible range of indigenous plant and animal communities, in appropriate habitats, to restore to the site its potential diversity of species.

Clearly stating the goals and principles of a project in a mission statement guides the overall development and focuses all participants. The mission should combine both vision and realism. The result is a cumulative building of the plan even where there is a wide range of disciplines or stakeholder interests. These guiding principles evolve out of what is learned during the design process, and should be revisited and reevaluated as the project proceeds.

THE PATTERN OF A PLACE—RECOGNIZING THE INHERENT NATURAL STRUCTURE

The way you observe the landscape determines what you see. This explains why, despite the fact that site evaluation and review have been an important part of design and planning processes for a long time, conventional evaluations have not led to responsive, ecologically sound plans or designs.

The phrase "a sense of place," although deceptively simple, is a nontechnical way of summing up the totality of a place and all the processes that shape it. When we talk about an English village or the Serengeti Plains we are summing up centuries of cultural history and eons of geological and biological evolution that created the places that these names represent. Our sense of place, although sometimes experienced as a single moment or image, is actually derived from a complex living community that is continuously responding to the forces that act on it, recognized as pattern. In nature, pattern is the result of process. As Frank Lloyd Wright said: "The pebble is a diagram of the forces that have acted upon it."[3] That diagram is a pattern, and these patterns are the end products of all the forces that have shaped a landscape to this moment. Landscapes reveal very complex patterns; they bring together and express an enormous amount of information about natural processes and the experience and influences of human culture in and on that place. When this sense of place and the natural and cultural information that it embodies is reduced to data collection—lists and descriptions of isolated phenomena, such as climatological data, soil types, and of endangered species—the picture of the living landscape, which is dynamic and interactive, is often lost.

As designers we are trained to see and work with forms and patterns. For the sustainable designer, pattern is the link between natural and social processes and design. Beyond data collection, mapping parameters, and creating overlays, sustainable design requires the designer to interpret the forms and patterns of a place and to tell its story—what the site was, how it has changed, and the directions in which it is likely to go. It is important to frame this story simply, accurately, dramatically, and without jargon. The more coherently the story portrays a place, the more deeply it uncovers connections, the more vividly it portrays site character, and the more dramatically it juxtaposes site themes—the better the finished design that will grow from it.

A useful way of summing up the knowledge revealed by an environmental analysis for a sustainable design may be expressed as a drawing of the "inherent natural structure" of a site, which is a representation of the intrinsic natural patterns of the place and includes the human modifications of these patterns. Such a drawing is shorthand for complex information and reveals the dynamic equilibrium that is the resolution of the interacting natural, social, and cultural forces of a site.

ADAPTIVE STRATEGIES FOR SUSTAINABLE DESIGN SOLUTIONS—TAKING ACCOUNT OF DIFFERENT CRITERIA

An adaptive strategy is a design solution that is tailored to a specific context and a specific problem. By definition, adaptive strategies are developed out of local contexts and local conditions; although they are not "universal solutions," they are based on universal concepts.

The sustainable designer reexamines conventional solutions in the light of environmental imperatives and asks, "Is there a better way of doing this task?" Adaptive strategies must solve more than one problem at a time, in an integrated way, using the most appropriate technology currently available. Single-focus solutions are, by definition, not strategic, because they do not account for the big picture. Only synergistic solutions can realize the efficiencies needed to resolve problems that are increasing exponentially. Sustainable strategies and sustainable design use a holistic, synergistic, and interactive approach.

Working with the forms and patterns of the natural world and the processes these forms and patterns express in the landscape is the prerequisite for sustainable design and is fundamental to the preservation of the integrity of a place. Civil engineers and designers usually consider their creations "improvements on nature" and often call them just that, but most engineering solutions rarely approach the efficiency of biological systems and are often sustainable only for short periods of time. Although there is no single magic technology that can solve environmental problems, conditions can be improved when the principle of using natural models is applied.

Looking closely at the natural systems of water, soil, and vegetation, we can examine our current treatment of them, identify trends, and review the specific implications, both moral and practical, for sustainable design. Although there are many ways to describe the land and the critical natural processes that sustain it, we can begin by examining three interrelated processes and looking at how the patterns of the larger systems are reflected in design:

1. Water—the hydrologic regimen
2. Soil—the cycling of mineral and organic nutrients
3. Vegetation—the structure, organization, and development of plant communities

Water—The Hydrologic Regimen

Increased runoff from development is one of the most pervasive problems in the landscape today. The engineering paradigm for drainage is to concentrate flow and velocity and carry water away from the place where it falls as quickly as possible. Conventional stormwater management relies heavily on curbs, pipes, inlets, dams, riprap, detention basins, and other "hard" engineering solutions. Where water from the uplands is collected in pipes that flow onto valley slopes, the result is gully formation. The gullies that form below outlet pipes not only prevent water from infiltrating into the ground to recharge groundwater, but also act as drains, pulling water out of the adjacent slopes. At the valley bottom, stream channels are recut in an effort to handle the increased sediment load and water volume and velocities. The result of our conventional management of stormwater is tree toppling, delta formation, and a stream in which the channel is migrating rapidly and undercutting and eroding its banks.

Most regulation today, despite some restrictions for wetlands, permits the destruction of nearly all existing upland terrain, soils, and plant communities on a site and the resulting severe disruption of hydrologic patterns. Both soil and water regulation in the United States have concentrated on "control" of problems, such as flood control, erosion control, "point" and now "nonpoint" pollution control. Conventional site design is by nature timid: It follows regulation rather than seeking to maintain whole site systems.

The sustainable design paradigm does not deal with single-focus goals, such as flood control or erosion control, but rather looks at the management of the whole resource. For example, all water, including wastewater, is treated as a resource—not as a problem—and is managed as a crucial component of the larger water system. This approach allows one to find solutions based on models that replicate the natural hydrology. Biological treatment of wastewater would not only allow it to be reabsorbed into the water system of the watershed, but also to provide the opportunity to expand and replace diminished wetland systems.

Drainage solutions should reduce runoff and maximize infiltration in the uplands, restore or maintain stream baseflow, provide groundwater recharge, and reestablish channel stability, regardless of the strength of the storm event. Vegetated swales slow water, trap sediment, and increase infiltration by using the natural system to accomplish these goals. Sustainable technologies such as "porous paving" foster infiltration and the reduction of contaminants, reinforcing natural functions.

Soil—The Cycling of Mineral and Organic Nutrients

Soil is the most hidden landscape problem of all. Soils are far more susceptible to damage than we realize. The function of soil in the biotic system is to recycle nutrients. Most of this work is done by plant roots, animal life, and microorganisms in the soil, all of which depend on a permeable soil crust, stratified soil layers, and appropriate amounts of organic matter. Much of what we do during the design and construction phase of a project destroys the life of the soil. Terrain modification, most of it unnecessary, is the greatest culprit. Grading destroys soil stratification and compacts soil, which limits root penetration, mycorrhizal growth, infiltration of water, and the exchange of atmospheric gases, chiefly oxygen and carbon dioxide.

Sustainable design must involve serious efforts to preserve soil resources, including the development of strict soil protection measures during construction, limits on the zone of disturbance, minimum-impact construction techniques, as well as innovative restoration measures such as making new soils from waste products, restoring soil tilth, and adding micronutrients and mycorrhizae to repair soil deficits.

Vegetation—The Structure, Organization, and Development of Plant Communities

Native plant communities are the most essential expression of the physical features of a place, and they support the richness of the wildlife with whom they have coevolved. What we are losing is not simply individual plant species, but the complex relationships of plants to other plants, to wildlife, and to place.

Plants, like people, live and develop as communities with characteristic companions. These communities can be described as "a distinctive group of plant species which may be expected to grow naturally together in more or less the same population proportions under similar habitat conditions."[4] The location of these communities, such as an oak-hickory forest, is largely determined by climate. If the earth were completely uniform there could perhaps be uniform bands of vegetation. Because the earth is broken into continents, there are instead, within the continents, physiographic provinces and climatic zones; the regional variations in vegetation within these climatic zones respond to variations in the landforms, and the local variations in vegetation respond to changes in topography and soils.

Vegetation is an exquisitely sensitive indicator of these conditions, growing in an almost infinite variety of recognizable patterns. For example, where there is a distinctive gradient of any sort—from dry to wet or from cold to warm or from toxic to normal conditions—we will observe plant species forming a series of concentric bands. As we become sensitive to patterns in vegetation, the relationship between form and function is underscored. To create patterns, at any scale, that are not representative of the patterns of a place "goes against the flow" and requires an additional input of energy in direct proportion to the movement away from the patterns of the place. In the northeastern United States, weekly summer mowings are required to maintain our lawns and beat back the forest that would otherwise grow in this region. This energy input is required because a forest, and not English turf grasses, is nature's expression of the fullest and most effective use of the resources available in this landscape.

The basic building block of ecological planting design is the plant community type, assembled in the patterns on and above the ground, that express plant life in that place. Planting plans that show plants simply as idealized circles with a dot in the center, placed in geometric relationships, cannot begin to capture the complexity of ecological relationships. For example, to represent the structure of a mature forest, the design drawings should reflect both the vertical layers (canopy trees, understory trees, shrubs, and ground layer) and the horizontal mosaics, distinguishing between growth forms of every species so that the canopy trees, often the largest plants, can be shown to occur in every layer and at every size somewhere within these mosaics. Variety in the size and in the shapes used to show plants will help to express the fact that the form of each plant is partially determined by its plant companions and partially by its response to local environmental conditions, such as its place within a gap in the canopy or along a forest edge.

Succession is the name given to the process of change and development in plant and animal communities, "the gradual replacement of one community by another" in which "a succession of plant communities is always accompanied by a succession of animal associations. Plant succession leads the way because plants are the foundation of every food chain."[5] The process of succession tends to proceed toward more complex interrelated communities of living things.

Today the impacts from development on our remaining native landscapes have inevitably meant environmental degradation. One of the most visible signs of environmental damage is the displacement of complex native ecosystems by a few invasive exotic plant species, which often form almost monospecific and nearly "static" plant communities. Takeover of a site by invasive exotic plant species disrupts the structure of the native ecosystems and interrupts the natural sequence of succession on a site, seriously diminishing both the health and diversity of native plant communities and the animals who are dependent on them.

Solving our biodiversity crisis inevitably involves the way we maintain our landscapes as well as the way we plan them. Understanding the process of succession—plant community development—is a key to long-term vegetation management and to creating and repairing native landscapes with minimal intervention. By using natural patterns we set the stage for nature to reestablish the functional relationships between plant and plant, and between plant and place. Ecological planting design offers a new vocabulary based on the language of landscapes—forest, woodland, prairie, desert, and tundra. It is a celebration of both the unique qualities of each individual place as well as the qualities that place may share with others similar to it. The attitude of the designer becomes one of continuous observation and increasing appreciation of the richness and complexity of these patterns within patterns—"worlds within worlds."

THE ECOLOGICAL AESTHETIC

Making art that is "expressive form" and that reveals and celebrates the patterns and processes of the landscape requires only that the ecological sensibility be married to an artistic one and that both sensibilities recognize the intrinsic design of the site as the highest value: "Again Lou Kahn has made clear to us the distinction between form and design. Cup is form and begins from the cupped hand. Design is the creation of the cup transmuted by the artist, but never denying its formal origins. As a profession, landscape architecture has exploited a pliant earth, tractable and docile plants to make much that was arbitrary, capricious, and inconsequential. We could not see the cupped hand as giving form to the cup, the earth, and its processes as giving form to our works."[6]

The designer attuned to sustainability accepts and respects the primacy of the natural patterns and processes of the landscape. The stream and wetland systems, the natural terrain, and the plant and animal communities are the given forms of a place. Such a designer works with them, does not violate them, and does not assume, for example, that a stream channel can be relocated or put into a pipe. With this approach, site resources are used to solve site problems. There is an economy of intervention and a minimization of destruction. In addition, there is respect for the integrity of patterns everywhere—ecological, historical, and cultural. The functional areas of a site—buildings, roads, and parking lots—adapt to the patterns of the place rather than obliterate them. Diminishing gradients of intervention allow as much of the site as possible to succeed to more complex ecosystems. No longer locked in the repetitive conventions of "bed, bosque, border, and allée," the designer discovers that natural patterns and the vocabulary of our indigenous landscapes are, like the natural world itself, infinite sources of form.

MONITORING

Sustainability is a goal that no one as yet knows how to achieve. The act of sustainable planning and design is a heuristic process; that is, one in which we learn by doing, observing, and recording the changing conditions and consequences of our actions. Observation, recording, and monitoring are crucial elements of the sustainable design process.

The function of monitoring is to tell the story of how the site has changed, is changing, and is likely to change. It continuously records and informs our actions and is the major vehicle by which "the site speaks to us," providing the information that allows the sustainable designer to work with the natural regenerative processes inherent in the patterns of each landscape.

Frequently, a major hurdle in sustainable design is our limited understanding of how landscape systems function. We often base our designs and policy decisions on landscape "myths." Examples of such myths that have influenced the design and management of forest ecosystems in the northeastern United States are that "the creation of forest edge will benefit wildlife" or "opening the canopy will stimulate forest reproduction." The creation of a site database through monitoring helps us to understand the local mechanisms that govern a site, to see long-term trends, and to determine the consequences of intervention—both past and present. Building a site database allows policy to be based on real science and helps to ensure that the most effective strategies are applied to the solution of site problems. Site monitoring feeds the continuous adaptation of the plan and management program, as information about the site is recorded and analyzed, and trends are observed. The plan, then, is not simply the initial design document, but, as Allan Savory says of his holistic resource management model, "the word plan must become a twenty-four-letter word: plan-monitor-repair-replan."[7] Restoring, assessing the site, and modifying our actions or our nonactions are ongoing activities without which a plan or management program cannot be truly sustainable.

EVERY ACTION IS SIGNIFICANT— EVERY PLACE IS IMPORTANT

A design ethic that accepts the preeminence of the natural patterns of a place—water, soil, and vegetation—may not solve all of our problems, but it will go a long way toward changing current trends. No landscape, no matter how apparently pristine, is beyond the reach of human impact. Sustainable design must embrace the entire spectrum of landscapes at every scale and in every place and include sustainable agriculture, sustainable industry, sustainable cities, and sustainable wild lands. There are success stories: For example, fish can now be caught and eaten in the river flowing by City Hall in Stockholm, Sweden, and the water is good enough for a four-kilometer downtown swimming course.

Sustainable design provides a design framework that seeks to address all ecological values, to create an ongoing partnership with the living landscape, and to reverse the trend of needless destruction of our landscape. It is the growing realization of the interconnectedness of development and environmental processes worldwide and within our communities that drives the evolution of sustainable design. At every scale, sustainable design is fundamentally about integrating the natural structure of the site with the built environment. Where a place is understood, preserved, repaired, and celebrated as an integrated whole, it can be experienced as powerful and memorable. What follows is a gallery of projects by Andropogon that reveals the application of sustainable ecological design

PROJECT:

CENTRAL PARK WOODLANDS MANAGEMENT
New York City, New York

THE PARTICIPATORY PROCESS

Despite great success in renewing the formal areas of Central Park, efforts to restore the more natural areas had been stymied by controversy. The Central Park Conservancy asked Andropogon to help break this deadlock and to develop a plan for restoration that would be agreeable to a constituent group that included multiple agencies, park donors, park users, and nonprofit organizations such as the New York City Audubon Society. In 1989, the Phase One Report, "Landscape Management and Restoration Program for the Woodlands of Central Park," outlined a new approach to manage and restore 130 acres of woodlands, which included the North Woods, the Ramble, and the Hallett Nature Sanctuary.

The report was the result of interviews with members of environmental groups, community board representatives, woodland users, and park managers about their perceptions and concerns. Out of the interviews, four major problems were identified: (1) Rogue trails created by off-path use by hikers and bikers, (2) trampling of the Woodlands, (3) the breakdown of the storm drainage system, and (4) the spread of exotic invasive plants.

The report recognized that these problems could not be addressed successfully by the conventional capital project approach. To ensure full participation, a Woodlands Advisory Board was established, including scientists, community members, members of environmental groups, and park managers. Anyone with a concern for the North Woods was welcome, and all decisions were made by consensus or no action was taken. The role of the landscape architect changed from outside consultant to in-house facilitator.

The restoration of the Loch—the little stream valley within the North Woods with its historic arches—became the first project designed and built in consort with the Advisory Board. Funds from the capital budget were shifted from an outside landscape contractor to hiring and training in-house construction crews to carry out in-house designs. A new position of "woodlands manager" was created. The crews rebuilt the rockwork directly associated with the Huddlestone and Glenspan Arches, the little pools within the

Volunteers removing invasive exotics in Central Park's Woodlands.

stream, as well as the steps and pathways alongside the stream. New pathways were designed and built to accommodate new "desire" lines and to recharge stormwater runoff eroding the hillsides. Woodland management techniques to restore an urban forest suffering from excessive erosion and compaction and overrun with exotic invasive plants were developed with this crew as the project progressed.

The current woodlands management crew removes litter and exotic invasives, collects native seeds and plants throughout the park, and plants native plants. They organize volunteers to assist them. This participation provides a new form of recreation and creates a growing constituency aware of the problems faced by this urban woodlands. While the woodlands management crew and the volunteers are at work, visitors have a sense of renewal and security in the park, thus making the public aware of park problems and constructive solutions.

PROJECT:

MORRIS ARBORETUM
OF THE UNIVERSITY OF PENNSYLVANIA

Philadelphia, Pennsylvania

USING NATURAL MODELS TO MANAGE STORMWATER

Andropogon's development of the design for a new entrance road and parking areas for the Morris Arboretum was seen as an opportunity to demonstrate new solutions to regional problems. Traditionally, roads and parking areas devour land, and they are often bleak, ugly, and insensitive to the landscapes they pass through. Instead of contributing to the solution of environmental problems, such as stormwater runoff, new construction of this type usually exacerbates them.

The new entrance road and parking lot for the Morris Arboretum were to serve multiple purposes. All aspects of these new facilities were designed to enhance the sense of place and deepen the visitor's experience of the landscape. The new entry experience reestablishes the historical context of meadow and forest, which had been lost with the suburbanization of the community. The alignment of the road reflects the scale and character of the broad, open limestone valley and dramatizes the topography and the spatial experience of the place. Each curve of the road frames and reveals specific views as the visitor climbs the hill, culminating in the arrival at the newly renovated Widener Education Center. Road drainage was designed to disperse rather than concentrate water and to maintain the natural hydrologic regimen by allowing water to soak into the ground where it falls. Along the road, cobble gutters provide a typical Victorian edge to the roadway. The rough surface of these gutters decreases water velocity and allows some water to soak into the soil through the open joints of the cobbles. Excess water is discharged through inlets within the gutter into perforated pipes laid in long infiltration trenches that carry water back into the hillside for recharge.

The new road brings the visitor to the site of the former Morris Mansion, which was demolished in the late 1960s. The road culminates in a new parking area that occupies the site of the turnaround and entrance to the mansion. This parking area is tucked just below the major ridge that forms a natural link between the Arboretum's two main buildings. The new arrival point allows visitors to begin their tour of the gardens from the original entrance. The parking bays are designed to incorporate groundwater recharge beds underneath

The parking lot at the Morris Arboretum of the University of Pennsylvania, where rain soaks into the porous asphalt bays.

porous asphalt paving and are considered to be an important outdoor exhibit. Because of its role as a water collector, the parking area is designed as a series of nearly level terraces, which gives it an elegant and formal quality. In plan and section the lots are carefully integrated into the existing topography and vegetation, curving to follow the contours and hidden from visitors in the garden below by the brow of the hill. A central pathway runs along the ridge, between the parking terraces, collecting visitors from the parking lot and leading them to the major buildings. During a rainstorm, water in the parking bays disappears into the porous paving and the process of water recharging into the ground becomes part of the aesthetic of this landscape.

PROJECT:

LOANTAKA BROOK RESERVATION
Morristown, New Jersey

PROTECTION, CONSTRUCTION, AND RESTORATION METHODS TO SAVE THE SOIL

Parks and natural areas, because of construction for utility lines and roads, are especially vulnerable to intrusion by right-of-ways and destruction of habitat. Typical pipeline construction utilizes a 75- to 100-foot construction zone and equipment that sometimes weighs more than twenty tons. This kind of conventional construction method causes serious soil compaction, which can damage the shallow roots of beech trees and destroy the soil as a living medium and reservoir of forest reproduction. In Morristown, New Jersey, the Federal Energy Regulatory Commission mandated that the Algonquin Gas Transmission Company route a new thirty-six-inch natural gas pipeline through the Loantaka Brook Reservation, a mature oak-beech forest, to avoid a residential neighborhood that already had two existing gas lines.

In protecting this site, the primary goal was to preserve the forest as an intact ecosystem. Protection measures focused on maintaining a continuous tree canopy overhead and preserving soil biota and structure. Working closely with the contractor and the pipeline engineers, several strategies were devised and implemented: (1) Realignment of the route. To overlay an existing seam of disturbance, the proposed route was realigned to follow existing park trails, which reduced the amount of forest to be cleared and the area of soil disturbed. (2) Minimized disturbance of the adjacent habitat. The construction zone was fenced along the entire route through the park before construction began. Trees were felled by qualified arborists and lowered with ropes into the construction zone to prevent damage to the adjacent forest. Wherever possible, tree stumps were left in the soil and cut flush. (3) Reduced construction zone. By using the soil from the trench to construct the access road for the pipe-laying equipment, soil compaction and the width of the corridor were substantially reduced. The pipe itself was welded in the trench instead of alongside it. These measures allowed the construction zone to be reduced to thirty-five feet.

In restoring the site, the goal was to reestablish the rich forest ground layer. This required that the soil structure and its reservoir of life remain intact. Regulatory agencies in charge of soil protection mandate only minimal restoration, concentrating primarily on separating topsoil from subsoil and stabilizing the bare ground with turf grasses after the soil is replaced. Andropogon's alternative restoration proposal was to harvest the upper soil layers in blocks before real digging began, to preserve their existing stratification, and to ensure the continuity of soil microorganisms, woody rootstocks, bulbs, corms, and seeds.

Napp-Grecco, the contractor, developed an especially adapted front-end loader blade to remove the soil blocks from the forest floor over the pipeline trench. These blocks were stored alongside the open trench and then replaced over the backfilled trench. The spaces between the reinstalled mats were mulched with decomposed leaf litter from the local Shade Tree Commission. After construction, the impact on the forest floor was limited, with the canopy cover largely maintained and a thick regrowth of ferns and wildflowers and resprouting of shrubs and small trees.

A bulldozer specially adapted to lift woodland soil blocks at Loantaka Brook Reservation in Morristown, New Jersey.

PROJECT:

SMITHKLINE BEECHAM ANIMAL HEALTH PRODUCTS

Worldwide Headquarters
West Chester, Pennsylvania

ESTABLISHING AND SUSTAINING NATURAL HABITATS ON A CORPORATE SITE

In rural communities in the East where we once expected to find landscapes of woodlands, hedgerows, and meadows, we find that much of what is left of our agricultural heritage is turf in poor condition with isolated ornamental trees and shrubs. SmithKline Beecham sited its Animal Health Products facilities on a portion of a swamp that had been drained and filled, leaving the remainder of the site, a farm, for future development. In 1986 the client requested a master plan for the entire site, including a delineation of the boundaries of the Animal Health property and a detailed site plan to include new buildings, new parking, roads, and the creation of a corporate campus that would build on the site's natural assets. The client was willing to go beyond a conventional "country club" image and rehabilitate this deteriorated agricultural landscape.

The goal for landscape design and management was to bring back to the site, in a connected fabric, the complete range of habitats available in the region. The strategy was to divide the 300-acre site into three landscape management zones: (1) A well-manicured campus zone; (2) a managed agricultural landscape, which was planted, maintained, and enriched over time; and (3) natural areas, which, once established, would require only limited management while providing a critical greenway for the property.

A wide range of environmental conditions at this site allowed the expression of many habitats, from dry, open fields to narrow, woodland floodplain corridors. In particular, the wetland systems of the site were treated as opportunities, rather than as problems. Because the facility was built on a swamp, the springs and seeps continued to flow, despite filling, creating major drainage problems throughout the site. To reestablish the natural patterns of water on the site, the drainage swales were treated as intermittent streams, restoring the natural drainage by removing the riprap, regrading the swales to follow the natural geometry of the flow of water, and

The original
drainage situation at
SmithKline Beecham,
showing conventional
repairs with riprap
and boulders.

Before restoration, 1986

replanting them with a wide range of wetland plants once typical of this area. With the intermittent streams restored, the entire wetland system—intermittent streams, stream, and wet meadow—could be linked.

The large and highly degraded wet meadow along the entry road had been so trampled by grazing animals that it supported only a single species—sweet flag. In the new design, farm animals were relocated and a wide range of woody and herbaceous wetland species were reintroduced. The stream banks had also been trampled to the degree that they had eroded and collapsed after heavy storms. After three years, the banks were stabilized and revegetated with a variety of soil-biotechnical techniques, including brush layers, fascines, and fiberschines. Removing invasive exotics and replanting the gaps along the stream corridor created a continuous forested floodplain corridor along the stream, connecting with the township's designated con-

The swale with its natural drainage patterns restored.

After restoration, 1989

servation areas, while providing privacy for the research facilities and recreation for the employees.

In this project, site design was integrated with the site's rehabilitation. The result was a beautiful evocation of the local countryside and the reestablishment and reconnection of plant and animal habitats of the region, which was both beautiful and functional.

PROJECT:

MANITOGA: RUSSEL WRIGHT'S FOREST GARDEN

Garrison, New York

DESIGNING WITH PLANT COMMUNITIES AND HABITATS

Russel Wright's Manitoga is a dynamic, ecological garden of native plant communities. At Manitoga, Wright, one of the founders of the industrial design profession in the 1920s, celebrated the American landscape as a natural extension of his pioneering work in industrial design. Although Wright was neither a scientist nor a naturalist, Manitoga is an ecological garden because he asked the question, "What is this place?" He then brought the skills and the sensitivity of a designer to the task of discovering and dramatizing the patterns and processes of this landscape.

Wright's intervention at Manitoga has produced a remarkable work of art that reveals to the visitor the unique qualities of the Hudson Highlands. Although many elements of this country estate are familiar—parking court, terraces, quarry pool, paths, and the house itself—nothing is conventional. Wright's integrating vision blended the built elements and the natural landscape so that each was made visible and was enhanced by the other. The house is an integral part of the landscape—the physical exploration of the garden and the psychological preparation for it.

Manitoga is a landscape that has been managed purposefully and innovatively for more than thirty years. It is a living laboratory demonstrating a sophisticated expertise with the management of natural systems. This management has had two goals: To return the landscape to a diverse, healthy, self-sustaining system, and to create dramatic and complex aesthetic effects.

The property that Wright bought in 1942 was sixty-nine acres on the side of a steep hillside, overlooking the Hudson River in New York State. On it were three abandoned quarries filled with rock debris and covered with brambles. The forests, cutover numerous times, were nearly uniform young woodlands, "dense, impenetrable, dry and uninviting." They created what Wright called "a garden of woodland paths."

He was inspired by the plant communities and his experiences in this forested landscape. Working with the closed, continuous quality of the forest, he discovered, enhanced, and created a variety of openings, from small

The house and quarry at Manitoga.

gaps such as those that occur when a tree falls, to the large holes made when the rock was quarried. These spaces are the special events within the fabric of the garden. Wright noticed and expressed the different ages of the forest—the almost monospecific woodland groves, the mixed ages and species, the mature forest, and the ancient "primeval" forest. He worked to reveal forest structure, elaborating the differences in each edge and exploring the contrast between the forest edge and the interior.

The laurel "meadow" set on a broad, gently sloping terrace at the edge of a steep cliff, one of Wright's most spectacular landscapes, is one of many different expressions of the theme of an "opening in the forest." Here, where bedrock is close to the surface, Wright found a dense understory of laurels in a relatively open oak-hemlock forest. To emphasize the shrub and ground layers, Wright thinned the canopy, removing the hemlocks and leaving

Laurel Meadows at Manitoga.

clumps of oak trees to evoke the qualities of a woodland glade in a dappled shade. In response to the diminished competition and the increased light, the shrub layer of laurel, lowbush blueberry, and huckleberry proliferated under the scattered canopy. The laurel, which gives this opening its name, is sculpted in a long "S" curve that snakes back up the hillside at the top of the terrace, drawing the eye deep into the forest beyond the edge. In the center of this space, Wright thinned the canopy and removed the laurels in the shrub layer to create an open area carpeted with moss, which emphasizes the topography. On the sides of the laurel meadow, the closed forest defines its boundaries. Wright recognized that this dry terrace was the site of occasional wildfires, and used a light winter burn to maintain the crisp quality of this landscape and to prevent the hemlocks and black birches from returning.

PINECOTE, CROSBY ARBORETUM

Picayune, Mississippi

PARTNERSHIP WITH PLACE

The mission of the Crosby Arboretum is to preserve, display, and interpret the native plant communities of the region—in particular, the plant communities and habitats of one of the Gulf's major tributaries, the Pearl River. Located within three southern Mississippi counties, the Crosby Arboretum now includes a network of natural areas covering 1,700 acres. The purpose of these natural areas is to preserve typical native habitats and to provide sites for long-term ecological research. These sites are considered to be genetic archives and are protected from any development.

In the design for Pinecote, the public facility for the larger Crosby Arboretum, Andropogon and the arboretum director, Edward Blake, who is a landscape architect, formed the core of the planning team. The role of the landscape architects was to create a bridge between scientific and artistic expertise, synthesizing the ideas of a wide variety of specialists—including horticulturists, botanists, ecologists, cultural anthropologists, graphic artists, and architects—and to translate these ideas into thematic, programmatic, and site design concepts. The goal of design at Pinecote was to marry the artistic values of drama, beauty, and expressiveness with the scientific values of the correct relationships between plant and plant, and between plant and place. The design was governed by respect for the reality of the place—the biome, the region, and the local plant communities and habitats. All design at Pinecote—thematic structure, site planning, interpretive paths, architecture, plant displays, and site management techniques—sought to reveal the major natural processes of the Piney Woods and to express their evocative qualities. Planting design, for example, reflects the "architecture of nature," the underlying structure and organization—expressed as pattern—of each type of plant community type.

This sixty-four-acre property was an abandoned strawberry field in the flat, low-lying southern coastal plain. It was, initially, a discouragingly undistinguished site for an arboretum with the goal of displaying a rich variety of native plant communities and habitats. Mapping the "potential natural vegetation" revealed that plant habitats occur here along two continuums: (1) A successional gradient, showing the development of plant communities over time; and (2) a moisture gradient, showing the changes in environmental condition, particularly in relationship to the depth of the water table. In addition, half of the site had been repeatedly burned, so it was divided into burned and unburned portions. The site structure, revealed in this initial exploration, provided the basis for the site design and for the themes and locations of the four major path loops: (1) The introductory path loop, which reveals the diversity of the site; (2) the lake path, which explores lowland habitats; (3) the long path, which contrasts the burned and unburned areas; and (4) the forest interior path at the gum pond.

Prescribed fire management at the Crosby Arboretum. The use of fire reinstates a traditional cultural practice in the southern pine woods. Working closely with Dr. William Platt, associate professor of botany at Louisiana State University, Blake used a program of pulsed burns of varying intensities, set at different seasons, to foster an open landscape of grasses and wildflowers in the pine savana exhibit. Photograph by Edward Blake.

The Pine Savannah and Wildflower Meadow established through Crosby's program of pulsed burns. Photograph by Edward Blake.

The view toward the "slough" and portion of the lake path at Crosby. Photograph by Edward Blake.

In developing the site in consort with the reality of the place, the human-made changes accentuated potential diversity but did not reflect atypical characteristics. The Piney Woods Lake, although not originally found on-site, was introduced to make a uniform lowland more dramatic and interesting to the public. However, the pond is neither arbitrary in location, unnatural in appearance, nor unusual on such a site. The presentation of the lake evokes the southern, rain-fed swamp with still, shallow, tea-colored water under a canopy of trees, with a foreground of rushes, sedges, and aquatic wildflowers. A small stream flowing from the north, which a farmer or a beaver might have dammed up, would take a configuration very similar in shape and character to the lake that was constructed.

Pinecote Pavilion, the first building on the site, was designed by Jones and Jennings of Fayetteville, Arkansas, and it is intended to evoke the structure of a southern pine forest. This open pavilion was designed with the long, hot summer months in mind, where evening and morning use is particularly appropriate. The master plan calls for a series of pavilions throughout the site, each to be located in the heart of a plant association that it interprets. As many of the proposed pavilions as possible will be open-air and use historically effective cooling devices, such as wind-collecting towers.

Planting at Pinecote reflects "plant community structure," and goes beyond establishing native plants in order to place them in ecological patterns. New plantings are treated as plant communities, not as individual specimens, and they are displayed in the habitats in which they actually occur, with characteristic companions and in representative organic patterns. Each plant community is described by a local name. A "buttercup flat," the local term for open lowlands where the yellow pitcher plant proliferates, was created at Pinecote in a location in which conditions would foster this particular plant community. Habitat management techniques included burning, introduction of the species, and removal of competing species. The goal of the design and management of each exhibit was to transform the latest and best scientific understanding into compelling visual images.

Piney Woods Lake, as seen from Pinecote Pavilion. Drawing by Ken Nakaba, 1994.

NOTES

1. The epigraph is from Aldo Leopold, *A Sand Country Almanac* (New York: Oxford University Press, 1949), p. 221.

2. Susan Maxman, former president of the American Institute of Architects and principal, Susan Maxman Architects, Philadelphia.

3. Frank Lloyd Wright, source unknown.

4. Beryl Robichaud and Murray Buell, *Vegetation of New Jersey* (New Brunswick, N.J.: Rutgers University Press, 1973), p. 98.

5. Jack McCormick, *The Life of the Forest* (New York City: McGraw-Hill, 1966), p. 59.

6. Ian McHarg, "An Ecological Method for Landscape Architecture," 1969. Reprinted in *The Subversive Science: Essays Towards An Ecology of Man,* Paul Shephard and Daniel McKinley, eds. (Boston: Houghton Mifflin, 1969), p. 332.

7. Allan Savory, *Holistic Resource Management* (Covello, Calif.: Island Press, 1988), p. 4.

11

IMAGES OF AN IDEAL LANDSCAPE AND THE CONSEQUENCES FOR DESIGN AND PLANNING

METO J. VROOM

The popular image of the Dutch landscape is that of a flat marshy expanse, engraved by straight ditches that are flanked by windmills, where sturdy farmers sporting wooden clogs mind their cows and tulips. Winding rivers and vast horizons dominated by dramatic skies complete the picture. These are the emblems of the Dutch national heritage. The promotion abroad of these images goes back to the seventeenth-century landscape painters.

As Simon Schama (1987) observed, the independent Dutch nation-state was formed during a time of "dramatic physical alteration of its landscape." The Dutch have needed to plan, reclaim, and manage land from the sea, lakes, and rivers to create places for people to live. Much of the wealth generated from their mercantile acumen and former colonial enterprises has been invested from the seventeenth century onward in making new lands called "polders." The resultant verdure landscape has proved to be fecund. Over fifteen million people inhabit a nation roughly the size of Massachusetts and Connecticut combined. This most densely populated nation in Europe ranks second in the world in agricultural exports after the United States, and it is highly industrialized as well. It is common to see, for example, industrial establishments adjoin pastoral rural landscapes with their windmills, ancient farms, and citizens dressed in traditional costumes. Photograph by H. van Aggelen.

Contemporary commercial advertising exploits this image in a vulgarized way: Miniature windmills and pretty blonds wearing traditional costumes and wooden clogs sell national products such as cheese and tulip bulbs. But the clichés are outworn in the eyes of some observers: "Stuck with windmills and tulips, the Dutch still cherish but nowadays seldom celebrate the dwindling compage of water meadows, copses, dairy holdings, and meandering rivers immortalized by Rembrandt and van Ruysdael."[1] In the meantime, KLM Airlines has shifted its advertising from Delft blue tiles and windmills to the icon of the graceful swan landing in marshy waters. What is there to celebrate?

Holland, or the hollow land, covers only part of the nation called the Netherlands, or the Low Countries. In the eastern provinces undulating higher sandy grounds with their irregular patterns bear resemblance to the adjoining German uplands and are much less commonly recognized as being Dutch. The origins of the western and northern lowlands are associated with the permanent struggle of its settlers against invading waters of the North Sea and the rivers. In recent geological history, the dynamic interaction between land and water created ever-changing scenes in space and time. Wind and wave action threw up dune ridges, causing a stagnation of the waters of the Rhine and Meuse rivers, and this resulted in vast marshes. The dunes never formed a continuous barrier, however, and during periods of high tides and stormy weather the sea entered these marshes and eroded away large parts, forming lakes that slowly would be filled by marine sediments. This resulted in a complicated pattern of sandy ridges, bogs, gullies, and mud flats. The sea and rivers alternated in building up and destroying land.

Human settlement on this soggy land was a hazardous undertaking. The eternal threat of flooding was countered by an increasingly complicated mechanism of surface drainage systems, supported by windmills and pumps. A landscape of polders and drained marshland, laid out in geometric patterns, came into being. All this required enormous investments, constant supervision, and a highly disciplined central organization.[2] Whenever internal strife or periods of war caused a lowering of the standard of maintenance and dikes were neglected over some time, punishment was inevitable: In the fifteenth century major floods destroyed much of the reclaimed landscapes of the southwestern part of the country. Land patterns resulting from these floods still dominate the map of the province of Zeeland.

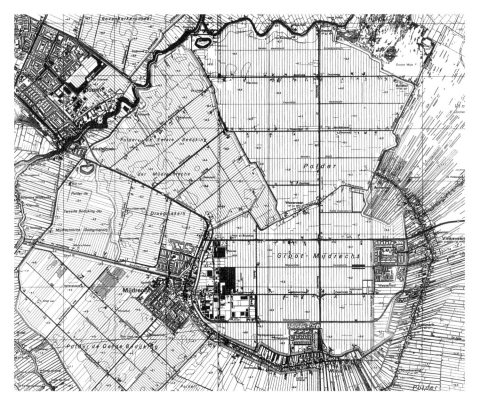

Polder Groot Mijdrecht and surroundings, Province of Utrecht, the Netherlands. The converging lines on the extreme right of the map represent remnants of peatland, mostly dug away. The polders in the center were cleared of their top layer of peat, beginning in the twelfth century, and the whole area was converted into a large inland lake. Reclamation of the land and the subdivision of the new clay polder occurred between 1789 and 1880. Source: © Topografische Dienst, The Netherlands.

When the North Sea last broke through the coastal defenses, in 1953, and destroyed thousands of homes and killed eighteen hundred people, the event became etched in the minds of the population and is remembered still as a national disaster.[3] A reminder occurred in January of 1995 when the Rhine threatened to burst its dikes, and 250,000 people plus an untold number of cattle were evacuated to higher grounds. A widespread hypothesis holds that these historic events have been ingrained in the minds of the Dutch and not only have strongly influenced some of their basic attitudes, values, and perceptions, but also have stimulated the maintenance of an efficient and orderly planning organization.

RULE AND ORDER IN PLANNING

It is not simply a set of standardized icons such as the polder, windmill, canal, and river that typifies contemporary Dutch landscape. There is an overall orderly appearance, a clear separation of town and country, with well-kept housing areas and landscapes that look as if they have been worked over by a giant rake. Holland is an orderly looking country, and Dutch planning authorities intend to keep it that way. "The edges of most Dutch towns and cities are clearly marked by canals, rows of trees, open space and the like. The edges signal the will to maintain the distinction between town and country. Above all they bear witness to the intention and the ability of the Dutch to keep development at bay."[4]

A comparison between the Dutch planning system and that of other countries reveals that the Netherlands probably is the most planned country in the world. Only a few democracies of the world can match the planning apparatus of the Dutch government.[5] In Dutch writings this circumstance is largely ignored, for the situation is considered to be normal.

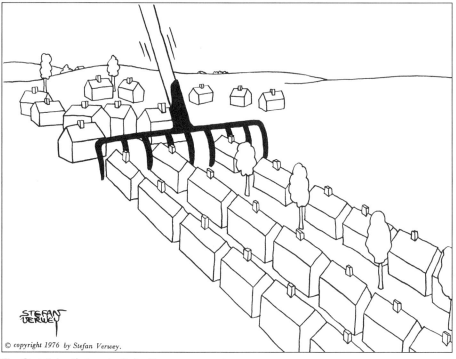

The Giant Rake. Cartoon by Stefan Verwey.

Visitors from abroad are impressed and sometimes delighted by the neatness of the Dutch landscape and tend to praise the Dutch planning system as an exemplary one. Even the enlightened mind of Lewis Mumford fell for the evident contrast between the well-contained development around Dutch cities and the urban sprawl elsewhere.[6]

Some observers are liable to base their conclusions on all-too-brief visits and fail to notice the underlying tensions and frustrations that are associated with what J. B. Jackson calls the "political landscape"; that is, a landscape that reflects or expresses the ideals and needs of government, of a powerful officialdom, rather than that of the ordinary citizen, and where the quality of private space is considered to be a matter of public concern.[7] This acceptance of order in a freedom-loving society is one of the paradoxes of life in the Netherlands. Whereas, for instance, the introduction of personal identity cards, a standard phenomenon in neighboring countries, is meeting strong resistance and is seen as an unacceptable invasion of privacy, the extremely strict planning and building codes are grudgingly accepted. A strict control over urban expansion and land use in rural areas is exercised by means of an elaborate set of zoning laws, building codes, and vast amounts of housing and other subsidies. No private citizen is allowed to build, add to, or alter the appearance of his or her house, dig a pond, fell a tree, or erect a shed or fence without written permission from local or provincial authorities. Seeking permission takes a long time, and requests are often refused on the grounds of aesthetic considerations and landscape amenity. A certain amount of arbitrariness is inevitable in these bureaucratic procedures.

This strict control over private initiatives is inverted in the realm of public planning, as the law requires a great deal of consensus on decisions affecting the implementation of communal projects. Any major project exceeding a certain amount of territory or investment requires public hearings, an environmental impact statement, and the cooperation of the national and provincial governments and local communities. As a result of these procedures, the time between a government initiative to construct a highway, bridge, tunnel, or railroad and the final and irrevocable decision to build may be twenty to thirty years. An overdose of public participation leads to an emphasis on private interests exemplified in the much-deplored NIMBY (Not in My Back Yard) syndrome. Apart from the manifold private interests, politically influential pressure groups also demand an orderly and well-kept landscape and town appearance. All this results in repeated revisions of plans, slows down the construction of building sites and the layout of infrastructure, and makes development very costly. Planning procedures have now been pronounced as being too "syrupy," and the government is preparing new legislation aimed at speeding up the decision-making process without losing public participation, a daunting task to say the least.

UNDERLYING VALUES AND PERCEPTIONS

The traditional struggle against the sea is reputed to have made the Dutch a highly disciplined people in terms of the planning and management of their environment.[8] Whether this is fact or folklore remains to be seen. After the major flood disaster in 1953 when the North Sea broke the sea dikes and flooded large parts of western Holland and Zeeland, public acceptance of drastic measures was very high indeed, and special legislation allowing for the strengthening of all dikes and the closing of the major seaways in the southwest was quickly passed in Parliament. Vast budgets became available overnight, and the project proceeded according to the original plan, even if some very expensive solutions had to be found in order to protect ecological processes in the eastern Scheldt.[9] Forty years later the fear of flooding had begun to ebb away, and the final stage of the project, which called for a reconstruction of all river dikes along the Rhine and Meuse rivers, met so much opposition that work was temporarily stopped in the fall of 1992, awaiting a renewed investigation of the why and how. The opposition, led by environmentalists, claimed that the heritage of the nation's river landscapes with their meandering dikes was under threat of total destruction. Nature struck back once again in January of 1995 when the water level in the Rhine rose to almost unprecedented heights. Some areas flooded, but the main dikes held—just barely. A state of national emergency was declared, and the population of a number of towns and villages was temporarily evacuated. The fear of water was suddenly back, and the impact, also due to the international media coverage, was tremendous. As a result, special legislation was passed again and quickly by Parliament, and the strengthening of the most vulnerable sections of river dikes commenced that same year. Environmentalists then went through a phase of low popularity. Many Dutch appear to be forgetful of their ancient enemy, and their proclaimed discipline seemingly is not founded primarily on the fear of water.

What do we know about prevailing attitudes? Attitudes to landscape quality always vary. There are some qualities, however, that seem to rank higher in the esteem of the Dutch than others. Surveys on environmental attitudes in three areas in the Netherlands, conducted between 1984 and 1987, yielded a number of dominant characteristics that come into play in the perception and evaluation of Dutch landscape scenes.[10] Some of these dominant characteristics are:

- *Unity:* The coherence of elements at different levels of scale; to fit and to belong
- *Land use:* The recognition of function; legibility, but also the opportunity to intervene and to change
- *"Naturalness":* Spontaneous growth and development and the absence of uniformity, large dimensions, or geometric patterns
- *Maintenance* or upkeep: An orderly, well-kept, or tidy appearance
- *Historical continuity:* Signs of the passing of time
- *Spaciousness:* An orderly subdivision of open space

There is an emphasis on tidiness and order. The respondents claim to love tidiness but at the same time they like naturalness because of the absence of straight lines and geometric patterns. They abhor a cluttered and polluted environment. But are they really all that tidy themselves? Illegal dumping of garbage is prevalent, and the famous canals of Amsterdam are loaded with debris. Dutch horticulture and especially bulb growers are reputed to hold the world's record in terms of pesticide use per acre. These facts seem to belie the claim of tidiness and cleanliness, and point to the same discrepancy between attitudes and real-life behavior as noted in other countries.[11] Historian Simon Schama describes how the seventeenth-century Dutch amazed foreign visitors by the amount of scrubbing and cleaning of both their homes and their doorsteps.[12] But the urban canals were cesspools at that time. In recent decades the Dutch government has succeeded in cleaning up some of the worst polluted waters and soils, at great cost. Industrial and urban pollution have diminished tremendously, but in the meantime agricultural production continues to threaten severely the nation's environmental quality.

AGRICULTURE AND ENVIRONMENT

The shaping and management of the Dutch landscapes has been predominantly in the hands of its farmers for many centuries. Most of the nation consists of highly productive farmland, and the intensity of use is high and increasing. While extensive areas of pastureland still cover most of the western parts, a more industrialized scene has emerged elsewhere. Beef cattle, hogs, and poultry are raised in large quantities in modern sheds that have replaced traditional farm buildings. Their visual and olfactory impact is strong, and the gigantic quantities of manure produced exceed demand and result in excessive dumping of nitrates, phosphates, and toxic minerals. Horticultural production in greenhouses (vegetables and cut flowers) and outdoors (bulbs and nursery stock) requires intensive spraying of pesticides. This sort of production is extremely important for the national economy, but the environmental impact is frightening: The pollution of soils and groundwater is reaching dangerous levels in certain areas. Deeper aquifers are being affected and the quality of drinking water is at risk. This process is almost irreversible, and the result is that we have a "time bomb" in the subsoil.[13] Both politicians and conservationists are convinced that something must be done to remedy this situation.

The discussion on the desirability either to separate or to interweave "nature and culture" in the rural landscape has been ongoing for decades in the Netherlands. The issue was complicated by the policy to combine the protection of natural vegetation and wildlife with that of historic patterns and settlements. The Dutch heritage is a combination of natural and cultural phenomena, and both need to be nursed carefully to survive. Attempts to interweave natural elements with productive farmland at a local scale have largely failed because economic interests always prevail. Some Dutch landscapes are, therefore, in danger of becoming internally disharmonious, and landscape design will be reduced to cosmetic treatment as long as hygienic standards are not improved. Non-Western anthropologists visiting Holland have commented: "Over here almost everything is created for its looks, the pretty flowers without fragrance, the large immaculate vegetables without any taste, the beautiful landscapes without any internal harmony."[14] This may be a somewhat exaggerated conclusion, but the warning is well taken.

The increasing degradation of agricultural landscapes since 1945 has led to the government's decision to set aside large areas of land where traditional scenery prevails and natural phenomena are still to be found. Farmers in these areas are subsidized to curtail production and assist in the protection of environmental and ecological quality. The result of these measures is not wholly satisfactory.[15] There are the problems of landscape image and costs. Selected landscapes of a certain age apparently are deemed fit for retirement and removed from the economic system. As a result, they no longer represent the interaction between contemporary people and land. In the long run the cost to the taxpayer becomes staggering: Landscape management becomes parkland management, while at the same time land values are tied to the extremely high production of Dutch agriculture.

A new policy, calling for a drastic separation of natural and cultural landscapes, represents a new outlook. After careful selection of valuable sites and zones throughout the country, the pattern of ecological corridors of varying width and hundreds of kilometers in length has been traced on the national maps. Some parts of this policy are actually being implemented. These corridors are separated from the adjoining farmland both in the visual and hydrological sense.[16] In some places controlled flooding of existing reclaimed polders has been proposed.[17]

THE LANDSCAPE OF ECOSYSTEMS

One interesting example of these corridors is the 1992 proposal called "Living Rivers" of the Dutch chapter of the World Wildlife Fund (WWF).[18] The intention is to dig up and remold the floodplains of the highly regulated stream flow of the Rhine. More diversity will be created by digging gullies and building up river islands, thereby forming a variety of wetlands and higher grounds. Nature is to be reconstructed. This costly project is proposed to be financed by the sale of clay sediment recovered from the plain to be used for the production of bricks and roof tiles. Within these ecological corridors an entirely new landscape is created. Or is it a re-creation of landscapes of the past?

The WWF initiative may be hailed as a marked progress in thinking, and it has been widely acclaimed in the Netherlands. It is good to see con-

The Living Rivers pilot project "Blauwe Kamer" near Wageningen, the Netherlands. Land has been dug away to create new habitats for wildfowl and specific vegetation types along the Rhine River. Photographs by M. J. Vroom.

servationists getting away from a seemingly hopeless defense of ever-diminishing nature areas and adopting an aggressive and creative stand. After a long period of strained relations between the doers and the protectors, landscape planners are again working happily side by side with ecologists in devising new ecosystems that will form interconnected linear patterns throughout the country.

Boar, deer, and elk are to be reintroduced in river landscapes, and waterfowl are expected to multiply, while rarer birds such as the black stork are expected to return. The image presented of the newly formed landscape resembles that of some centuries ago, at the time when the Rhine followed its own meandering course. In the meantime one or two pilot projects are in an advanced stage of construction. Grazing areas for wild horses and a selected breed of cattle adjoin areas for waterfowl and denser stands of poplars. Abandoned brick plants complete the picture of a landscape à la Jean-Jacques Rousseau's Ermenonville. But in this case the ruins are real, not follies.

All seems well, albeit not in the eyes of everyone concerned. The layout of these eco-landscapes shows a highly complex array of adjoining habitats. Paths are traced to allow visitors to behold the wonders of nature, but there is an overall lack of coherence, and no thought is given to the creation of a sequence of spaces and viewpoints. The overall atmosphere is that of cultural regression: The visitor is reminded of times long ago. The edict "Design with Nature" as practiced by ecologists is a rather one-sided affair and results in the landscape of the ecocrat, the counterbalance of the landscape of the technocrat. There are conflicts with other interests as well: Digging up large parts of existing farmland for the sake of new variety in habitats means erasing traces of natural landforms, which makes geomorphologists unhappy. Existing settlement patterns, some of which date to pre-Roman times, are also lost in the process, and historians and archeologists are in an uproar. Some cynical critics view the result of this "nature construction" activity as some kind of Disneyland-type, make-believe world.

The basic questions are, of course: What is our perception of the relation between people and nature? Are we satisfied when we have set aside—or created—certain areas where wild animals may frolic behind fences in the midst of a highly exploited agricultural and urbanized landscape? Is this activity in agreement with a proclaimed stewardship of the land? Or is it to be viewed as a mere letter of indulgence allowing us to proceed at will outside nature areas?[19]

NATURAL VALUES, NATURE PROTECTION, AND DEFINITIONS OF LANDSCAPE

One might wonder if the pursuit of nature conservation in one of the most densely populated and precisely planned countries in the world is worthwhile or even feasible. The expansion of built-up areas, the constant modernization of farming, and the improvement of infrastructure are creating unfavorable conditions for the survival of natural systems in general. Natural processes are discernible in a subdued and controlled way, except in a number of nature reserves set aside and managed by the government or private conservation societies. New initiatives for the layout of so-called urban ecosystems are found in many cities, but these are largely symbolic phenomena. At the same time geographic conditions provide enormous opportunities for wildlife: The vast coastal mud flats, with their gullies and sand banks; the estuaries of the Rhine and the Scheldt; and the inland marshy grasslands constitute wetlands of international status. These areas require careful control and management, based on a well-conceived overall policy on the conservation and development of nature and landscape.

This brief description of some of the planning and management problems in rural areas of the Netherlands so far demonstrates that the control over the environment is less efficient than it is reputed to be. There are various reasons for this. From the point of view of landscape architectural theory, the most interesting aspect is the circumstance that planners appear to have different perceptions of the nature of their tasks and use varying definitions of the object they are confronted with—that is, the Dutch landscape. As a result, communication between planners, landscape architects, and politicians is difficult, and policies vary.

Government agencies and private consultants use their own definitions, consciously or unconsciously, openly or by implication. Some definitions are based on high-minded principles or tasks perceived, whereas others serve the interests of certain professional groups, providing them with the most convenient opportunities to implement or counter change. The theoretical foundation is not always adequate and forms a poor basis for a consistent landscape policy.

In the Netherlands the main responsibility for town and country planning is shared by the Ministry of Planning and Environment and the provincial governments. The Ministry of Agriculture, however, has always claimed the responsibility for the planning and management of rural areas, this in view of the circumstance that Dutch farmers control most of our territory. During the 1980s the agricultural ministry's tasks were expanded and now include the conservation of nature and landscape. This implies responsibility for a simultaneous safeguarding of conflicting interests: Production, development, and conservation. Policymakers and landscape planners must, therefore, tread their way carefully. According to the latest official policy document on landscape, the agricultural ministry states its objective as "to promote a long-term maintenance and conservation of a landscape of high quality." And landscape is defined as follows: "Landscape is the visible part of the earth's surface, as determined by the interdependence and the interrelation between factors like soils, topography, water, climate, flora and wildlife, as well as human activities."[20]

The definition given here seems like a sound basis for a well-conceived landscape policy. The simultaneous conservation and development of landscape, however, has proved to be extremely difficult because of the conflicting interests associated with the two objectives. It is even more difficult to implement for a government department internally divided in outlook and ideology.

LANDSCAPE AS A SYSTEM

To define landscape as all that we see and as an expression of all that happens is to view landscape as a system composed of a vast number of interrelated subsystems. This definition implies a step forward from the previously held notion that the outward appearance of a landscape can be manipulated as an independent characteristic, conforming to some cosmetic standard of quality. The systems view has provided us with a basis for understanding some of the economic, cultural, and natural processes, and it is helpful in dealing with change.

But not all is well with this approach nor with the way it has been applied to comprehensive planning in the Netherlands. It poses quite a challenge for planners and designers, a challenge that might be more than they can cope with. A careful approach is required when one is faced with the overwhelming amount of information to be processed. This approach has not always been apparent. One consequence of the systems view is the need to know and understand the extremely complex interrelationships in space and time of all processes in the natural and the human-made world. Landscape viewed this way becomes synonymous with "a history of total environment."[21] So far we have only a limited understanding of some of the subsystems, important as this may be. The functioning of a production system such as horticulture, or the management of water control systems, may be understood much better than in the past, but their interconnectedness is often ignored. The ramifications of natural ecosystems need much more research in terms of cause and effect, and our comprehension of social systems is scant indeed.

There is, also, the ethical aspect. What sort of planning and design results from a growing understanding of these matters, or perhaps the illusion of such insight? It is apt to lead to an arrogant centralistic type of planning in which the experts mold society into a physical environment they have conceived.

The ideal of centralistic planning was dominant in Dutch planning in the early post–World War II years when the first National Planning Agency saw its task as (literally) drawing up a National Plan, which would regulate or fix all land use throughout the country. This idea was quickly abandoned on the basis of the experience that changes in economic development and in values and behavior made every national plan outdated at the moment of its publication. The concept reemerged in 1973—in different wording—when the Third Report on Physical Planning was published. In this report the national landscape was viewed as a system, essentially composed of four subsystems, identified as economic, ecological, management, and visual.[22]

The underlying motive is a "quest for certainty" leading to a "quest for control." This is a socialist ideal that has proved to be unattainable in authoritarian states and is unthinkable in a democracy.[23] As long as we are unable to control natural processes because of inadequate knowledge, we certainly should not assume the arrogant posture of wanting to exert social control over the human world. In a democratic society people express their own will and want to shape their own world. A better approach is to try and plan in a flexible way, sticking to the main issues and allowing for unexpected developments. This may be seen as the philosophy underlying the proposals to introduce "framework planning," as exemplified in the pattern of ecological corridors described above.[24]

In recent years planning philosophies in the Netherlands changed in outlook, albeit not wholeheartedly. There is a growing awareness that total control is impossible and that many decisions should, perhaps, be left to market forces. A careful planning and management of subsystems, such as that represented by the interaction of plants and soils, and based on an understanding of some of the complexities of the environment, is of vital importance. The systems approach in comprehensive planning, however, when based on an authoritarian ideology, leads to unwanted consequences. It certainly does not tell us how to design. It cannot serve as the only way to look at landscape.

THE LANDSCAPE OF ADDED VALUES

Landscape analysis techniques, which have emerged since the early 1960s and are still being applied, are based on the notion that landscape as a whole is too complex a notion to be understood with an eye on planning interventions and, therefore, must be dissected into certain component parts. Landscape is subdivided in a number of territorial units, characterized by some form of continuity or coherence, expressed in types of land use, landform, or vegetation, all depending on the characteristics of the area studied and the planning objectives stated. These units are described and their quality is assessed. This type of analysis has helped a great deal in predicting the impact of new development in particular places, but the problem of how to combine and unify what was taken apart seems to be baffling the analysts.

Another problem lies in the evaluation methods used. Some land values can be expressed in terms of money, whereas others must be rated on the basis of more abstract parameters. Both the choice and the combination of these categories leads to arbitrary decisions. Ecological criteria such as diversity, uniqueness, and exchangeability of species are frequently used for the rating of scenic elements. These ratings are added up in numerical form or by overlay maps.[25] This type of landscape evaluation is internationally well known and has acquired a respected standing in the Netherlands because it has a scientific ring to it; its application is still popular in regional planning.[26] Landscape values appear to be suitable for mathematical treatment and can be calculated systematically. This approach not only is based on a lack of insight in human perception and behavior, but also betrays logic.

Apart from the obvious problems associated with the establishment of boundaries between units, the adding up of apples and pears, and the synthesis of parts into wholes, pitfalls abound. Some studies show that the landscape analyst does not know how to rate high-tension wires or rural gas stations, with the result that these objects are not included in the survey. There are "hidden values" that this approach does not recognize.

The approach has some merits for conservation policies in certain areas where the protection of existing elements is of prime importance, but it has a strongly negative effect on planning, especially in a densely populated country such as the Netherlands. Once an area is pronounced as having a certain "value" it becomes very difficult to change this assessment. New development always must go to places that show the least value. Planning is reduced to weighing and balancing, and to the avoidance of conflicts between the new and the existing. Making a leap forward by imaginative design is an apparently unheard of possibility.

THE LANDSCAPE OF SPACE

Landscape architecture is concerned, in part, with the layout of open space. Dimensions of space are important attributes of any landscape.[27] The conscious design of types of outdoor space, however, as practiced in urban parks, has its limitations in the layout of multifunctional landscapes.

In the relatively flat landscapes of the Netherlands the enclosure of space is mostly defined by buildings and trees and, in principle, is subject to planning control. Dutch landscape planners have attempted to implement form concepts in their plans, with varying success. The difficulty of molding landscapes into a preconceived form, even in a country where central planning is based on such powerful instruments, was demonstrated in the reclaimed polders of the former Zuiderzee, which presented a chance to form a new landscape by the siting of towns and villages and the planting of shelterbelts and woodland. As J. H. Meeus has demonstrated, the original idea to create a hierarchy in spatial configuration in the Northeast Polder by means of a planting plan is only visible in the original drawings.[28] After its implementation the plan already had been changed considerably, because the cooperation of local communities and independent individuals was required to effect the concept. In later years further changes came about, and presently little of the original character of the planting plan remains. Landscape plans cannot precisely prescribe landscape form in the long run; one cannot control or fix space in a living landscape. Only the main outlines have some degree of permanence.

On the basis of extensive map studies in which buildings, woodland, and tree plantings were registered all over the country, the Dutch Physical Planning Agency has concluded that the degree of enclosure in different areas in the Netherlands has changed considerably during the twentieth century. Small-scale landscapes in the eastern part of the country, where all land-lots used to be enclosed by hedgerows in the early decades of the twentieth century, are disappearing. Farm machinery requires larger land-lots, and trees and hedgerows have been removed. The landscape has become more open.[29] From an ecological view this is a negative development: Diversity in habitats has decreased. There is, also, a tendency toward visual uniformity. At the same time a reversed process is going on in the open pastureland in the western provinces. Building activities and the layout of infrastructure and recreation areas have led to more vertical elements and boundaries. The resulting alarm over the apparently increasing uniformity in scale and character of the Dutch landscape as a whole is understandable but not entirely justified. This is so not only because the perspective at eye level differs from impressions gained from maps, but also because boundary lines may, in reality, be transparent screens, and isolated objects may improve the perception of depth. Equally important is the circumstance that differentiation in landscape units is not solely determined by its degree of enclosure. It is the total impression of a landscape character that allows the experience of differences.

The notion of space is intimately connected with that of place.[30] Space is the result of the boundaries that define place in a given period of time.[31]

THE LANDSCAPE OF PLACE

The specific Dutch landscape of place in the western lowlands is associated with the need to keep one's feet dry and one's house from drowning in a soggy land. Its origins can be deducted through historical analysis. The reclaimed marshlands and polders of the Netherlands may appear to be uniform at first glance, but a closer study reveals a great deal of subtle change in topography. Both the military and the landscape designer are trained to

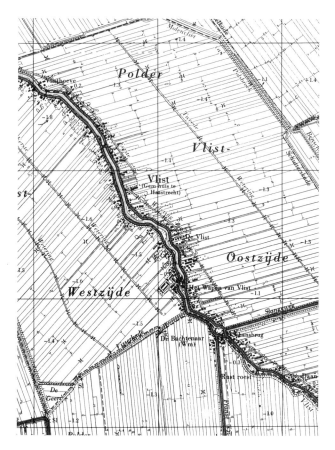

A cartographic example of the Dutch landscape of place. De Vlist in Zuid Holland is a creek that runs through former marshland. Repeated flooding in the past resulted in sedimentation of clay along the banks, creating higher, dryer, and more stable ground. This was the physical basis for a linear settlement with its characteristic frontage and rear parts of farmsteads. A natural gradient runs from high to low, from dry to wet, from clay to peat. Source: © Topografische Dienst, The Netherlands.

observe this unevenness. Dutch topographic maps used to be surveyed and drawn by the Department of Defense to show all the spots where the soldier can hide. Landscape architects learn to compare these elevations with soil maps: Any change in level is related to changes in the composition of the subsoil and in the groundwater level. In the coastal marshlands, sandbanks, almost imperceptible, protrude through the upper layers of peat and form a stable foundation for buildings and clumps of trees. At the same time, this higher ground makes these areas less susceptible to periodic flooding. This is the natural basis for centuries-old settlements that are so typical in parts of the western provinces. Similar developments have occurred elsewhere— along former or existing creeks, on fossil riverbanks along the Rhine. Physical conditions are never identical, nor are the settlements that adapt in form and size to these conditions. This is the landscape of vertical relations where every place has its own face. Older towns and hamlets mostly show a central district in which natural conditions have created a strong identity in layout.[32] There is also an ecological aspect: This type of settlement has created diversity in natural conditions; for instance, in places where farms occupy higher grounds in linear patterns, showing front and rear yards, with a diminishing intensity of land use toward the rear of lots. Dutch landscape architecture students are trained to make use of such natural conditions to create new variety. They also try and fit new patterns into the old, creating as little disturbance as possible. In the layout of some parks and recreation areas the geometry of surrounding land patterns penetrates the site, thereby weaving the new into the existing. This approach can only be applied in places where development is of a modest scale and character. Whenever the size of new elements such as housing areas exceeds the limits of the soil type units, a different approach is called for.[33]

THE FUNCTIONAL LANDSCAPE

Modern development occurs at a large scale and changes are sudden, in contrast to the continued slow development of landscapes of the past. The strengthening of vertical relationships, even if possible, fails to solve the problems one must confront. Landscape, therefore, should be looked at with different eyes. Horizontal relations now dominate conditions for settlement: It is the vicinity of the highway or the seaport rather than the soil conditions that govern decisions affecting new development. Functionalism has emerged as the new basis for landscape design. A "good" landscape is a landscape that functions in an optimal way, in social, economic, and ecological spheres. This approach overlaps with the holistic view described above, but the emphasis in a functional view is on the expression of meaning in which some elements might be emphasized and visual contrast consciously created.

During the 1950s a small group of landscape architects, working with the renowned Nico de Jonge, advocated a type of functionalism that in later years was associated with the notion of "legibility": Show what the various types of land use are and let individual elements stand out and be recognized. Adaptation to landscape patterns dating from the past is not the right answer, according to this view; rather, the new should stand out in sharp

Some of the contemporary Dutch parks are simple in layout and spatial sequencing. The Zevenkamp neighborhood is situated on the eastern outskirts of Rotterdam. It was built in the 1960s, is of fairly high density (sixty dwellings per hectare), and lies in a former polder four meters below sea level. This circumstance required the raising of the land by layers of sand. The park zone, designed by landscape architects Riek Bakker and Ank Bleeker, runs from south to north, where it opens up in a continuous greenbelt on the northern outskirts. It demonstrates the use of simple design elements such as open rectangular meadows, straight rows of trees, and reintroduced sections of dikes, canals, and ditches reminiscent of the former polder landscape. The combination of these elements forms a strong entity. The parkland is of a robust character and is designed for little maintenance and rough use. A former polder canal was converted into a moat with green embankments between housing units. Photograph by H. van Aggelen.

contrast to the old. This contrast heightens the awareness of the change over time and the existing land-use conflicts. This functionalist view may underlie a moralistic attitude; for example, farm buildings and farm yards should look good and need no sheltering plant screens to satisfy the need for an orderly and aesthetic looking landscape. This attitude caused a great deal of irritation on the part of the Ministry of Agriculture, and a certain professor of landscape architecture got a dressing down from a top government official for training his students not to corrupt themselves by being exploited as camouflage experts. This highly principled stand helped to frustrate government attempts toward what was called a "reconciliation of modern farming and landscape amenity." The real government objective, however, was to reduce the opposition to the expansion and modernization of agriculture. Frustrating this objective was considered to be a serious offense.

A typical example of this functionalist approach was exemplified in a scheme originating in the 1950s involving the layout of large drinking water reservoirs adjoining the river Meuse (Maas). Existing low-lying polders in the Biesbosch Estuary were to be surrounded by high dikes and used to store drinking water to be pumped to Rotterdam in times of need. De Jonge and fellow landscape architect Alle Hosper designed high, black, asphalt-covered dikes in geometric patterns, which stood out as artificial elements against the surrounding seminatural estuary landscape. The scheme was deemed unacceptable and authorities commissioned a different design in which they attempted to fit sinuous greened dikes into the existing environment.

OTHER VIEWS OF LANDSCAPE

The views and definitions of landscape discussed so far have originated in the professional world of landscape planners and architects. There are, also, more traditional views of what the Dutch landscape should look like, views that have had, and still have, consequences for the way landscape architects are able to operate. There are, also, consequences in terms of design quality and planning logic.

During the 1970s, when all authority was challenged, the notion that planners and designers could shape the daily environment of citizens came under fire. It was believed that the role of professional experts should be reduced to that of counselors of groups and individuals who wanted to make up their own minds about the sort of environment they wanted. Some students in landscape architecture devised their own notion of a "democratic landscape." When charged with the design of a park zone in a southern Dutch town they started off by ringing doorbells and asking people what they wanted. To their utmost dismay—and their instructor's delight—the response was strongly negative. "You are supposed to be the professional expert; we want you to come up with ideas and proposals," was the general response. However democratic one's attitude might be, there is always the challenge to invent and compose, to delight and stimulate, especially in park design. In the 1980s the design professions bounced back and happily resumed their self-proclaimed task of cultural renovators.

Dutch civil engineers who plan and design roads, canals, dikes, and bridges think of "landscape" in terms of a green cloth of trees, shrubs, and herbaceous vegetation that blissfully covers human-made form, blends the new into the old, and hides the ungainly and the shameful parts. Their ideas about "fitting in" new construction to an existing environment are limited to attempts to dig in, to screen off. They cannot conceive their work as one of the constituent parts of a landscape. In their eyes the landscape is reduced to a green mantle. This attitude has resulted in some awkward design solutions.

Agricultural engineers have similar problems in viewing landscape as an expression of the interaction between land use and natural factors. While carrying out their task in improving the layout of the land as part of a nation-wide Land Reconsolidation Program, their prime concern used to be more efficient agricultural production. Now the objectives have been expanded to include the needs of outdoor recreation, nature conservation, and landscape.[34] These four "functions" are seen as types of land use and are called "planning sectors." A sector is defined as a specific activity requiring a certain area of land suitable for this particular use. One needs a plan and a budget to achieve this goal. "Landscape" is one of these sectors and, therefore, is defined as the total amount of land surface needed to plant trees and shrubs (to be distributed, of course, in an agreeable pattern). There is a special "landscape budget" set aside for this purpose. The total area as well as the budget available for the landscape sector are predetermined. Here again there is little idea of the circumstance that a new layout of the land is the backbone of the architecture of landscape, creating far more change than any additional plant materials could support or compensate.

Both in civil engineering and agricultural land-use planning definitions of landscape are made subservient to a procedure in which the engineer traditionally dominates the planning process. The task of the landscape architect is limited in this view to aligning roads with trees, to embellishing and to hiding objects whenever deemed necessary. The result is a cosmetic landscape that has lost its legibility.

CONCLUSION

Varying views, images, and definitions of landscape influence the way rural landscapes are planned in the Netherlands and around the world. Inversely, the varying conditions that landscape architects must confront invite an approach to planning and design that is adapted to local or regional condi-

The Dutch have developed many types of parks during the twentieth century. Among the many examples is the vernacular botanical garden, or heempark, which originated in the Netherlands. This type of small park was first conceived and laid out by landscape architects C. P. Broerse and J. Landwehr of the parks depart-ment of the town of Amstelveen near Amsterdam. It is characterized by a planting plan consisting entirely of native species, gathered from all corners of the country, and planted on a site on which soils and water tables were meticulously adapted to the conditions posed by individual plants or plant communities. The resulting semi-natural composition is pleasing to the eye and useful for the teacher of botany. Nature is controlled, and the ongoing maintenance of heemparks requires specific expertise: After all, what is the difference between a weed and a prized native specimen of the native flora? This type of park has become popular in the Netherlands, and examples are found in several communities today. Photograph by H. van Aggelen.

tions. The *systems view* of landscape, if it is applied with some restraint, may help in understanding the relationship between interacting processes and landscape form. A combination of the landscape as organization of *space and place in time,* applied in planning, may result in a diversity of landscape character. The *functional landscape* poses a challenge to the creative design of new development, whereas the landscapes of *added values,* of *separate sectors,* and of *covered-up shame* are leading nowhere.

What would be the most appropriate approach to landscape planning in the Netherlands? The answer must be found in a reconciliation between what was and what is needed now. Historic patterns may serve as a basis for new development, both in terms of the fitting of the new into the existing, or the deliberate and sensitive creation of contrasting form. In doing so one should be aware of the circumstance that the landscapes the Dutch have inherited are among the most human-made of the world.

Early settlers were obliged to adapt to difficult site conditions, a circumstance that helped to create a strong identity in many places. The Dutch alluvial landscapes are also quite flat, and most of the visible vertical elements have been planted or constructed: The landscape of space is based on human decisions. Finally, the functional use of the land has always been the predominant factor in determining its layout and its image. Landscape planners should aim at maintaining and reinforcing these national characteristics, which implies an emphasis on a functional approach, combined with a search for local characteristics. Such an approach poses quite a challenge to the creativity of landscape architects, however, for the increasing standardization of built environments, and the growing emphasis on horizontal relations in an expanding economy, limit opportunities to maintain or create a much-needed variety.

A legible landscape expresses the way the land is used. It shows what people do, how they live and make a living, and also reveals their standards of maintenance, their sense of propriety, their values, and how they deal with change over time. The Dutch landscapes express a centuries-old and successful battle against natural constraints. Nature has been subdued, even if it is still present, and remnants of formerly existing vegetation and wildlife are now carefully nursed. This is natural for the Dutch, and it should stay that way. A policy to reintroduce (quasi-) nature images by means of large-scale interventions along our rivers, as described above, will result in falsified images. Any attempt at make-believe worlds, whether in the shape of human-made natural environments or historic showpieces, creates fake landscapes that deny the existence of a national culture.

On the other hand, there is more to the design of new landscapes than a mere "following of functions" in order to create legibility. Landscape as a whole remains an imprecise and ambiguous concept. As S. C. Bourassa states: "A further analysis of the concept leads from an objectively comprehensible entity to something which has primarily subjective meaning."[35] To create landscapes in which sustainable use and harmonious form are the expression of the hopes and beliefs within a certain society is a daunting task indeed.

NOTES

1. Lowenthal 1992, pp. 15–23.
2. Lambert 1971.
3. Kohl 1986.
4. Faludi 1992, p. 93. Faludi is a planner trained in the United Kingdom and presently with the University of Amsterdam. He combines the view of the outsider with that of the knowledgeable insider.
5. Dutt and Costa 1985, p. 1.
6. Mumford 1938, p. 137.
7. Jackson 1984, p. 12.
8. Faludi 1992, p. 98.
9. Kohl 1986, pp. 527–37.
10. Coeterier 1987, chap. 4.
11. See Yi-Fu Tuan 1972.
12. Schama 1987.
13. Sijmons 1990, p. 265.
14. Achterhuis 1992.
15. Sijmons 1990, p. 270.
16. Van Buuren and Kerkstra (1993) describe the hydrological aspects of these proposals.
17. These drastic measures have attracted international attention. The issue was extensively discussed in the *New York Times* (Simons 1993).
18. Helmer et al. 1992.
19. The real answer to these problems lies in a change in human lifestyle, with less consumption, less waste, and less travel, resulting in less environmental pollution. But this seems to go against some fundamental human desires, and the answer is, therefore, sought in technical innovation, which may be helpful but rarely is enough.
20. Ministerie van Landbouw 1990, pp. 5–7.

21. Vanderbilt 1992, p. 122.

22. Ministerie van Volkshuisvesting en Ruimtelijke Ordening 1974, pp. 22–23. It was proposed that the four systems be studied and interrelated. How this should be done was not explained. Especially the notion of a "visual system" with its cultural connotation was poorly defined and ill-conceived. A few years after the publication of this document the whole idea was abandoned.

23. Koningsveld 1988.

24. Kerkstra and Vrijlandt (1990) describe and simulate some of these corridors in real-life situations in the eastern part of the Netherlands.

25. This is what Pirsig (1991) calls "static quality." The scientific mind distinguishes between subject and object. The subject (an expert or a group of experts) assesses the quality of objects in various levels and expresses this in a numerical form. Once a quality has been assessed it becomes the property of the object (or landscape), and the numbers indicating levels of quality are used as quantities one can add up, subtract, or multiply.

26. Vroom 1990, p. 143.

27. Lynch 1960; Vroom 1986.

28. Meeus 1984. See, also, Vroom and Meeus 1986, pp. 281–85.

29. This phenomenon is also illustrated in Kerkstra and Vrijlandt 1990, pp. 277 and 278.

30. Norberg-Schulz 1980, p. 11.

31. This idea is beautifully explored in J. B. Jackson 1995. See especially pp. 48–50.

32. Burke 1956, chaps. 4 and 7; see, also, Vroom 1976, pp. 377–80.

33. Pohl 1992.

34. Beun et al. 1989.

35. Bourassa 1991, chap. 1.

REFERENCES

Achterhuis, J. 1992. *De Illusie van Groen: Over milieuzaken en de fixatie op de techniek.* Amsterdam: De Balie.

Beun, N. J., E. G. M. Dessing and Th. W. H. de Vos. 1989. "Planning, organisatie en uitvoering van landinrichtingsprojecten." Pp. 194–251 in J. J. Vonk and R. T. de Boer, eds., *Inleiding tot de inrichting van het landelijk gebied.* Wageningen: Pudoc.

Bourassa, S. C. 1991. *The Aesthetics of Landscape.* London: Belhaven Press.

Burke, G. L. 1956. *The Making of Dutch Towns: A Study of Urban Development from the Tenth to the Seventeenth Centuries.* London: Clever-Hume Press Ltd.

Buuren, M. van, and K. Kerkstra. 1993. "The Framework Concept and the Hydrological Landscape Structure: A New Perspective in the Design of Multifunctional Landscapes." Pp. 219–43 in C. Vos and P. Opdam, eds., *Landscape Ecology of a Stressed Environment.* London: Chapman & Hall.

Coeterier, J. F. 1987. *De Waarneming en Waardering van Landschappen: Resultaten van een omgevingspsychologisch onderzoek*. PhD diss., Wageningen Agricultural University.

Dutt, A., and J. Costa. 1985. *Public Planning in the Netherlands: Perspectives and Changes since the Second World War*. New York: Oxford University Press.

Faludi, A. 1992. "Dutch Growth Management: The Two Faces of Success." *Landscape and Urban Planning* 22: 93–106.

Helmer, W., G. Litjens, W. Overmars, A. Klink, and H. Barneveld. 1992. *Levende Rivieren: Studie in opdracht van het Wereld Natuur Fonds*. Baarn: Bosch & Keuning.

Jackson, J. B. 1984. *Discovering the Vernacular Landscape*. New Haven: Yale University Press.

———. 1995. "In Search of the Proto-Landscape." In G. F. Thompson, ed., *Landscape in America*. Austin: University of Texas Press, pp. 43–50.

Kerkstra, K., and P. Vrijlandt. 1990. "Landscape Planning for Industrial Agriculture: A Proposed Framework for Rural Areas." *Landscape and Urban Planning* 18: 275–87.

Kohl, L. 1986. "Man against the Sea: The Oosterschelde Barrier." *National Geographic* (4): 527–37.

Koningsveld, H. 1988. "Planning en (on)zekerheid: De samenleving als experiment of als technocratie." *PLAN* 1–2: 32–38.

Lambert, A. 1971. *The Making of the Dutch Landscape: A Historical Geography of the Netherlands*. London: Seminar Press.

Lowenthal, D. 1992. "European Landscapes as National Emblems." *Paysage & Aménagement/ Landscape Research* 21 (Special Issue): 14–23.

Lynch, K. 1960. *The Image of the City*. Cambridge: MIT Press.

Meeus, J. H. 1984. *Op zoek naar een instrumentarium voor ontwerpkritiek in de Landschapsarchitectuur*. PhD diss., Wageningen Agricultural University.

Meinig, D. W. 1979. "Symbolic Landscapes: Some Idealizations of American Communities." Pp 164–92 in D. W. Meinig, ed., *The Interpretation of Ordinary Landscapes*. New York: Oxford University Press.

Ministerie van Landbouw, Natuurbeheer en Visserij. 1990. *Visie Landschap: Beleidsvoornemen*. (Policy Document on Landscape). Den Haag: Staatsuitgeverij.

Ministerie van Volkshuisvesting, Orienteringsnota Ruimtelijke Ordening. 1974. *Eerste deel van de Derde Nota Ruimtelijke Ordening*. Den Haag: Staatsuitgeverij.

Mumford, L. 1938. *The Culture of Cities*. New York: Harcourt, Brace and Co.

Norberg-Schulz, C. 1980. *Genius Loci: Towards a Phenomenology of Architecture*. London: Academy Editions.

Pirsig, R. M. 1991. *LILA*. New York: Bantam Books.

Pohl, N. 1992. "Horizontal Articulation in Landscape." *TOPOS* 1 (September): 42–52.

Schama, Simon. 1987. *The Embarrassment of Riches: An Interpretation of Dutch Culture in the Golden Age*. New York: Knopf.

Sijmons, D. 1990. "Regional Planning as a Strategy." *Landscape and Urban Planning* 18: 265–73.

Simons, M. 1993. "A Dutch Reversal: Letting the Sea Back In." *The New York Times,* 7 March.

Tuan, Yi-Fu. 1972. "Discrepancies between Environmental Attitudes and Behavior: Examples from Europe and China." Pp 68–81 in P. W. English and R. C. Mayfield, eds., *Man, Space, and Environment.* London: Oxford University Press.

Vanderbilt, P. 1992. *Between the Landscape and Its Other.* Baltimore: Johns Hopkins University Press.

Vroom, M. J. 1976. "Landscape Planning: A Cooperative Effort, A Professional Activity." *Landscape Planning* 3: 371–82.

———. 1986. "The Perception of Dimensions of Space and Levels of Infrastructure and Its Application in Landscape Planning." *Landscape Planning* 12: 337–52.

———. 1990. "Landscape Planning in the Netherlands: The Role of Competitions." *Built Environment* 16: 141–61.

———, ed. 1992. *Buitenruimten/Outdoor Space: Environments Designed by Dutch Landscape Architects in the Period since 1945.* Amsterdam: THOTH publishers.

Vroom, M. J., and J. H. Meeus. 1986. "Critique and Theory in Dutch Landscape Architecture." *Landscape and Urban Planning* 13: 277–302.

12

ECOLOGY AND DESIGN

IAN L. McHARG

I am unabashedly committed to the imperative *design with nature,* or ecological design and planning. Indeed, I conceive of non-ecological design as either capricious, arbitrary, or idiosyncratic, and it is certainly irrelevant. Ecology, the study of environments and organisms, among them people, is totally inclusive. What falls outside this definition? Not content, perhaps only attitude. Non-ecological design and planning disdains reason and emphasizes intuition. It is antiscientific by assertion.

There is no doubt about my attitude toward this topic. I invented *ecological planning* during the early 1960s and became an advocate of *ecological design* thereafter. This was explicit in *Design with Nature;* it was not only an explanation, but also a command.[1]

Ecological planning is that process whereby a region is understood as a biophysical and social process comprehensible through the operation of laws and time. This can be reinterpreted as having explicit opportunities and constraints for any particular human use. A survey will reveal the most fit locations and processes.

Ecological design follows planning and introduces the subject of form. There should be an intrinsically suitable location, processes with appropriate materials, and forms. Design requires an informed designer with a visual imagination, as well as graphic and creative skills. It selects for creative fitting revealed in intrinsic and expressive form.

The deterioration of the global environment, at every scale, has reinforced my advocacy of ecological design and planning. Degradation has reached such proportions that I now conclude that non-ecological design and planning is likely to be trivial and irrelevant and a desperate deprivation. I suggest that to ignore natural processes is to be ignorant, to exclude life-threatening hazards—volcanism, earthquakes, floods, and pervasive environmental destruction—is either idiocy or criminal negligence. Avoiding ecological considerations will not enhance the profession of landscape architecture. In contrast, it will erode the modest but significant advances that ecology has contributed to landscape architecture and planning since the 1960s.

Yet, you ask, What of art? I have no doubt on this subject either. The giving of meaningful form is crucial; indeed, this might well be the most precious skill of all. It is rare in society, yet it is clearly identifiable where it exists. Art is indispensable for society and culture.

Does art exclude science? Does art reject knowledge? Would a lobotomy improve human competence, or is the brain the indispensable organ?

There is a new tendency by some landscape architects to reject ecology, to emphasize art exclusively. This I deplore and reject. Such an approach is tragically ironic when so many world leaders are calling for sustainable development, when architects are issuing green manifestos, and professional associations in architecture and engineering are refocusing their attention on the environment.

We have been at this impasse before; it was not beneficial, and the result was calamitous. We have only to remember that, by the end of World War I, landscape architecture was firmly established at Harvard University. It was the world center for this subject. It had inherited the concepts and accomplishments of Frederick Law Olmsted and Charles Eliot, but all was not well: There was dissension.

It transpired that there were opposing camps within landscape architecture. The Olmsted disciples wished to emphasize conservation and regional and town planning. They included Henry Hubbard and Theodora Kimball, Harland Bartholomew, John Nolen, Warren Manning, and, later, Howard Mennhenick. The remainder were oriented to Beaux Arts; they were self-proclaimed aesthetes, interested in designing estates for the rich and famous: Bremer Whidden Pond, James Sturgis Pray, Steven Hamblin, and Robert Wheelwright. The aesthetes defined landscape architecture design between the world wars at Harvard and elsewhere. Meanwhile the Olmsted disciples founded the field of planning during the 1920s, and inadvertently created a schism between design and planning that persists to this day.[2] Brains and knowledge abandoned landscape architecture, which experienced a massive decline from the peaks of Olmsted and Eliot to an abyss with little intelligence, skill, or passion.

This antagonism between art and science, as well as between design and planning, has lasted too long. It is now a serious obstruction to education and the earth's well-being. Both art and science have their antique, prepared positions, their mandarin advocates, their lines of competence defined, and their proprietary jargons. Yet, when stripped of pomp and pretensions, at root art merely means skill and science means knowledge. Can we imagine, in the challenging environment we occupy, the rejection of either art or science? Surely knowledge needs skill to give form and significance to our landscapes and our adaptations. Surely skill needs knowledge just as a solver needs a problem. Surely, once and for all time, art and science, skill and knowledge, ecology and design and planning should unite.

What the world needs from landscape architecture is an enlarged vision, greater knowledge, and commensurate skill. Landscape architects are engaged in the challenge of adaptation. They must acquire the accomplishments that can make a significant contribution to preserving, managing, planning, and restoring the biosphere, to designing human environments.

And, thanks to Charles Darwin and Lawrence Henderson, we have a theory. Darwin said: "The surviving organism is fit for the environment." Henderson, another biologist and author of *The Fitness of the Environment* (1913), wrote that Darwin's assertion was insufficient. He concluded that, as there are infinite environments and organisms, the evolutionary challenge for every participant is to seek and find the fittest available environment, to adapt that environment and the self to accomplish a better fit. Moreover, Henderson's writing defined a fit environment as one in which most of a consumer's needs exist in the environment as found, requiring less work for adaptation than for any competitor. The thermodynamic challenge implies that successful adaptation is creative.[3]

What are the instruments for adaptation? The universal adaptations—mutation and natural selection—while manipulated extensively for food, plants, and animals, are not widely applied to human breeding (thank goodness). Mutation and natural selection are slow processes. And innate behavior in living organisms is similarly difficult to manipulate. Cultural adaptation is the more pliant and useful. Language, philosophy, science, art, and technology are such instruments. If one is to ask which aspect of cultural adaptation most clearly meets the Darwin-Henderson challenge—to find the fittest environment and then to engage in adaptation—surely the most direct response is landscape planning and design.

But we need an appropriate criterion for guiding and evaluating landscape architecture in the twenty-first century. Art critics evaluate the contribution of painting, sculpture, dance, photography, and other art forms. Can their appreciation extend from the product to the source of creation, the painter, his or her brain, eye, hand, bones, sinews, arteries, and veins? Beauty alone is an inappropriate criterion for evaluating art or the organs that create it, so why should beauty be used exclusively to evaluate a landscape? Fitness, as explained by Henderson, for me is a thoroughly suitable criterion. We have, then, not only a theory, but also criteria for performance and fitness.

If one is fit, then one is healthy, and this applies equally to a landscape. Furthermore, if being healthy enables one to seek and solve problems, or provides the ability to recover from insult or assault, then fitness confers health. Therefore, fitness is an index of health. Extending this thought to landscape architectural theory and practice, do we have a method for accomplishing creative planning and design and, more simply, an ecological method for adaptation?

We live in a physical world, a biological world, and a social world, and our investigations must include them all. As matter preceded life and the human species was late in biological evolution, we can employ chronology as a unifying force. We can recapitulate events and retrace time. Thus, when we design and plan, we should begin with the geological history of a landscape, working in concert with an understanding of climate. Bedrock and surficial geology as well as climatic processes can be reinterpreted to explain geomorphology and hydrology. These processes set the stage for soil formation. Now, the relationships among the constituent parts of a landscape become clear: The past informs the present, and each feature is only comprehensible from understanding its earlier layers. After we learn about a landscape's geology, climate, hydrology, and soils, then vegetation patterns become more apparent, as does the resultant wildlife. At which point we can ask the human occupants who they are, how they distinguish themselves from others, how they view the environment and its occupants, and what are their needs and desires, their preferences and aversions.

I wish to emphasize my belief that ecological study includes natural and cultural processes. We will find that discrete value systems are associated with distinct human constituencies, and we can associate these groups with their needs and values. This approach allows landscape architects to inter-

4

5

6

7

The Greenfield Garden, a rock and water garden for Mrs. Albert M. Greenfield. These sketches illustrating (4) the main rock face and cascade with four "sentinel" rocks in foreground, framing the "Rock Pool," and stone bridge at left; (5) the stepped pools between two existing weeping hemlocks; (6) the rapids tumbling into the "Hemlock Pool"; (7) the "canyon" and "copse" below the Beech Pool. Landscape architect: Ian L. McHarg, Philadelphia, 1959–1960; drawings by Anthony J. Walmsley.

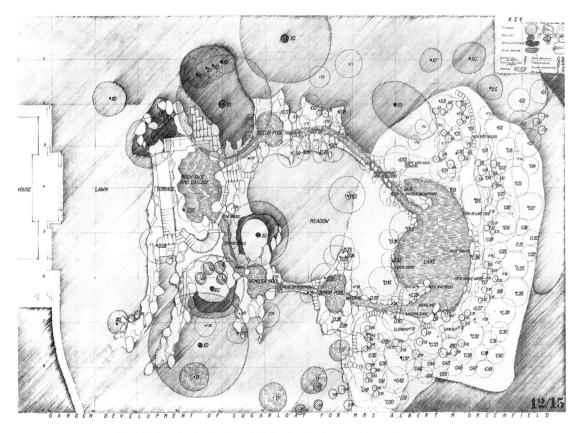

The planting plan for the Greenfield Garden. Landscape architect: Ian L. McHarg, Philadelphia, 1959–1960; drawing by Anthony J. Walmsley.

pret all phenomena in the light of these systems. With such vision and knowledge, we can plan, because we have developed the context for planning and design.

This is the biophysical model I developed more than three decades ago for ecological design and planning. This is the model I live by. It can be reinterpreted to explain social values, technological competence, an ethnographic history of human settlements—urban as well as rural. We then are able to see the primeval landscape successively modified, through history, in order to arrive at the present.

Ecological study is indispensable to planning, but it also produces a context for a regional design vocabulary. The settlements of Dogon, the Berbers in Morocco, the settlement of the Greek islands, Italian hill villages, and pueblo communities in New Mexico and the Colorado Plateau are fitting examples of ecological responses in planning and design. Contemporary examples of ecological designers are too few. I am able, however, to select three firms.

The first is Andropogon in Philadelphia, whose principals are Carol and Colin Franklin, Leslie and Rolf Sauer. These landscape architects possess unchallenged primacy in ecological design and restoration. Their science is impeccable, their applications cross the threshold of art, and their realizations of design and planning are wonderfully effective, fitting, and, even for the uninitiated, beautiful.[4] Coe Lee Robinson Roesch in Philadelphia is the second example; the third is Jones & Jones in Seattle. Both firms have built sterling reputations designing and building appropriate exhibits for zoos. Their science, too, is elegant, employing inventories of the native environments of animals, replicating these environments with consummate skill. Their creations include ecological and psychological factors never before employed, to my knowledge, for human habitations. It is more difficult to find other examples. These three exceptions simply prove the rule. Ecological design is still an aspiration, not yet a practice, within landscape architecture.

A major obstruction to ecological design is the architecturally derived mode of representation by drawings. This is paper-oriented, two-dimensional, and orthogonal. In contrast nature is multi-dimensional, living, growing, moving with forms that tend to be amorphous or amoebic. They can grow, expand, interact, and alternate. Field design would be a marvelous improvement over designing on paper removed from the site. Yet new representations must be developed to supersede the limitations of paper-oriented, orthogonal investigations with their limited formal solutions. We should be committed in our work to designing living landscapes in urban, rural, and wild settings. Yet there are infinite opportunities afforded to those who would study natural systems, their components, rules, succession, and, not least, their forms. This should be the basis for an emerging ecological design.

This system does not need invention. Forms, materials, and processes have evolved by trial and error over eons of time and represent the finest solutions of materials and form that nature could invent. Such ecosystems

The greensward at La Paloma resort in Tucson, Arizona, utilizes indigenous plants and a xerophytic design to accommodate the region's soils, climate, and natural of beauty. Photograph by George F. Thompson, 1987.

are exquisitely adapted and provide an example for people to design and plan.

Strangely, the area where art and science have been most successfully employed is neither architecture nor landscape architecture. It is in the creation of prostheses. Here biological knowledge is indispensable, but skill produces the adaptation. The purposes are to amplify the performance of a biological function—to see small and far, we have the microscope and the telescope; to speak far, we have the telephone and the microphone; to move far and fast, we have the plane and the rocket. Our major prosthesis is the expansion of power from muscle to tools, mechanical equipment to atom bomb.

Consider the steps to improve sight—spectacles, bifocals, magnifying glasses, laser operations for cataracts and glaucoma, and soft contact lenses—a miracle of adaptive design. Or walking—first a shoe, then a crutch, a walker, the wheelchair, now titanium hips and Teflon knees. The computer may be the prosthesis for the brain.

Should we pursue this track we would reconsider membranes. The giant clam and nudibranch have incorporated chloroplasts; those animals can now photosynthesize. Why not build membranes, walls, and roofs? Could they do so? Consider vegetation on walls and roofs to add carbon, fixing and minimizing carbon dioxide. Consider creating calcium carbonate, with electric charges in seawater.

Membranes modulate freshwater and saltwater. They facilitate the transport of nutrients. Consider the adaptations to cold in plants, reduction in water content, hairy surfaces, corrugations, and color. Wastes in nature are often nutrients, not problems. The route that Andropogon, Coe Lee Robinson Roesch, and Jones & Jones have developed is superb but needs to be augmented. The example of prosthetic development is a fitting analog. It is indisputably ecological, without caprice.

Of course, the best example of successful adaptation is the coral. The ocean floor is generally sterile. Coral transforms such areas into some of the most fertile and beautiful environments on earth. Would that landscape architects could equal this.

When the training of landscape architects includes at least an introduction to all of the relevant natural and social sciences, as well as design proficiency, then a new proposal can provide them with an exceptional opportunity to design and plan ecologically and artfully.

There are moves afoot to initiate a National Biological Survey. I recommended this in 1974 to Russell Train, then of the U.S. Environmental Protection Agency (EPA). When William Reilly became EPA administrator in 1990, he asked me to advise him on the reorganization of the EPA, and the conduct of the Environmental Monitoring and Assessment Program (EMAP), the proposed inventory. EMAP was proposed to be a broadly conceived ecosystem inventory integrating regional and national scales, allowing for monitoring and assessment, and designed to influence decision making. With my colleagues John Radke, Jonathan Berger, and Kathleen Wallace, I produced a document, "A Prototype Database for a National

Ecological Inventory" (1992). This recommended a three-part process, a national inventory at 1:2,000,000 with all natural and social regions delineated; a regional scale inventory at 1:250,000; and, finally, samples at the scale of 1:24,000.

Our first assertion was that the resolve to undertake a National Ecological Inventory should be recognized as the most important governmental action ever taken in the history of the American environment. This resolve contains implicit resolutions: That inventory, monitoring, and modeling are indispensable to the EPA and essential to the fulfillment of its regulatory roles.

This first requires the reconstitution of the EPA to include leadership from all environmental sciences. To provide such leadership, we recommended the creation of an executive committee composed of leading officers in all of the scientific societies. Regional groups of environmental scientists and planners would be assembled to undertake regional inventories. And landscape architects, being among the most competent professionals to decide on the appropriate data to be incorporated and its contribution to planning and design, would participate in the content of these inventories. For the crystalline piedmont and adjacent coastal plain in Pennsylvania and New Jersey, for example, we would assume that landscape architects and regional planners at the University of Pennsylvania, Rutgers University, and Pennsylvania State University would be part of a central group to that association of regional scientists. This model would be replicated throughout the country with other university landscape architecture faculties, professional designers, and planners contributing to the regional groups. By such an involvement the landscape architecture profession would vastly enhance its social contribution and academic reputation.

It is then necessary to produce a plan for the process to undertake the inventory as well as to monitor its progress. This would involve the recommended scientific committee, an expanded staff representing all of the environmental sciences, and an appropriate organizational structure. When the plan is completed, we advocate a massive public relations and advertising campaign to inform the general public, conservation groups, the scientific community, and government officials at all levels of the significance of the enterprise.[5]

Our proposed inventory must include physical, biological, and social systems. The last is indispensable for understanding human environments. We suggested a demonstration ethnographic survey to illustrate that these are crucial for understanding human ecology. In our recommendation to the EPA, we observed that the greatest problem lies not in data collection, but rather with integration, synthesis, and evaluation.

Now, there is a new development. Secretary of the Interior Bruce Babbitt announced, shortly after his appointment by President Clinton in 1992, his intention to undertake a National Biological Survey. This may supersede EMAP. There is another possibility: NASA, the Defense Mapping Agency, and the federal departments of defense and energy have collected global environmental data since the onset of the Nuclear Age, employing instrumentalism that is unavailable to civilians. There is discussion of declassifying these data, which, of course, could be included in a National Ecological Inventory or a National Biological survey. There is, also, the possibility that this capability could be invested in the United Nations as the U.S. arm of the U.N. Environmental Program and employed for a global inventory. Others are recommending the creation of a National Institute of the Environment in which the inventorying and modeling might be invested.

Clearly massive data will soon become available, ultimately in digital form, globally and locally. Whoever has access to this cornucopia will have immense power. Landscape architects should become advocates for such ecological inventories and become primary users of these data for planning and design. Landscape architects must learn to lead.

In 1992 I received a signal honor from President George Bush, the National Medal of Art. The noteworthy aspect of this act was the inclusion of landscape architecture as a category eligible for this high honor. As preface to the award President Bush stated, "It is my hope that the art of the twenty-first century will be devoted to restoring the earth."

This will require a fusion of science and art. There can be no finer challenge. Will the profession of landscape architecture elevate itself to contribute to this incredible opportunity? Let us hope so. The future of our planet—and the quest for a better life—may depend on it. So let us resolve to green the earth, to restore the earth, and to heal the earth with the greatest expression of science and art we can muster. We are running out of time and opportunities.

NOTES

1. Ian L. McHarg, *Design with Nature* (Garden City, N.Y.: Doubleday/Natural History Press, 1969; reprint, New York: John Wiley & Sons, 1992).

2. Frederick Law Olmsted was an amateur farmer, familiar with science, and Charles Eliot consorted with the leading scientists of his time, but their influence was bred out of city planning, which became the applied social science department that I encountered as a student at Harvard University in 1946. The natural sciences were banished. It is barely credible that the accomplishments of that giant, Olmsted, and the opportunities presented by Eliot were disregarded—first, by landscape architecture and, then, by city planning at Harvard. Nor were either replaced by a superior doctrine. We have yet to rediscover their significance.

3. I use the word *consumer* because the roots of *ecology* and *economics* both lie in the Greek word, *oikos,* or "a dwelling place." Henderson used terms such as *consumer* close to this root meaning.

4. See Carol Franklin's essay in this book.

5. It is worthwhile to remember that Charles E. Little and David Brower, among other leading conservationists, have for decades advocated the necessity of employing advertising and public relations techniques in the cause to inform the public, industry, and government and university officials about environmental matters. Also of note is Richard Beamish's important book, *Getting the Word Out in the Fight to Save the Earth* (Baltimore: Johns Hopkins University Press, 1995). Beamish is one of the unsung heroes of the modern environmental movement, especially for his work on saving the Adirondacks.

THE CONTRIBUTORS

James Corner, M.L.A., is an associate professor of landscape architecture and regional planning at the University of Pennsylvania. He is the coauthor with Alex MacLean of *Taking Measures Across the American Landscape* (Yale University Press, 1996). His graphic work has been widely exhibited and his articles on landscape architectural theory have appeared in *Landscape Journal, Architectural Design,* and *AA Files.*

Carol Franklin, M.L.A., is a founding principal of Andropogon Associates, Ltd., an ecological planning and design firm in Philadelphia, Pennsylvania. Andropogon is a national and international leader in the field of sustainable design. The firm is known for its innovative ecological design strategies at all scales and for its pioneering work in the management and restoration of natural habitats in environments ranging from nearly pristine areas to the most disturbed urban and rural environments.

Mark Johnson, M.L.A., is a principal of Civitas, a landscape architecture and design firm in Denver, Colorado, which has pioneered a new vocabulary for urban landscapes, especially in the American West. He is, also, an adjunct professor in the New College of Architecture and Planning at the University of Colorado.

Michael Laurie, M.L.A., is a professor of landscape architecture at the University of California, Berkeley. He is the author of *An Introduction to Landscape Architecture* (Elsevier, 1975; 2d ed., Prentice Hall, 1986). For many years, he has been associated as an editorial board member and illustrator for *Landscape* magazine in Berkeley, the magazine founded in 1951 by John Brinckerhoff Jackson.

Ian L. McHarg, M.L.A. and M.C.P., is founder, professor emeritus, and former chairman of the department of landscape architecture and regional planning at the University of Pennsylvania. He was, also, a founding partner of the acclaimed international firm, Wallace, McHarg, Roberts and Todd, and author of *Design with Nature* (Doubleday/Natural History Press, 1969; reprint, John Wiley & Sons, 1992) and *A Quest for Life: An Autobiography* (John Wiley & Sons, 1996). In 1992 President George Bush awarded Professor McHarg the National Medal of Art, making him the first landscape architect or planner to receive this high honor.

Steve Martino, Fellow, A.S.L.A., is a landscape architect in Phoenix, Arizona. He has won six national American Society of Landscape Architects design awards for his innovative work in the Sonoran region, in particular for pioneering the use of desert plants to create a new aesthetic that is being emulated throughout the Southwest and in other arid regions of the world.

Elizabeth K. Meyer, M.L.A., is associate professor and chairwoman of the department of landscape architecture at the University of Virginia. Through her teaching and research, she is recovering the theories of modern landscape architecture from their relative obscurity. Those discoveries are chronicled in a book in progress entitled *The Margins of Modernity.*

Forster Ndubisi, Ph.D. and M.L.A., is an associate professor of landscape architecture at the University of Georgia and an urban planner in the University's Institute of Community and Area Development. His articles on the application of human ecology to landscape management and planning have appeared in leading professional journals in the United States and abroad, and his book, *Approaches to Ecological Planning,* is forthcoming from Johns Hopkins University Press.

Laurie Olin, B. Arch., is a founding partner of The Olin Partnership, formerly Hanna/Olin, an international design practice in Philadelphia, and the former chairman of the department of landscape architecture at Harvard University. His designs have attracted international acclaim and attention, and his honors include a Rome Prize, the Thomas Jefferson Professorship at the University of Virginia, and a John Simon Guggenheim Memorial Foundation

Fellowship. He is a Fellow of the American Academy of Arts and Sciences and a member of the National Academy of Design.

Clair Reiniger, M.L.A., is principal of Clair Reiniger and Associates, a design and planning firm, and president of Designwrights Collaborative, a nonprofit planning organization, both in Santa Fe. She is New Mexico's first registered landscape architect and is best known for her bioregional approaches to ecological planning and design.

Sally Schauman, M.S., is a professor and former chairwoman of the department of landscape architecture at the University of Washington. She previously was the chief landscape architect of the U.S. Soil Conservation Service, Washington, D.C. Her honors include a Loeb Fellowship in advanced environmental studies at Harvard University. She has long been a leader in the development of visual assessment and rural planning in landscape architecture.

Meto J. Vroom, M.L.A., is professor emeritus and former chairman of landscape architecture at the Agricultural University, Wageningen, The Netherlands. He was instrumental in developing the international journal *Landscape Planning* (now known as *Landscape and Urban Planning*), and he is editor of *Outdoor Space: Environments Designed by Dutch Landscape Architects since 1945* (Thoth, 1992) and coeditor of *Learning from Rotterdam* (Nichols, 1990).

Joan Hirschman Woodward, M.L.A., is an associate professor of landscape architecture at California State Polytechnic University, Pomona, and a former park planner and landscape architect with the National Park Service in Colorado, Alaska, and other western states. Her work involves the linkage of regional landscape ecology with site-specific design.

ABOUT THE EDITORS

Gᴇᴏʀɢᴇ F. Tʜᴏᴍᴘsᴏɴ is founder and president of the Center for American Places, a nonprofit organization based in Harrisonburg, Virginia, and Mesilla, New Mexico, that is dedicated to enhancing the public's understanding of geography, landscape, and the values of place, through research, education, and through book publications. He previously worked as an acquisitions editor for Johns Hopkins University Press, was the first book review editor for *Landscape Journal*, has taught on numerous occasions at The Colorado College and University of Wisconsin–Madison, and has won an Honor Award and a Merit Award from the American Society of Landscape Architects for his editorial work. His books include *Landscape in America* (Texas, 1995); *Registered Places of New Mexico: The Land of Enchantment*, with Cotton Mather (New Mexico Geographical Society, 1995), and *Beyond the Great Divide*, with Cotton Mather and P. P. Karan (Rutgers, 1992). He is, also, founder and director of numerous book series, among them *Creating the North American Landscape, Center Books on Space, Place, and Time, Landscapes of the Night, The Road and American Culture, Center Books in Natural History*, and *American Land Classics*.

Fʀᴇᴅᴇʀɪᴄᴋ R. Sᴛᴇɪɴᴇʀ is professor and director of the School of Planning and Landscape Architecture at Arizona State University in Tempe. He previously taught at the University of Colorado, Washington State University, and the University of Pennsylvania. In 1980 he was a Fulbright-Hays scholar at the Agricultural University, Wageningen, The Netherlands. He is the author and editor of eight books, among them *The Living Landscape: An Ecological Approach to Landscape Planning* (McGraw-Hill, 1991) and

Soil Conservation in the United States: Policy and Planning (Johns Hopkins, 1990), for which he was awarded, respectively, two Merit Awards from the American Society of Landscape Architects for Communication and Research. His articles have appeared in numerous professional journals and magazines around the world, including *Landscape Architecture, Landscape Journal, Landscape and Urban Planning,* and *American Land Forum.*

INDEX

Page numbers in italics refer to illustrations or illustration captions.